*LIFE
INSURANCE*

LIFE

INSURANCE

How to Buy the Right Policy
from the Right Company
at the Right Price

The Editors of Consumer Reports Books
with Trudy Lieberman

Consumers Union   Mount Vernon, New York

Copyright © 1988 by Consumers Union of United States, Inc.,
Mount Vernon, New York 10553
All rights reserved, including the right of reproduction in whole or in part in any
form.
Library of Congress Cataloging-in-Publication Data

Life insurance.

Includes index.
1. Insurance, Life—United States.   I. Lieberman, Trudy.   II. Consumer Reports
Books.   III. Consumers Union of United States.
HG8951.L527   1988   368.3′2′00202   87-71006
ISBN: 0-89043-095-0
Design by Jeff Ward
First printing, April 1988
Manufactured in the United States of America

Life Insurance is a Consumer Reports Book published by Consumers Union, the nonprofit organization that publishes *Consumer Reports*, the monthly magazine of test reports, product Ratings, and buying guidance. Established in 1936, Consumers Union is chartered under the Not-For-Profit Corporation Law of the State of New York.

The purposes of Consumers Union, as stated in its charter, are to provide consumers with information and counsel on consumer goods and services, to give information on all matters relating to the expenditure of the family income, and to initiate and cooperate with individual and group efforts seeking to create and maintain decent living standards.

Contents

Foreword

Life insurance has been an important topic for Consumers Union since 1937, when we published our first report on the subject. In 1946, 1967, 1974, and 1980 we published major insurance reports, and in 1967 we published our first book on life insurance. In 1986 *Consumer Reports* featured a three-part series on the subject, which attracted wide attention from both the insurance industry and consumers, winning two prestigious national magazine awards. Those articles form the basis of this book.

Life insurance has undergone many changes since our 1980 report. New types of policies, such as universal and variable life, have further complicated an already confusing marketplace. Today the consumer is confronted with a myriad of options and questions: How much life insurance is enough? What kind of policy should I buy? Are policy riders worth the money? Is life insurance a good investment? Does it pay to switch policies? Are all insurance companies the same? It's obvious to us that buyers badly need accurate and up-to-date information that goes beyond the usual industry hype. We hope this book will meet that need.

In our most recent survey, we found that too many agents selling life insurance today show a startling lack of knowledge of their own field, and too many prefer to use overbearing and emotional methods of sales persuasion rather than a careful analysis and evaluation of available products. Selling life insurance is often a difficult and frustrating experience, but it is our belief that the informed professional agent can play a key role in successfully assisting the consumer to make one of the more important purchases of a lifetime.

Consumers Union has benefited extensively from the help of consultants, including a team of actuaries, and from suggestions and criticisms made by members of the life insurance industry. The final recommendations, judgments, and opinions, however, are those of Consumers Union.

The Editors of Consumer Reports Books

Acknowledgments

Special thanks to consulting actuary J. Ross Hanson, and to Harold Skipper, director of the Center for Risk Management and Insurance Research, Georgia State University, for their careful review of the manuscript and consultation during its preparation. Trudy Lieberman would also like to thank Julie Henderson, editorial associate at Consumer Reports Books, for her assistance, patience, and many helpful suggestions for polishing the manuscript; and Bruce Booker, vice president and actuary, The Life Insurance Company of Virginia; Thomas Eason, senior vice president and chief actuary, The Union Central Life Insurance Co.; Jerome S. Golden, chairman of the Golden Financial Group; Lowell Lamb, assistant actuary, Metropolitan Life Insurance Co.; and James Reiskytl, vice president, The Northwestern Mutual Life Insurance Co., for the many hours they spent explaining the technical points of life insurance.

Introduction

A life insurance agent prospecting for new business paid a call on a man whose only life insurance coverage was a $20,000 group policy provided by his employer. His wife had only $25,000 of coverage. The couple had also bought their one-year-old son a $100,000 policy, which would provide a substantial windfall to them if he died, but it was hardly what the family needed for its current financial security.

Unfortunately, this is not an isolated case. According to a recent study by the American Council of Life Insurance, 42 percent of all adults carried less than $25,000 of life insurance coverage. The median coverage was only $15,000. Ironically, though, Americans seem to spare no expense when it comes to insuring their children, whose chances of dying are slim at best, and whose deaths would not cause great financial hardship for their families. In 1984 the median coverage on children was $5,000, one-third of the coverage for all adults.

Many people pay $400, $1,000, or even $2,000 a year for life insurance, often without much idea of what they are getting for their money. Reluctant to probe the complexities of death benefits, cash values, and ledger statements, consumers too often leave the buying decisions to their insurance agents. "Insurance is a trust-me product," says one industry official. Frequently that trust is misplaced, for most agents are paid to sell policies that generate the most money for their companies, rather than affordable policies that meet consumers' needs.

Although the insurance world may seem mysterious, it's well worth investigating. Life insurance is one of the most important and costly purchases a family makes. If you buy the wrong type of policy, you may be dangerously underinsured and may pay thousands of dollars more for your coverage than is necessary. A 35-year-old woman buying $200,000 worth of life insurance, for example, could save $15,000 or more over a 20-year period if she knew how to shop carefully for a policy. But chances are she wouldn't know where to get the correct information or, if she found it, how to interpret it for her own personal needs.

Insurance companies often succeed in making consumers believe that one policy is much like another. "Most of these companies have been in business for a hundred years," says a marketing official of the Prudential Insurance Company. "You're not going to get big differences in costs." But each time we've rated life insurance policies, we've found huge price differences. Unfortunately the insurance industry discourages cost comparisons. One agent, for example, told us that teaching consumers how to calculate the best buy in life insurance is a waste of time and only confuses the reader. "Most people cannot decide whether or not to buy, and how much," he said. "Asking them to analyze cost factors only delays the act of purchasing." It can also lose the agent a chance for a commission: Agents know they must close a sale immediately, or there may be no sale at all.

Currently, about 650 companies sell most of the life insurance in the United States. Ideally, so many sellers should mean a lot of price competition. But a few years ago, the Federal Trade Commission found that "price competition is so ineffective in the life insurance industry that companies paying 20-year rates of return of 2 percent or less compete successfully against companies paying 4 to 6 percent. This disparity should be contrasted with the banking industry, where differences of a quarter of a percent are considered to be competitively crucial." For the most part, the life insurance industry doesn't sell by price. Recently, however, some companies offering new products have promoted high rates of return on these policies, so buyers may have noticed some rate competition. But, as we point out throughout this book, shopping for the highest rate will not necessarily get you the cheapest policy.

HOW TO USE THIS BOOK

Consumers Union has reported on life insurance since 1937, and has conducted major cost comparison surveys in 1946, 1967, 1974, 1980, and 1986. This book, our fifth on the subject, is based on our latest survey.

When we began our 1986 report, we found an industry that had changed dramatically since our last study in 1980. Companies had dressed up their traditional policies to make them more attractive to buyers—for instance, offering interest rates that fluctuated with market conditions. They had even invented brand-new policies that were designed to compete handily in the market with other financial instruments. These concessions to the marketplace, however, have also enormously increased the potential for buyer confusion. It is our hope that this book—up-to-date and relatively free of industry jargon—will help to guide you through the frustrating maze of the new and not-so-new life insurance policies and practices.

The organization of this book follows the sequence of steps the consumer takes when setting out to buy a life insurance policy. Part I helps you decide whether you need life insurance—and if you do, how much. We explain how an insurance company evaluates you as a prospective customer, and discuss the difficulties in obtaining coverage faced by consumers who have certain health problems. We also show you how to estimate the amount of one kind of insurance that wage earners already have: their Social Security benefits.

Part II describes the four major types of life insurance policies available today: term, whole life, universal life, and variable life. We explain how each of these types of policies works and how to decide which one is right for you. A checklist at the end of each chapter is designed to help you make your own comparisons among the policies agents may offer you. We also discuss insurance riders—features that agents like to tack onto policies at an extra cost to you—and tell you which ones are worth buying.

Part III gives you advice on how to cope with today's insurance marketplace. We explore the wisdom of switching insurance policies and help you cut through the hype of the agent's sales pitch.

We also discuss life insurance companies and how the consumer can select among them. What does it mean when an agent says he or she represents a "quality" company? What do the ratings in Best's Insurance Reports ratings mean? What is the likelihood of your present insurance company becoming insolvent just when you need it most? Finally, we provide sample letters you can use when you encounter a problem with a life insurance policy. Use these letters to write to an insurance company about its failure to settle a claim, for instance, or to write to an insurance regulator about an agent's failure to give you cost information. The letters are easy to follow, and you can adapt them to your own circumstances.

In Part IV, appendix A supplies the Ratings for the term, whole life, and universal life policies that appeared in *Consumer Reports* in June, July, and August of 1986. Because the life insurance industry today is changing so rapidly, we realize these Ratings may be out of date by the time you read this book. But they will give you a way to compare policies, as well as provide you with some idea of the huge cost differences among policies on the market today. Moreover, even if some of the information is obsolete, you won't find any other comparable source of life insurance information in bookstores.

Part IV also contains six other appendixes that supply important information on calculating the real cost of policies, as well as a list of states that have cost disclosure regulations and guaranty associations that protect policyholders in case their insurance company becomes insolvent. The glossary that follows defines commonly used insurance terms.

Buying life insurance isn't one of life's pleasures, but we hope this book will make the task a little easier. Too often life insurance is sold, not bought. We'd like to change that. If you read each chapter carefully and use the worksheets provided, you'll be able to buy the policy you really need and want at a price you can afford, not the policy an agent wants to sell you.

PART I

Before You Buy

1

Why Have Life Insurance?

Life insurance isn't fun to buy. You can't wear it, eat it, or decorate your house with it. It doesn't bring you the same pleasure as a new dress, fine chocolates, or Japanese prints on the wall. In fact, buying life insurance can be painful. It forces you to think about your own death, a subject most people prefer not to confront.

Sometimes even people who know they need life insurance are too passive about shopping for a policy. A Prudential agent in Chicago put it this way: "In twenty-four years I've had no more than five or perhaps ten people call me up and say 'I need life insurance,' but I've had hundreds of calls for auto and homeowners insurance." Or people put off the decision until they meet an agent who then sells them a policy that may not be right for their needs. All too often, when agents do call on prospects, they sell them policies that provide too little coverage at too high a premium. Sometimes, too, because it's hard to say no to an agent, many buyers build an inventory of several small policies that don't add up to much coverage. One 59-year-old woman in Chicago, who was providing income for her dependent grandchildren, owned thirty-eight policies totalling only about $60,000. That's hardly an efficient way of providing coverage for a family.

The overriding reason for buying life insurance is to provide an income for your dependents should you die prematurely. Of course, you can also use life insurance as an investment, as a tax shelter, and to help pay estate taxes. In this chapter we'll briefly discuss all these uses, but we can't emphasize strongly enough that the paramount need for insurance is as a replacement for the family breadwinner's salary should he or she die tomorrow.

LIFE INSURANCE AS INCOME REPLACEMENT

Most American families are underinsured. The median amount of life insurance on all adults in 1984 was only $15,000. Try to put yourself in your survivors' shoes, and imagine having to stretch that sum to cover the house payments and the children's college educations, not to mention everyday living expenses. Of course, you *can* forgo buying life insurance on the chance you'll live to be 99. But that's a gamble you probably shouldn't take.

Who, then, needs life insurance?

Families with Young Children

If you have young children, you definitely need a lot of life insurance. The younger your children, the more years they'll need to be supported—sometimes past their twenty-second birthdays if you intend to pay for their college educations.

Do both parents need life insurance? Historically, companies have viewed life insurance as a man's product, because traditionally the husband worked while his wife stayed home with the children. But today many wives are wage earners. Almost half of all women with a child less than one year old are in the work force, either as one provider in a two-income family or, in many cases, as the sole breadwinner. These women need insurance.

If your family is a traditional one, is it necessary to insure the person staying at home with the children? Unquestionably, the premature death of the homemaker brings many additional expenses to the family. There will be funeral costs and possibly medical expenses, and the surviving spouse often has to hire a full-time person to care for the house and the children.

The family's savings may be adequate to cover these additional expenses. If they aren't, then insuring the homemaker's life is probably wise. But before buying life insurance on a nonworking spouse, ask yourself first: Are you, the breadwinner, adequately insured? The wage earner must have sufficient coverage before buying a policy on the nonworking spouse. Unfortunately, it's often a struggle for many families to pay the premiums on one life insurance policy. Paying an additional premium can drain away money needed for essentials such as food, clothing, and health care. Necessities come first in the family budget.

Families Without Young Children

Couples without children may or may not need life insurance. The test is whether your mate would suffer financial hardship if you died tomorrow. If he or she can earn a reasonable living without you, don't waste your money on insurance premiums. (Many of today's white-collar professional couples fall into this group.) But if your mate depends on your income, by all means consider buying insurance to provide an income for him or her after your death.

Recently insurance companies and their agents have begun targeting a new market for life insurance: couples who are approaching retirement and whose children are grown. More than likely these couples had traditional families in which the wife stayed home and raised the children and the husband worked. The wife may still be at home, or may have entered the work force late in life. She probably will not have an adequate retirement income of her own.

If you're in your fifties and still working, you may want to consider buying life insurance to provide an income for your spouse after your death. But before you do, pay close attention to the section "Life Insurance or a Joint and Survivor Annuity?" in chapter 2 (page 20).

Families in Retirement

Insurance agents try to make a strong case for owning life insurance after retirement; one agent even suggested to us that old age is the best time to buy a policy. They reason that if one spouse dies, the other can live on the proceeds of the policy. We disagree. We view the primary purpose of life insurance as protecting dependents against the consequences of the loss of income should the breadwinner(s) die prematurely. Once a person or a couple reaches retirement age, the situation changes. Then, the primary need in most cases becomes adequate retirement income.

Most—though not all—people who have cash value life insurance should cash it in when they reach retirement age, invest the money, and use the proceeds for their living expenses. It's usually an unwise financial move to continue paying for life insurance when you're no longer earning an income, and you're gambling that one spouse will die early enough to supplement the otherwise inadequate financial resources of the other. Of course, insurance agents say you may want to use life insurance for other purposes—to build an estate for your heirs, for example. But many retirees don't have enough money to pay for life's necessities. For these people, spending money on an insurance premium is not practical.

A few couples in retirement may want to keep their cash value policies if the policy is paid up, provides a very high rate of return, or if cashing in the policy results in a large tax bill they may have trouble paying. If the policy is not paid up, these couples may want to stop paying premiums and take a reduced amount of paid-up insurance, or take out a policy loan if they are strapped for living expenses.

Single People

If you're a single person supporting an aged parent who would suffer financial distress if you died, you need life insurance. But if you have no dependents, you may be better off spending the money on a Caribbean vacation or investing it for your future needs.

Agents have a vast arsenal of sales pitches meant to encourage single people to buy life insurance. For example: Buy insurance now so you'll have it later when you really need it. After all, they say, the rates are cheaper when you're young and healthy. Later on, you might get sick and become uninsurable. The odds, however, are against that happening. Even if you did get sick, many illnesses that once would have disqualified you from getting adequate coverage, such as mild forms of diabetes, no longer do. Buying insurance when you don't need it is a waste of money, no matter how cheap the rates. Unless you have a family history of some chronic and crippling disease and there's a high probability you may contract it, ignore this argument.

An agent may also try to persuade you that you need insurance to pay for your burial expenses. Before taking out a policy for this purpose, check the balance in your savings account. When you die, your savings may well be adequate to cover this expense. Also check with your employer; you may have minimal life insurance as one of your benefits. And don't fall for the argument that you need life insurance in order to benefit your favorite charity. Leaving money to the Anywhereville Boys Home is a generous act on your part, but it hardly constitutes a real need for life insurance.

Children

Children generally don't need life insurance, because they have no incomes to replace and their parents normally don't count on them for support. Nevertheless, children are a favorite target of life insurance salespeople. As we've noted, the median coverage on children in 1984 was $5,000, not an insignificant amount when you consider that the median coverage for all adults was only $15,000. Because the odds are against children dying, the rates are low, and agents often suggest tacking children's coverage onto the parents' policies for a very small additional premium. Buy enough to bury the child and you'll rest easier at night, agents argue. But funeral costs are minimal compared with the cost of raising a child over a number of years. Money spent on children's coverage would be better spent to increase the often inadequate coverage on the family wage earner.

LIFE INSURANCE AS A TAX SHELTER

In an age when almost everyone is looking for tax breaks, insurance agents have their own version. Cash value life insurance policies, which we'll discuss in detail in chapters 5, 6, and 7, do offer certain tax advantages. The money you accumulate in those policies over the years is tax-deferred until it is withdrawn. At that time, you'll probably pay taxes only on the amount withdrawn that exceeds the premiums you've paid and dividends (if any) you've received. And if your heirs collect a death benefit from the policy, they'll pay no taxes on the money they receive. The insurance industry has lobbied long and hard to retain this tax advantage, which Congress left untouched when it rewrote the tax laws in 1986.

Should you then buy life insurance as a tax shelter? Consider the tax advantages of life insurance only after you've purchased enough coverage to provide for your family should you die prematurely. And even then you may find other tax-advantaged investments that are more attractive. The new tax law lowers everyone's marginal rate, so if you were in the 45-percent tax bracket and are now in the 28-percent bracket, you may have less need to shelter your money. On page 83 we discuss how to determine whether a particular life insurance policy is a good tax shelter.

LIFE INSURANCE AS AN INVESTMENT

When you buy a cash value policy, the life insurance company, like all financial intermediaries, takes your money, invests it at a profit, and pays you for the use of it. Although we discuss several kinds of cash value policies you can use as an investment, the basic principle is the same: Companies collect your premium, deduct their expenses and charges for insurance protection, and invest the rest.

If a company's investments do well, the company has extra earnings to share with its policyholders. These extra earnings are called *excess interest*, and companies share it in different ways depending on the kind of policy you own. If you own a participating whole life policy, extra interest is shared through higher dividends. If you own a universal life policy, excess interest is credited directly to cash values. If you own a variable life policy, excess interest buys a larger death benefit and is credited directly to cash values. In fact, how companies distribute excess interest is the key to understanding the policies we describe in this book.

The life insurance industry has traditionally pushed its cash value policies as "forced" savings plans. But, as savings plans go, they have historically ranked somewhere near the bottom of the heap because of the extra fees and charges built into the policy that affect the actual return. Investing through a life insurance policy was also expensive because companies built their agents' commissions into the premium. Also, for the most part, insurance investments are not very liquid. That's a point worth considering if you decide to combine insurance protection with the investment aspects of a life insurance policy.

Today, new kinds of policies have rates of return that are closer to those of other savings instruments, and an agent may try to impress you with a policy's investment potential. Indeed, sales pitches now tend to emphasize insurance more as a lucrative investment than as a form of death protection. But don't let such sales arguments sidetrack you. Insurance as death protection always comes before insurance as an investment.

Should you consider insurance as an investment once your family protection needs have been met? Perhaps, but remember that some policies are better investments than others. In chapter 5 we'll discuss in detail how to find the best ones.

INSURANCE IN ESTATE PLANNING

For a number of years, agents have promoted insurance policies as a way of passing money on to your heirs tax-free. After all, death benefits from insurance policies are not subject to federal or state income taxes. Agents have also argued that the proceeds from a policy can help your survivors pay estate settlement costs, including estate taxes. However, for the average family, estate tax arguments have little relevance. Congress has significantly lowered estate taxes over the years, and you must accumulate an estate of more than $600,000 before Uncle Sam takes his share. Most families don't have estates anywhere near that amount. The U.S. Census Bureau found that the median net worth of all white households in 1984 was only $39,000, while for black families it was $3,400. Consequently, in 1987 only one percent of all estates owed any federal taxes. As you can see, buying insurance as a form of tax-free estate planning for your heirs is hardly worth the trouble or expense for the average family.

2

How Much Insurance Is Enough?

When our reporter shopped around for life insurance, one agent told her she needed insurance equal to five times her income, which would have given her $245,000 of coverage. Another agent recommended $250,000 to $300,000. A third plucked the figure $100,000 out of the air. Actually, after analyzing her own insurance needs, she found that about $200,000 of coverage was adequate.

Too often agents fail to analyze a customer's insurance needs properly. Rule-of-thumb estimates such as five or eight times your income are simply guesses that may produce too little or too much coverage. Carry too little insurance and you may not be able to provide a reasonable standard of living for your family after your death. Carry too much and you may not enjoy a reasonable standard of living while you're alive.

The only way you can accurately figure out how much insurance to buy is to analyze your needs using worksheet 1 on page 13. Don't be alarmed if the analysis reveals that you need $100,000, $200,000, or even $300,000 of coverage. Many families with young children do. In 1986 we conducted a survey of our readers' finances and weren't surprised to find that many of our subscribers were inadequately insured. Among the households we surveyed, 39 percent carried less than $50,000 of coverage. Only 40 percent carried $100,000 or more, a figure more in line with our recommendations over the years.

Some agents have told us that even when they do a thorough needs analysis, many consumers resist buying the amount of insurance indicated. "It's hard to convince a factory worker that his wife needs $200,000 of coverage," one State Farm agent told us. Researchers have found that it's difficult for people to grasp the idea of insuring against an uncertainty. When you buy life insurance, you're asked to commit hard cash to protect your family against an event you'd rather not think about and believe can't possibly happen, at least not for a long while. But if you should die suddenly and your family is left without adequate support, you can't learn from your mistake. There's no substitute for a thorough evaluation of your financial needs and the purchase of the right amount of insurance.

WHO SHOULD FILL OUT THE WORKSHEET?

Anyone who has income to protect should complete the needs analysis worksheet. That means *both* husbands and wives. Married people may have completely different insurance needs, depending on how much they earn. A wife, for example, who earns less than her husband will need less insurance coverage, but she'll require coverage nonetheless.

USING THE WORKSHEET

The first part of worksheet 1 helps you figure what your family's expenses would be if you died tomorrow. The expenses fall into two broad categories: final expenses such as estate taxes, probate costs, and funeral expenses, and funds for future needs such as daily living expenses and future educational costs for the children. The second part of the worksheet analyzes your assets and any income sources your family can use to cover expenses. Once you've calculated both your family's income needs and your assets, subtract the assets from the needs. The result is the amount of additional life insurance you should buy.

The worksheet is personal; there are no right or wrong answers. The answers depend on your goals and the assumptions you make about your job, education plans, and so on. Don't forget to include Social Security benefits. We discuss those on page 22.

We've used, as an example, an analysis of the insurance needs of a working mother. We'll call her Kristine Hill.

Your Family's Immediate Expenses

The first part of the worksheet has entries for the immediate expenses your family would face after your death. These could include estate taxes, probate costs, funeral expenses, and uninsured final medical expenses.

Estate Taxes. Generally, everything you own—your house, bank accounts, stocks, jewelry, automobiles—becomes part of your estate. Property you bequeath to your spouse, however, is not subject to estate tax. (If your estate exceeds $600,000, you can figure your tax obligation with the help of government publication 448, "Federal Estate and Gift Taxes." Call 1-800-424-1040 to request a copy.)

Keep in mind that state inheritance taxes or state estate taxes can be substantial if you leave a large estate. An *inheritance* tax is levied on each heir's share of the estate. An *estate* tax is levied on the total value of the estate. Some states follow federal law and allow you to pass your estate to a spouse tax-free. Check with your lawyer or tax advisor to find out whether your estate would be subject to these state taxes. Kristine Hill's estate, for instance, would owe no tax because New York permits an estate to pass tax-free to a spouse, and her husband is the sole beneficiary.

You can decide whether to include your life insurance policies in your estate. Under current tax law, you can exclude them if you allow someone else to own the policy and if the policy's death proceeds don't pay off a debt of your estate or benefit your estate in any way. Transferring the ownership of the policy, however, means that you can't borrow on it, use it as collateral for a loan, or even name the beneficiary. In other words, you have completely relinquished control over the policy. Another common technique for keeping life insurance proceeds out of an estate is to set up an irrevocable trust, contributing the insurance policy to the trust. In that case, you would be able to designate the beneficiary of the policy (i.e., of the trust) but you would lose control over other aspects of the policy, such as borrowing against it, or changing the beneficiary.

Of course, the borrowing feature may be one of the reasons why you selected a cash value policy in the first place. If you expect to have

WORKSHEET 1
HOW MUCH LIFE INSURANCE DO YOU NEED?

	Kristine Hill	Your needs
What you need		
Immediate expenses		
Federal estate taxes	$_____*0*_____	$_____
State inheritance taxes	_____*0*_____	_____
Probate costs	_____*0*_____	_____
Funeral costs	_*5,000*_	_____
Uninsured medical costs	_*1,000*_	_____
Total final expenses	$_*6,000*_	$_____
Future expenses		
Family expense fund	_*179,800*_	_____
Emergency fund	_*10,000*_	_____
Child-care expenses	_____*0*_____	_____
College fund	_*61,200*_	_____
Fund for repayment of debts	_*500*_	_____
Total future expenses	$_*251,500*_	$_____
Total needs	$_*257,500*_	$_____

	Kristine Hill	Your assets
What you have now		
Cash and savings	$_*20,000*_	$_____
Equity in real estate	_____*0*_____	_____
Securities	_*38,000*_	_____
IRA and Keogh plans	_*9,000*_	_____
Employer savings plans [e.g. 401 (k) plans]	_*5,400*_	_____
Lump-sum employer pension benefits	_*7,300*_	_____
Current life insurance	_*66,000*_	_____
Other assets	_____*0*_____	_____
Total assets	$_*145,700*_	$_____

Extra insurance needed		
Total needs minus total assets		
Total needs	$_*257,500*_	$_____
Total assets	− _*145,700*_	− _____
Additional insurance needed	$_*111,800*_	$_____

a large estate and want to keep your taxable assets down by excluding a life insurance policy, think carefully before buying one. It also follows that if you are giving up the right to borrow on a policy as a strategy for minimizing your estate, an agent's argument for a policy that builds cash values may be less than persuasive.

Kristine Hill kept life insurance in her estate because it didn't affect the amount of estate taxes her heirs might have to pay.

Probate Costs. Assuming you have made a will, it may have to go through probate after your death. Probate is the legal process by which the state validates your will and makes sure all your debts are paid and your last wishes are carried out. Your will may be probated, especially if you have property in your own name, make special bequests, give property to your children, or set up trusts. The procedure can involve lawyers' fees, filing and administrative fees, and fees to your executor. A family member named as executor may choose not to take a fee.

Attorneys' fees vary from state to state and from lawyer to lawyer. Some states set a maximum fee based on a percentage of the estate's value. These are frequently measured on a sliding scale—for example, 10 percent on the first $20,000 of an estate's value, 4 percent on the next $50,000, and so on. Other states allow lawyers to charge "reasonable fees" based on the actual work they do. If your estate is complicated or relatives contest your will, probate costs can be high.

Discuss probate costs with your lawyer or tax advisor. Kristine Hill consulted her attorney and determined that her will probably would not have to go through probate because she is leaving everything to her husband and all of their property is jointly held. So she excluded probate expenses.

If you don't have a will—and we believe everyone should have one—the state will distribute your property and charge your estate for its work.

Funeral Expenses. If you want to go out in grand style, your funeral expenses can be staggering. But with intelligent cost-saving measures, your survivors can keep the funeral costs fairly low. The National Funeral Directors Association says that in 1988 individual funeral charges and casket costs will average about $3,000 across the country. Those figures don't include cemetery expenses, monuments, or miscellaneous items such as flowers, clergy fees, and transportation, which can double that figure. In our example, Kristine Hill allowed $5,000 for funeral expenses.

Social Security provides a token amount toward your funeral expenses. It will make that payment—currently $255—to your surviving spouse, providing he or she is living with you at the time of your death. Payment can also be made to a surviving child who is eligible for survivors benefits.

If you're a veteran, you might consider cutting your funeral expenses by opting for burial in one of sixty-four national cemeteries that still have available space. Veterans who were honorably discharged from the service, as well as their spouses and dependent children, can be buried there. The Veterans Administration (VA) picks up the tab for the burial, the headstone, and the perpetual care of the grave site. Even if you want to be buried in a private cemetery, the VA will provide a free headstone. If you don't want the free burial or free headstone, the VA provides an allowance for a headstone of your choice. In 1987, that allowance was $71, but the amount changes yearly.

The VA also provides other allowances if certain requirements are met. It will pay a veteran's survivors a burial allowance of $300 and a plot allowance of $150 if the veteran died as a result of a service-related disability, was entitled to a VA pension or compensation at the time of death, or died in a VA hospital.

Uninsured Medical Expenses. A terminal illness can be very costly, particularly if you don't have adequate medical insurance coverage. If you do, your medical and hospital coverage will probably pay almost all your medical expenses. Failing that, it's wise to budget several thousand dollars, perhaps as much as $10,000, for uninsured medical costs. Kristine Hill has a good medical plan where she works, so she thought $1,000 was enough to cover any uninsured expenses.

Your Family's Future Expenses

These expenses, which represent the bulk of your life insurance needs, include a family expense fund, an emergency fund, in some cases a child-care fund, a college fund, and a fund for repayment of debts.

Family Expense Fund. This is the estimated amount of money your family will need for its daily expenses. Here's how to figure it out:

STEP 1. Calculate your monthly take-home pay by multiplying your weekly take-home pay by 4.33 (the average number of weeks in a month). If your spouse has income, make the same calculation. Add the two figures to arrive at the family's total monthly take-home pay.

Kristine Hill figured her family's total monthly take-home pay was $3,378.

STEP 2. Decide how much of that amount your family would need to cover its expenses after your death. Most people estimate that about 75 percent of their current take-home pay is adequate because it costs two people more to live than one, but not twice as much. Kristine Hill figured that her family would need $2,534 per month. That included day-care costs, apartment rent, food, clothing, and transportation expenses.

If you want the family expense fund to cover mortgage payments, your survivors will keep on making monthly mortgage payments just as you do now. You may decide, though, that your insurance proceeds should pay off the mortgage entirely. In that case, include the outstanding amount under repayment of debts. If you have a separate mortgage insurance policy, consider your mortgage paid up for the purposes of the worksheet.

STEP 3. Determine the amount of monthly income your family will receive after you die. Include your spouse's take-home pay as well as survivors benefits from Social Security. (Most people can determine these benefits by looking at the table on page 26.) It is possible that survivors benefits from Social Security will provide all the income your family needs after your death. Include in this calculation any survivors benefits from company pensions. For most workers under 55, company pension benefits will be small. Ask your pension administrator to estimate them for you.

Kristine Hill figured her family could count on her husband's monthly take-home pay ($1,146) and Social Security survivors benefits (expected to be $833 a month). So, after her death, the family would have a monthly income of about $1,979.

STEP 4. Figure out the monthly shortfall—the amount by which your family's monthly income after you die falls short of the amount it needs—by subtracting the total in step 3 from the total in step 2.

Hill calculated that her family would need $2,534 per month after her death, but they could count on only $1,979. Her family would be about $555 a month short.

STEP 5. Multiply the monthly shortfall by 12 to arrive at an annual figure. In our example, that figure is $6,660 ($555 × 12).

STEP 6. Decide how many years your survivors will need the yearly income you determined in step 5. If your spouse is working and has a good company pension and substantial private savings (IRAs and Keoghs, for example), you may not need insurance proceeds for his or her retirement income. Many young two-career couples will probably fall into this category. If you want the fund to last longer—perhaps because your spouse doesn't work or has few prospects for a good retirement income—use a larger number of years. In effect, your insurance policy will provide part of your spouse's retirement income if you die. If you are older and no longer have insurance, see page 20.

Keep in mind that Social Security benefits to children end when they turn 18, and Social Security benefits to nonworking surviving spouses (the so-called mothers' or fathers' benefits) end when the youngest child reaches 16. A nonworking spouse will receive Social Security benefits again at age 60.

The Hills' only child is one year old now, so they need to provide seventeen years' worth of income for her support. Our couple wanted the wife's insurance to supplement her husband's retirement income for ten years. So Kristine Hill planned on buying enough insurance to make the family expense fund last for 27 years.

STEP 7. Multiply the number of years by the amount of annual income you need, determined in step 5. The Hills wanted 27 years of income, and figured the annual shortfall at $6,666. Multiplying the two figures, Kristine Hill concluded that the family expense fund should total $179,820.

We assume that the insurance fund would be invested upon Kristine Hill's death, and earn interest at a rate that exactly equals the rate of inflation. That's a fairly conservative assumption, but if you overestimate your needs it could balance an underestimate elsewhere, such as unanticipated medical expenses, unforeseen probate expenses, or the need for major repairs on the family home after your death. Keep in mind that the amount of the overestimate increases the more years you build into your calculation.

Emergency Fund. Every family should have an emergency fund. Some financial experts recommend $10,000 or $15,000. Others suggest two to six months' after-tax income. The Hills thought $10,000 was enough.

Child-Care Fund. For many couples, child-care expenses will already be factored into the family expense fund. That was the case for the Hills. But if one spouse is currently staying at home with the children, add an appropriate amount to the wage earner's coverage for possible child-care expenses if the surviving spouse must go to work. In 1986 the Conference Board, a business research organization, found that most parents were paying about $3,000 a year per child for out-of-home care. In some large cities the cost ran as high as $13,000. Figure how much the yearly child-care costs are likely to be in your area, and multiply that number by the number of years until your children can take care of themselves.

College Fund. You may want to provide a sum for your children's college education. The College Board, an organization that monitors college costs, says that for the 1986–87 school year, the *average* annual cost of a four-year private college was $10,199. That figure includes room and board, books, tuition, personal expenses, and some transportation costs. A comparable figure for a four-year public institution was $5,604.

If your children are nearing college age, those figures should remain reasonably accurate. If college is a long way off, interest earned on the insurance proceeds should help to offset future cost increases. Nevertheless, if college costs keep rising, it's best to update your life insurance needs analysis every five years or so.

The Hills wanted to provide for six years of college and postgraduate education for their daughter. They multiplied today's cost of $10,199 by 6 and got $61,194.

If your children attend private elementary or high schools, you may want your insurance proceeds to pay for their continuing education at those schools. If so, add an appropriate sum to your education fund.

Fund for Repayment of Debts. Because you probably want to leave your survivors as debt-free as possible, you could budget some insurance money for this purpose. A mortgage loan will probably be your biggest debt, but you may not want to enter it here. If you have a mortgage insurance policy that will pay off your mortgage when you die, or if you want your spouse to keep making the monthly payments, don't list your mortgage as a debt.

Do include other debts such as car loans and credit card purchases, unless they're already covered by separate credit life insurance policies. Check your loan agreements to see if credit life insurance has been included. (Credit life insurance is often very expensive. It's generally better to buy one big insurance policy than several small policies.)

Total Need. Add up all your immediate and future expenses and enter that figure on the appropriate line of the worksheet. Kristine Hill estimated her total insurance needs at $257,500.

What You Already Have

The next step is to add up all your assets that could be turned into cash in the event of your death. These may include cash and savings, equity in real estate, securities, IRA and Keogh plans, employer savings plans, employer lump-sum pension benefits, current life insurance, and miscellaneous assets such as art collections or assets from a business. Don't count any particular asset unless you expect your survivors to turn it into cash. For example, if you want your survivors to continue living in the family home, then don't count the equity that's been built up.

If your spouse uses the IRA or Keogh proceeds right away, he or she has to pay ordinary income taxes on the money. You may want to include among your assets the after-tax amount of your IRA or Keogh funds. To arrive at that amount, multiply your marginal tax rate by the total value of your account. Subtract that number from the total value, and the result will be the approximate after-tax amount your survivors could use. If your spouse doesn't need that money immediately, he or she could keep the money in the IRA or Keogh account, and the tax deferment will continue until the spouse reaches age 70½. If you're covered by a pension plan at work, check with your pension administrator to see if there will be a lump-sum survivors benefit payable upon your death. If there is, include it in your assets. If you've already listed a monthly pension benefit in step 3 of your family expense fund calculation, you probably won't have a lump-sum pension benefit. You normally get one or the other, but not both.

List any life insurance policies you already own. Like many people, you may have more than one. Include employer-provided group insurance and any policies you might have bought through the mail.

Kristine Hill catalogued her family's assets this way: cash and investments, $57,986; IRAs, $9,000 (she used before-tax value); employer 401(k) plan, $5,381; employer pension lump sum benefit, $7,270;

life insurance, $66,000, including $16,000 in group insurance from her employer. She owns no real estate and doesn't want her husband to sell their art and antique collections if she dies. The grand total of her assets is $145,700.

Extra Insurance Needed

Once you've determined your total needs and total assets, subtract the assets from the needs to arrive at the amount of additional insurance required. For most people, this amount is likely to be quite high. Kristine Hill needed about $257,500, but her total assets, including existing life insurance, came to only $145,700. The worksheet shows she needs an additional $111,800 of coverage to provide adequately for her family.

We recommend that you review your insurance needs every five years, and more frequently if your financial situation has changed significantly. The birth of a baby or the purchase of a house might mean you need more coverage. If you inherit money or if a child grows up and leaves home, you'll probably need less.

LIFE INSURANCE
OR A JOINT AND SURVIVOR ANNUITY?

If you are married and about to retire with a sizable pension, should you seriously consider buying a life insurance policy to take the place of the pension for your spouse when you die? Let's examine the various options available to the prospective retiree.

If you are married when you retire, you usually can take your pension in one of two ways. Under a *straight life annuity*, you receive the pension in equal monthly payments as long as you live, but your spouse receives nothing after your death. Under a *joint and survivor annuity*, you receive monthly payments that are less than those under a straight life annuity, but if your spouse survives you, he or she will continue to receive monthly payments until death.

The amount of those payments depends on the type of joint and survivor annuity you select. A *joint and 50-percent survivor annuity* provides your surviving spouse with half the monthly income you received when you were alive, and is the most common type of joint and survivor annuity. Under this option, your monthly payments at age

65 are usually reduced by 10 percent. A monthly pension of $1,000 would become $900 under such a joint and survivor annuity, and your surviving spouse would receive $450 monthly.

A *joint and 66²/₃-percent survivor annuity* provides your surviving spouse with two-thirds of the monthly income you received. A *joint and 100-percent survivor annuity* gives your surviving spouse the same monthly payments you received but produces the greatest reduction in your monthly pension payments when you are alive. A person eligible for a $1,000 monthly pension under a straight life annuity would receive only about $800 if he or she selected the joint and 100-percent survivor annuity.

In the past, husbands frequently rejected the joint and survivor option, leaving their widows stranded with little income in their later years. Furthermore, many women were totally unaware that their husbands had opted for a straight life annuity. The Retirement Equity Act of 1984 assured that both husbands and wives would have the chance to share in their spouses' pensions. Under this law, an employee can decline the joint and survivor option only with the consent of his or her spouse.

Where does insurance come in? Many companies and agents are trying to persuade employees that sharing a pension with a spouse is costly and financially unwise. Agents also want to make sure the surviving spouse is protected—but with a life insurance policy instead of a joint and survivor annuity. We disagree. Unless you know that your spouse is terminally ill at the time you retire, you're better off taking the joint and survivor annuity. If you're virtually certain you will outlive your dependent spouse, take a straight life annuity that will give you the highest monthly payment.

There are several reasons why buying life insurance may be far more costly in the long run than the difference between a pension from a straight life annuity and a pension from a joint and survivor annuity:

1. The insurance company has to pay its usual acquisition expenses, including the agent's commission, and these expenses can add up to as much as 100 percent of your first-year premium. Why pay these fees when you can get an annuity virtually free? There are no comparable expenses associated with the joint and survivor annuity.

2. Companies charge higher premiums to people who have health problems that often come with advancing years. You may not be as

insurable as you were in your younger days. If you *are* a substandard insurance risk, you should certainly choose the annuity option that provides your spouse with the most income until his or her death.

3. You may not be able to afford a very large policy because life insurance is always more expensive when you are older. An annuity is also a more efficient way of providing sufficient income for a surviving spouse because monthly income is reduced when you die. Life insurance in force at the time of your death may be far more than is necessary for your spouse's needs.

If these reasons don't convince you to take the annuity option, we suggest you fill out worksheet 2 to determine whether a life insurance policy is better than a joint and survivor annuity. We have used as our example an employee eligible for a $1,000 monthly pension taken as a straight life annuity or a $900 monthly pension taken as a joint and 50-percent survivor annuity. The employee is 65 years old and the spouse is 62. (We have used rates from a major life insurance company whose whole life policy does not pay dividends. If you're offered a lower cost whole life policy than the one we've used here, the results from the following calculation might be slightly more favorable for the life insurance option. But it's still doubtful that life insurance will turn out to be better than a joint and survivor annuity in the long run.)

In this example, the joint and survivor annuity pays $450 a month; the annuity bought with the life insurance proceeds pays $200 a month. Obviously, if the insurance buys less monthly income than the joint and survivor annuity, which often is the case, the joint and survivor option is the better buy.

WHAT SOCIAL SECURITY PAYS YOUR SURVIVORS

For most families, Social Security benefits are a major source of income when the breadwinner dies. If you don't consider them when estimating your life insurance needs, your calculation will lead you to purchase far more insurance than you actually need. Apparently some life insurance agents, taking advantage of the alleged uncertainty surrounding the Social Security system and its funding, are encouraging buyers to ignore these benefits when figuring their insurance requirements. Of course, it follows that if buyers don't count on Social Security sur-

WORKSHEET 2
COMPARISON OF PROCEEDS FROM LIFE INSURANCE
AND JOINT AND SURVIVOR ANNUITY

	Example		Your situation	
	Monthly	*Annual*	*Monthly*	*Annual*
Amount of monthly pension to employee (life annuity)	$1,000	$12,000	$	$
Amount of monthly pension to employee (joint and 50-percent survivor)	$900	$10,800	$	$
Amount of monthly pension to spouse (joint and 50-percent survivor)	$450	$5,400	$	$

STEP 1. Find the difference between your annual pension if you take a straight life annuity or if you take a joint and survivor annuity. In our example, the difference is $1,200. ($12,000 − $10,800 = $1,200)

STEP 2. Ask your insurance agent how large a policy you can buy with the difference. (You might want to compare several companies.) Enter the amounts in the columns below. (The agent will probably try to sell you whole life or universal life, arguing that term insurance premiums are too expensive at your age. We should add, however, that whole life premiums aren't exactly low-cost.) In our example we have assumed the $1,200 buys a $20,000 whole life policy.

Example	*Company A*	*Company B*	*Company C*
$20,000	$	$	$

STEP 3. How large an annuity guaranteed for your spouse's life will the face amount of the policy buy? Ask the agent. (You are converting the policy into monthly payments for your spouse.) Be sure to use the annuity rates for your spouse's sex and age at retirement and enter the amounts in the spaces below. In our example, the $20,000 death benefit could be converted into a straight life annuity paying $200 a month.

Example	*Company A*	*Company B*	*Company C*
$200	$	$	$

STEP 4. Compare these amounts to the amount of monthly income your spouse will receive if you take the joint and survivor annuity. In this example, the joint and survivor annuity pays $450 a month; the annuity bought with the life insurance proceeds pays $200 a month. Obviously, if the insurance buys less monthly income than the joint and survivor annuity, which often is the case, the joint and survivor option is the better buy.

vivors payments, the sales agent gets the chance to sell even bigger policies. Despite occasional rumors in the media, there is no indication that the Social Security system will fail in the near future or even later. It is on a sound financial footing well into the twenty-first century.

The monthly payments to survivors are a percentage of a certain "magic number" the Social Security Administration (SSA) calculates for you, based on your earnings record over a lifetime. That number is called your *primary insurance amount.* The actual amount your survivors receive depends on several factors: the amount of your past earnings, your age when you die, the ages of surviving family members, and the amount of income your spouse earns.

WHO RECEIVES THESE BENEFITS

Social Security survivors benefits are available for (1) surviving spouses 60 or older; (2) disabled surviving spouses 50 or older; (3) some surviving divorced spouses; (4) young children and their mothers and fathers; and (5) other family members in unusual circumstances.

Surviving Spouses

A surviving spouse under 60 receives benefits only if he or she is caring for young children and does not have substantial earnings. These benefits stop when the youngest child reaches 16, but they may start again when the spouse turns 60. Disabled spouses can receive benefits at 50.

If the surviving spouse earns less than a specified amount ($6,120 in 1988, or $8,400 for people age 65 to 69), Social Security pays the full benefit. (The earnings test does not apply for people age 70 and older.) If the spouse earns more than $6,120, the benefit is reduced by $1 for every $2 of earnings above that amount. In most cases, an employed spouse earning around $20,000 or more would receive no survivors benefits. The Social Security survivors benefits aren't affected if a surviving spouse gets investment income, pension benefits, or insurance proceeds.

If the spouse is caring for a child who was disabled before age 22, he or she receives a benefit for as long as the child remains disabled. A divorced spouse who was married to you for at least ten years (and isn't married to someone else now) is also eligible for survivors benefits.

Children

Social Security also pays benefits to surviving children until they are 18, whether or not their mother or father gets a benefit. Children can continue to receive benefits until their nineteenth birthday if they are still in high school. Unmarried children who were disabled before age 22 receive survivors benefits as long as they remain disabled. (The Social Security system used to provide benefits for college students, but gradually phased them out beginning in 1981.) If your child has sufficiently high earnings, his or her benefit could be reduced according to the earnings test. But few children have annual earnings of more than $6,120.

If you have three or more family members eligible for benefits, Social Security doesn't pay full benefits to each one. In that case, the family receives a *maximum* benefit, which is the highest amount any family is eligible for under the current law.

FIGURING THE BENEFIT

Because the formula that determines your primary insurance amount is complex, CU asked the Social Security Administration (SSA) to devise a simple table you can use to estimate what your survivors benefits would be if you died in 1988. See table 1 on page 26. It gives you an accurate estimate if (1) you have worked steadily since entering the work force at about age 22 or earlier, and (2) have received regular pay increases of average size. The estimates will be off if you've received either very small or unusually high pay raises over the years or if you've had many years without any earnings at all. The SSA estimates that about 60 to 70 percent of all workers can get a sufficiently accurate estimate from this table in order to figure their insurance needs. (That means the estimate should be within $25 to $75 of the actual monthly survivors benefit.)

If your work history does not fit the typical pattern, the table will give you only a rough approximation. You can, however, visit your local Social Security office and try to persuade a staff member to figure the benefit for you, or you can request help from SSA headquarters in Baltimore. Although in 1986 SSA officials told us they would gladly figure benefits for people whose wage patterns didn't neatly fit our table, the agency seems to have changed its mind since then. We urge

TABLE 1. SOCIAL SECURITY SURVIVORS BENEFITS

Approximate monthly benefit your family would receive if you died in 1988. The amounts shown are close approximations only if you have been employed steadily throughout your career and have had average wage increases.

Your age	Your family	Your earnings in 1987					
		$15,000	$20,000	$25,000	$30,000	$35,000	$43,800+
25	Spouse and 1 child[a]	$864	$1,060	$1,234	$1,324	$1,416	$1,582
	Spouse and 2 children[b]	1,064	1,266	1,441	1,547	1,654	1,847
	1 child only	432	530	617	662	708	791
	Spouse at age 60[c]	412	505	588	631	675	754
30	Spouse and 1 child[a]	$858	$1,052	$1,230	$1,320	$1,410	$1,572
	Spouse and 2 children[b]	1,055	1,260	1,436	1,542	1,647	1,836
	1 child only	429	526	615	660	705	786
	Spouse at age 60[c]	409	501	586	629	672	749
35	Spouse and 1 child[a]	$852	$1,044	$1,224	$1,314	$1,404	$1,534
	Spouse and 2 children[b]	1,043	1,252	1,430	1,534	1,639	1,791
	1 child only	426	522	612	657	702	767
	Spouse at age 60[c]	406	497	584	626	669	731
40	Spouse and 1 child[a]	$850	$1,042	$1,224	$1,312	$1,380	$1,462
	Spouse and 2 children[b]	1,040	1,251	1,429	1,533	1,611	1,708
	1 child only	425	521	612	656	690	731
	Spouse at age 60[c]	405	496	583	626	657	697
45	Spouse and 1 child[a]	$850	$1,040	$1,222	$1,294	$1,342	$1,402
	Spouse and 2 children[b]	1,039	1,250	1,427	1,511	1,568	1,638
	1 child only	425	520	611	647	671	701
	Spouse at age 60[c]	405	496	582	617	640	668
55	Spouse and 1 child[a]	$850	$1,040	$1,196	$1,254	$1,284	$1,322
	Spouse and 2 children[b]	1,038	1,249	1,398	1,464	1,500	1,545
	1 child only	425	520	598	627	642	661
	Spouse at age 60[c]	405	495	570	597	612	630
65	Spouse and 1 child[a]	$812	$996	$1,148	$1,192	$1,222	$1,260
	Spouse and 2 children[b]	998	1,192	1,340	1,392	1,427	1,471
	1 child only	406	498	574	596	611	630
	Spouse at age 60[c]	387	474	547	568	583	601

Your estimated survivors benefits: $_____

[a] Amount shown here also equals the benefit paid to two children if no parent survives. The same amount is also payable to a family with two children and a surviving parent who has substantial earnings.

[b] Equals the maximum family benefit.

[c] Amounts payable in 1988. Spouses turning 60 in the future will receive higher benefits.

you to write to the SSA anyway and see if the agency will help you.

The table shows benefits payable to various categories of survivors. All the examples assume the beneficiaries have either low earnings or no earnings and thus are eligible for full benefits. The "spouse with two children" category shows the maximum family benefit. The "spouse at age 60" category shows the amount payable in 1988. For a spouse turning 60 in the future, the benefit will be greater.

A surviving spouse who has worked and has an earnings record can receive Social Security retirement benefits based on that record. But people can't get both the retirement benefit and the survivors benefit at the same time. A spouse who has worked will receive an amount equal to either the survivors benefit or the retirement benefit, whichever is greater. Also, all Social Security benefits are automatically increased each year to match increases in the cost of living. This is a valuable adjustment not normally available from private insurance benefits.

To determine which family category to use, estimate how much your spouse will earn after your death. If he or she will earn less than $6,120 per year, use the "spouse and one child" or "spouse and two children" benefit, whichever is appropriate. Remember, the "spouse with two children" category is the maximum family benefit.

If your spouse will earn about $20,000 or more and you have one child, use the benefits for "one child only." If you have two or more children, use the category "spouse and one child" which, as we point out, is also the benefit for two children when a spouse earns substantial income.

Once you've estimated what your survivors would get from Social Security, enter that amount at the bottom of the table and in step 3 of the needs calculation on page 16.

Social Security may replace at least 75 percent of your family's take-home pay, and possibly more. Do you still need life insurance? It's quite possible that if you have the right combination of family members, Social Security will provide enough income, at certain times. But family circumstances can change. Remember, Social Security benefits stop when children reach 18. If the children go to college, your family will have even greater expenses, and any insurance proceeds will come in handy.

3

Are You a Good Insurance Risk?

Applying for a life insurance policy turns your medical history and daily health habits into an open book for the insurance industry. Obviously, no one will insure you if you are terminally ill. But companies and agents will race to insure you if you are vigorous and healthy because the chances of their having to pay off on your policy in the future are statistically very low.

How soon are you likely to die? American men who were 35 in 1986 can expect to live to age 74; women to age 78. Not everyone will live that long, of course, so the insurance industry tries to find clues that pinpoint when that event is likely to happen. You may smoke or drink too much, or recently had coronary-bypass surgery. Your occupation may be the problem—a crop duster or a miner may die sooner than a lawyer or an insurance agent. Your health, your parents' health, your occupation, and even your marital status can affect how insurance companies view you as a customer. If the company thinks you're a high risk, you will pay more for your insurance, or have trouble getting it at all. So a company often plays detective trying to learn as much as it can about your health and current life-style; it looks in a number of places for evidence.

THE APPLICATION

Buying insurance begins with the application. An eager agent may treat the application lightly and minimize its importance, but the answers you give determine whether the company decides to probe further. Different companies ask different questions, depending on how stringent their underwriting practices are and on how much insurance is involved. Generally, the questions on the application focus on your general health and your medical history. A company may want to know whether a doctor has treated you in the past twelve months for heart disease, stroke, or cancer. It may want to know whether you've recently had an electrocardiogram or are on medication for high blood pressure. One company may ask whether you've ever been treated for alcoholism, while another may simply ask how many drinks you regularly have per week. (An underwriter won't raise his eyebrows if you drink a few glasses of wine every day, but he might if you admit to drinking a bottle of scotch.) Some companies ask if another insurance company has ever rejected you, and if so, why.

Almost all applications ask whether you smoke, because your smoking habits are a key determinant of the rates you'll have to pay.

Occasionally a company will ask its agents to provide more information about you. Prudential, for example, wants to know whether a prospective customer races cars or skydives as a hobby. Prudential also expects to be informed when its agents know or suspect that an applicant drinks to excess, uses habit-forming drugs, or has a criminal record.

Many companies today ask questions about acquired immune deficiency syndrome (AIDS), and more will do so in the future. (If you have the disease or have tested positive for AIDS antibodies, you may as well forget about buying life insurance.) Insurance companies claim they haven't priced their policies to take into account the deaths resulting from the current AIDS epidemic, but they talk apprehensively about staggering losses if they are hit in the future with a large amount of AIDS-related claims from people who were insured before contracting the disease. Several companies, in fact, are now reducing the amount of insurance they offer to men and women who refuse to take blood tests for the AIDS virus.

The application also asks how much life insurance you want. The amount you specify must bear some relation to your income or other justifiable financial needs. If you make $10,000 a year and want $1 million of coverage, the company will probably decline.

Sometimes your answers to the questions on the application are enough for an insurance underwriter to assess you as a risk. If they aren't, the underwriter will request that you take a physical examination given by a medical doctor or by a paramedic who comes to your home. But the company pays, no matter who performs the exam.

THE MEDICAL EXAM

A person's age and the amount of insurance applied for usually determine whether the company will ask for a medical exam and how thorough it will be. "If a person is 45 or 50, a company may not offer as much insurance without an exam as it would if he were 25," says an officer of the Home Office Reference Laboratory in Kansas City, which performs laboratory tests for most of the insurance industry.

A doctor or a paramedic will measure your weight and height, take your blood pressure, collect blood and urine samples, and sometimes administer an electrocardiogram. A company may want to check the cholesterol or triglyceride levels in your blood or look for traces of nicotine in your urine. At some companies, nicotine screens are becoming routine as a way of tracking down people who lie about their smoking habits. Some companies are also testing blood samples for traces of drugs and for AIDS antibodies, especially from applicants they consider risky. Many companies are now requiring blood tests even if a person applies for as little as $150,000 of coverage.

Companies differ on how much insurance they will write for a customer without a medical exam. "There's continual competitive pressure to make the limits higher and bring in as much business as possible," says a senior officer at Northwestern Mutual. Companies try to balance the competitive pressures for new business with the risk of attracting some people who might be in poor health or with high-risk habits such as smoking. In fact, how a company strikes this balance determines the amount of life insurance you can buy without taking a medical exam. As you can see from table 2, some companies are far more liberal than others. You can't buy insurance at age 42 from Northwestern

Mutual without taking an exam, but at New York Life you usually can buy as much as $75,000.

MEDICAL INFORMATION BUREAU REPORTS

If the company underwriter is suspicious about something on your application, or if it doesn't match the results of a medical examination, he may check to see if there's a file on you at the Medical Information Bureau. This is an insurance company–sponsored computer data bank whose members exchange pertinent information about prospective policyholders. When you apply for life, health, or disability insurance, you usually sign a form giving the company permission to turn over to the Bureau information about your medical condition. A Bureau report, however, won't tell the new insurance company whether another company accepted or declined your application. Although the Bureau has been around for eighty-four years, the information in its files is fairly current—a computer automatically erases reports that are more than seven years old.

TABLE 2. AMOUNT OF INSURANCE GENERALLY AVAILABLE WITHOUT A MEDICAL EXAM FROM SELECTED COMPANIES

Company	Age 0–30	Age 31–35	Age 36–40	Age 41–45	Age 46–50
Connecticut Mutual	$300,000[a]	$199,999	$199,999	$50,000	$50,000
Kemper Investors Life	300,000[b]	300,000[b]	300,000[b]	150,000[b]	150,000[b]
Lincoln National	200,000[c]	200,000	150,000	75,000	50,000
Massachusetts Mutual	200,000	100,000	50,000	25,000	0
New York Life[d]	1,000,000	500,000	150,000	75,000	35,000
Northwestern Mutual	200,000	100,000	50,000	0	0
Prudential	500,000	250,000	100,000	50,000	25,000
Union Central	300,000	300,000	200,000	100,000	100,000

[a] $350,000 for ages 0–20.
[b] Net amount at risk, not face amount.
[c] $150,000 for ages 0–15.
[d] Blood tests required for all policies above $150,000, regardless of applicant's age.

YOUR OCCUPATION

An insurance company will also consider your occupation. In life insurance, rating you by your current occupation is not as common as it once was, although it is still important if you apply for an individual health insurance policy. Most companies judge a few occupations as more hazardous than others. Smoke jumpers, underground miners, rodeo riders, and high climbers in the lumber industry, for instance, obviously will pay more for life insurance. If you're in one of these risky occupations, a company tacks an extra flat charge onto the basic premium each year. Businessmen's Assurance Company, for instance, will charge an underground miner an extra $2 per $1,000 of insurance or $200 on a $100,000 policy, but a smoke jumper will pay an extra $5 per $1,000 or $500 on a $100,000 policy.

YOUR SMOKING HABITS

If you don't smoke, most insurance companies will give you a price break because, as a group, nonsmokers are likely to live longer than smokers. Nonsmokers will often pay as much as 40 or 50 percent less for a life insurance policy than smokers, depending on the kind of policy and the company's rating schemes. Some companies have smoker and nonsmoker rates in their standard class, while others have both in their preferred class. At some companies, the nonsmoker rate is the preferred rate. (For an explanation of these classifications, see pages 34–35.) Lately, many companies are classifying users of chewing tobacco as smokers. Former smokers, however, can usually qualify for nonsmoker rates if they have completely stopped smoking for at least a year.

Occasionally you may find a company that gives initial discounts to smokers as a marketing incentive. Crown Life, based in Toronto, offered a "smokers discount" to buyers of its universal life policy. For the first two years of the policy's life, smokers got a price break. If they stopped smoking for twelve months, the company continued to charge them the same premium as it did nonsmokers. But policyholders who didn't stop smoking had to pay higher premiums after the first two years.

INVESTIGATIVE REPORTS

A company may conduct its own research on your daily habits and medical history, or it may ask an outside agency to furnish the information. If you are applying for $500,000 worth of insurance, for instance, the company will want a thorough report, although sometimes even requests for less insurance can trigger such an investigation.

The investigator interviews you in person or on the phone to confirm the data on your application. He or she may talk to your spouse, friends, or business associates about your daily habits and sometimes your financial affairs. According to Equifax Services, a prominent investigative agency based in Atlanta, investigators may ask about your current marital situation; if you are applying for $1 million of insurance while in the midst of a divorce action, the insurance company would like to know about it.

Occasionally, according to Equifax, an investigator uncovers something an applicant forgot to mention: frequent trips to the Middle East, for example, or too many martinis for lunch every day. Such facts may be red flags to an insurance company. Besides scrutinizing your smoking habits, the company may also check your driving record. Companies aren't keen on insuring drunk drivers or chronic speeders.

MEASURING THE RISK

When the company feels it has sufficient information, it "underwrites" you—that is, it determines the rate you'll pay: standard, substandard, or preferred. To do that, it views you as a sort of balance sheet. Every applicant starts with 100 points; the underwriter subtracts credits for favorable findings and adds debits for unfavorable ones. For example, you might get 30 credits if you've never smoked, but only 20 credits if you've stopped for a year. You might get 10 credits if your blood pressure is normal and 20 credits for a favorable cholesterol level. If your cholesterol level is abnormally high, a company might dock you 20 debits, or, if your father died of a heart attack at age 47, you'd lose 20 more points. The underwriter then adds up the debits and subtracts the credits to arrive at your final score.

Standard Rates

If your score is low, you'll be rated *standard*. That means you have no significant health problems and your chances of dying are about average for your age group. One company may include more people in its standard class than another company, and therefore sets lower requirements for obtaining a standard policy. Over the last few years, about 87 percent of all life insurance policies were issued at standard rates.

Substandard Rates

If your score is high, that means you have a greater than average chance of dying in the next few years, and the company's underwriter will classify you as *substandard*. The higher your score, the higher your classification, and the more you'll pay for your insurance. Someone with mildly elevated blood pressure, for instance, will pay less than someone whose blood pressure is extremely high and uncontrolled. If you're a poor risk, the company may also restrict the amount of coverage you can buy, or may even decline to insure you at all.

Most companies use rating tables to determine the extra premium for substandard applicants who buy term or universal life policies. (If you buy whole life, companies add a predetermined extra amount to the basic premium to reflect the extra risk an applicant represents. This extra cost is leveled out over the life of the policyholder.) Table 3 shows how the severity of a chronic illness or impairment affects the cost of a $100 term insurance premium.

Different companies don't necessarily view particular illnesses or impairments the same way. One company may charge a higher premium for a particular illness than another. Table 4 shows how two companies rate people with various forms of diabetes.

A company's rating table as well as its overall rate structure determine what you will ultimately pay if you're a substandard risk. At Company A, for example, a 35-year-old male nonsmoker who had an illness that placed him in the insurance company's Table 2 would pay a first-year premium of $198 for $100,000 of term insurance. At Company B, he would pay $292 for the same coverage. Company B charges more for its standard policy than Company A, so it follows that its substandard policies will cost more. As shown on table 4 (page 36),

TABLE 3. RELATIONSHIP BETWEEN SEVERITY OF ILLNESS AND COST OF A TERM INSURANCE PREMIUM

Rating table	Percentage increase in term insurance cost	Effect on a $100 term insurance premium
Standard	0%	$100
1	25	125
2	50	150
3	75	175
4	100	200
5	125	225
6	150	250
7	175	275
8	200	300
10	250	350
12	300	400
16	400	500

Company B also rates certain kinds of diabetics higher than Company A does.

If you're a substandard risk, you may have to shop several companies before you find one that will accept you at a rate you can afford.

Preferred Rates

The score on your balance sheet may be so low that a company will offer you its *preferred* rate, which is the best rate a company can offer its customers. Not every company has a preferred rate, but those that do have stringent qualifying requirements. Southern Farm Bureau, for example, usually considers your driving record, and prefers that you maintain a regular exercise program. At the North American Company for Life and Health, a successful applicant for a preferred rate cannot hold a pilot's license, and his or her parents must not have contracted cardiovascular disease before their 60th birthday. At John Hancock, preferred means that you are in exceptionally good physical condition with normal build and average weight and height; your family history indicates above-average longevity; and "your financial stability,

TABLE 4. HOW TWO INSURANCE COMPANIES RATE DIABETIC CONDITIONS

Age at onset (years)	Current age (years)	Severity of illness	Company A's rating table	Company B's rating table
55	60	Well controlled, regular doctors' visits	Standard	Standard to 2
45	50	Controlled by diet alone, no associated impairments or complications	Standard	1–4
45	50	Controlled by diet alone, only associated impairment is hypertension	4	3–4
25	30	Well controlled, regular doctors' visits	3	6
25	30	Regular doctors' visits, only complications have been two episodes of acidosis or coma within past three years	5	12
15	20	Well controlled, regular doctors' visits	8	14
Any	Any	Major complications or impairments such as several recent episodes of acidosis or coma, severe hypertension, frequent severe insulin reactions, or chronic kidney disease	Decline	Decline

habits, character, business, and home environments [are] of a high standard."

Even if you qualify for a particular company's preferred rate, however, it may not be the lowest rate available. One company's standard rate may be lower than another's preferred rate. Look at the Ratings in the back of this book and you'll see that preferred policies are not clustered at the top, but are scattered throughout the tables.

Guaranteed Acceptance Policies

Over the past few years, some companies have been promoting life insurance policies aimed at those who have serious health problems and who normally may be uninsurable. Using celebrities to pitch the insurance, these companies offer guaranteed acceptance to virtually anyone who can pay the premium. Although the companies themselves do little or no underwriting on these policies, the coverage is usually much more expensive than life insurance provided by other companies. The benefits may be limited as well. A policyholder, for example, may have no coverage during the first two policy years.

We urge you to look carefully at these policies. If you have a health problem, you might be better off paying the substandard rates offered by another carrier than investing your money in these costly policies. Learn to compare policies using the interest-adjusted net cost indexes discussed in chapters 4 and 5.

TELLING THE TRUTH

If you deliberately omit or lie about something important on your insurance application, and you die during the contestable period— within two years of buying the policy—you can put your surviving dependents in financial jeopardy. The insurance company can deny all or part of the claim.

Companies complain, for example, that applicants don't always tell the truth about their smoking habits. Based on the percentage of people in the general population who smoke, companies say there should be more smokers among their applicants. "We're seeing a higher percentage of people applying for nonsmoker rates than we believe qualify," says a vice president at State Mutual of America, the company that pioneered nonsmoker rates. Today, many companies are testing applicants for cotinine, a byproduct of nicotine that lingers in the urine for several days. Others are keeping close tabs on agents to make sure they are reporting accurate information.

If you lie about your smoking habits and subsequently die of lung cancer or a smoking-related disease, a company can reduce the amount it will pay your survivors. Instead of receiving the full face amount of the policy, your beneficiaries may only get a sum that represents what your paid premiums would have bought at the company's smoker rate.

The Canadian Life and Health Insurance Association, a trade group of 100 insurance companies in Canada, recommends that its members simply void a policy if it discovers, during the contestable period, that the policyholder has lied. After the contestable period is over, the Association suggests that companies void the policy if there's a reasonable chance of proving fraud. Many Canadian companies write policies in the United States.

CHECKING YOUR RECORDS

While you have an obligation to tell the truth when you apply for insurance, the investigative companies that keep files on you also have an obligation to collect and maintain accurate information. To see that they do, the Fair Credit Reporting Act gives you the right to see the information in the files and to make corrections if necessary.

To obtain a copy of your record at the Medical Information Bureau, write to the Bureau at P.O. Box 105, Essex Station, Boston, MA 02112, or phone 617-426-3660. The Bureau will disclose medical information only to a medical professional you designate, but will give nonmedical information directly to you. To obtain a copy of your investigative report from Equifax Services, contact the local Equifax office listed in the telephone directory. There are 600 of them around the country. You can also write to the Director of Consumer Affairs, Equifax Services, P.O. Box 4081, Atlanta, GA 30302.

PART II

The Different Types
of Policies

4

Term Insurance

Term insurance is the poor cousin of the insurance industry. Few companies want to sell it, and few agents will suggest that you buy it. Some won't even tell you about it. If they do, they may say that term insurance is just not good enough for you. The truth is that most companies would rather sell the more profitable whole life or universal life policies, even if these types of policies leave you underinsured.

Even the supposedly impartial insurance regulators may make term insurance difficult to buy. Some years ago, Jeffrey Miller, a Colorado agent representing several insurance companies, placed an ad in a local newspaper explaining term and urging consumers to seriously consider buying this type of life insurance. The state's insurance commissioner, a longtime opponent of term, wrote to the companies Miller represented, asking them if they would have participated in the ad if the agent had included their names in it. Miller was fired from five of the ten companies he represented; one of the companies admitted that the letter was pressure it couldn't afford to ignore. Miller sued the commissioner and eventually won $40,000 in damages.

For nearly fifty years, we have recommended that most buyers choose term insurance for their families' needs. With other types of life insurance, you might not be able to afford adequate coverage. For example, when we conducted our insurance cost survey in 1986, we found that a 35-year-old woman buying the top-rated term policy would pay $200 the first year for $200,000 of protection. She would pay $2,000 for the same amount of coverage from one of the top-rated whole life policies in the study.

True, term insurance premiums increase as you get older. But the annual premium for the lowest-cost term policy in our study doesn't exceed $2,000 until the twenty-first year. Long before then, the typical family may find that its insurance needs have declined substantially.

WHAT IS TERM INSURANCE?

Term insurance provides coverage for a specific time period or term— often as short as one year, or as long as ten or fifteen years. If you die during that time, the insurance company promises to pay the face amount of the policy to your beneficiaries, provided, of course, that you've continued to pay your premiums.

The insurance company may guarantee in advance that it will renew the policy for another term, without any need for you to prove you're still insurable. Many term policies potentially provide coverage for life—that is, they can be renewed until age 100. Some can be renewed only until 65 or 70. Still others are nonrenewable.

The amount of coverage during the term usually remains level. In other words, if you bought a $50,000 *level term* policy for five years, your coverage would always be $50,000. Sometimes, though, the coverage can increase or decrease. If, for example, you bought a $50,000 *decreasing term* policy to cover a mortgage loan, your coverage would decline as the outstanding amount of the mortgage declined.

Your annual premiums usually stay constant during each policy term. With each renewal, though, the premiums go up. That's because you're older and your chances of dying during the new term of the policy are greater. Actuaries call this *attained-age* pricing. For example, a 42-year-old man who bought a term policy five years ago would pay the same premium as a 42-year-old who bought the same policy today.

The new premiums you'll pay under an attained-age pricing scheme may be guaranteed or nonguaranteed. If the premiums are guaranteed, you know in advance exactly what you'll pay at each renewal, and the company can't change that amount. If they are not guaranteed (which is the case with many of the new term policies on the market), the company reserves the right to change the amount you are scheduled to pay at each renewal. These policies are called *indeterminate-premium* policies. Although the company may lower or raise the premiums you will pay at each renewal, it will never raise them more than the maximum amount specified in the policy. Sometimes these stated maximums are high enough to deter you from buying this particular type of policy. For example, a policy issued in 1986 to a 39-year-old woman by Bankers Security Life Insurance Society shows that she could pay a yearly premium of $605 when she reaches age 49, $1,045 at age 54, or $3,100 at age 64.

The chances of Bankers Security or any other company charging the maximum premium are very small. Nevertheless, if you've bought an indeterminate premium policy, you may well see the scheduled premium amount go up or down when your policy comes up for renewal, depending on the company's financial picture and other market conditions at that time. Most of these policies reached the market in the early 1980s, and so far, most companies have increased the premiums according to the scheduled rates rather than the maximum ones they can charge.

A term policy may be either *participating* (dividend-paying) or *nonparticipating* (nondividend paying). Participating policies are issued mainly by mutual companies, which are nominally owned and controlled by their policyholders. Nonparticipating policies are usually issued by stock companies—those organized to make a profit for stockholders. Because dividends on term policies tend to be small, it usually doesn't make a big difference whether you choose a participating or a nonparticipating policy. Dividends assume much greater importance in whole life policies (see chapter 5). If you have an indeterminate premium policy, there probably will be few dividends because the company's financial and mortality experience is reflected in the premium changes instead.

Participating policies generally have higher initial premiums, although with term policies the differences are small, if there are any at all. When you buy a *par* policy, you are hoping that the company's experience as reflected in the dividends it pays will reduce your net cost below what it would have been had you chosen a *nonpar* policy. In the years since World War II that hope has generally been realized. On the whole, participating policies have been better buys in the long run than nonparticipating policies. Over the last three decades, mortality trends and interest rates have been favorable to insurance companies, which, in many cases, have paid dividends that were far more generous than those illustrated when the policies were first presented and sold. (An *illustration* is a computer-generated printout that supplies information about a particular policy. See glossary.)

In recent years, actuaries have used *select and ultimate* pricing schemes as well as *attained-age* pricing for their term policies. Select and ultimate schemes assume that a healthy insurance buyer taking out a new policy is a better risk than someone the same age who bought a policy from the company years before and has not been medically examined since then. New policyholders get a price break—they pay less than existing policyholders who are renewing at the same age. (This kind of pricing is at the heart of the *revertible* policies we discuss on page 53.)

As a rule, term policies offer a death benefit only, and don't build cash values. Most of the time, though, they can be converted to cash value policies such as whole life or universal life. When you see the word "convertible" associated with a term policy, you will know that under certain conditions you can make a conversion to a cash value form of life insurance. (For more about convertibility, see page 52.)

WHY THE INDUSTRY DOESN'T PUSH TERM

Although most companies offer term policies, selling term rarely brings in big profits, and companies discourage their agents from selling it. Compensation schedules tell the story. Some agents can earn as much as 100 percent of the first-year premium for selling a whole life policy, but only 70 percent of a smaller amount for selling term. Other agents may earn even less, but they almost always earn more for selling cash value policies.

Agents—like most people—will sell the products that earn them the largest commission. Consequently, many agents tend to color term insurance with negative overtones to discourage people from buying it. For instance, some call it "temporary" insurance as opposed to the "permanent" coverages offered by whole life and universal life. Others insist that buying term is like renting a house. "You don't rent your house or your car so why should you rent your life insurance?" asks one agent. Other agents make it seem as if you're settling for less than you deserve if you buy term. "You buy term if you're broke," one New York Life agent flatly told our reporter.

Some agents go to great lengths to avoid selling term, even if their company offers a good policy. National Life of Vermont's *yearly renewable term-15* policy placed at or near the top of the rankings for term insurance in our 1986 survey. One of the company's general agents took it upon himself to tell the other agents in his region that the policy was not available, that there was virtually no commission for selling it, and that the policy was not convertible—all untrue statements. A *Consumer Reports* subscriber alerted us to the agent's letter, and our reporter contacted the company. The general agent was reprimanded, but by then he had discouraged many of his agents from selling this highly rated policy to the public.

HOW TO COMPARE COSTS

When you buy life insurance, it's relatively easy to compare the first-year premium costs with other policies on the market. But that figure tells you nothing about how much the policy will cost in the long run. Some policies with similar premiums over a period of years can cost thousands of dollars more than others. Ferreting out a good buy requires more information than an insurance company usually gives an ordinary customer, and involves more calculations than most people can do conveniently with a calculator or a home computer. That's why we conduct our own life insurance cost surveys every few years.

To see how the policies in our survey compared with one another, we calculated a number called the *interest-adjusted net cost index* for each policy. That index is an industry-accepted method for determining the true cost of insurance to the consumer. The index itself isn't hard to understand, although the actual calculation is more complex.

A term insurance policy has two obvious elements: the premiums you pay each year and the dividends (if any) you get back. The premiums are usually fixed, but they may not be in the case of indeterminate premium policies. In any case, the premiums for those policies won't rise above a stated maximum. The dividends are not fixed; nor are they guaranteed. The dividend is a partial refund of premium payments from prior years, paid at the discretion of the company.

You may think that the net cost of the policy is simply the premiums paid minus the dividends received over the years. Close, but not correct. There's a third, less obvious element—the *timing* of your payments and receipts. Suppose two policies have equal total premium payments over twenty years. The one with lower payments in the early years is a better deal because you can bank or invest the money you saved by paying the initially lower premium. By the same token, a dividend paid earlier on is worth more to you than one paid in a later year.

So instead of simply adding up all the premiums and subtracting all the dividends, the interest-adjusted net cost method of comparison accumulates premiums and dividends at a stated rate of interest—by custom, 5 percent. That takes timing into account and gives a more accurate picture of the policy's projected true costs.

This index is often expressed as a cost per $1,000 of insurance. Thus, a policy with a ten-year, interest-adjusted net cost index of 4.32, for example, is estimated to cost an average of $4.32 per $1,000 of coverage per year, or about $432 annually for a $100,000 policy.

What matters most to the prospective buyer is not the index number as such, but how it compares with the index numbers for competing policies. The lower the index number, the better the buy. We have included the Ratings of policies from our 1986 survey in this book, even though some of the information may be out of date by the time you read it. Nevertheless, our Ratings give you information you will find nowhere else. They also will help you understand the key points in buying term insurance, and they will serve as a base from which you can conduct your own price survey for term insurance. In our survey we also calculated the interest-adjusted net cost index for each policy for three periods—five, ten, and twenty years. A policy's performance over these three time periods determined its overall ranking.

HOW TO SHOP FOR TERM INSURANCE

"Don't knock yourself out going to too many companies," a New York Life agent advised our reporter when she shopped for life insurance. "They're all the same, especially the top four companies." New York Life's policy wasn't a particularly good buy, and, contrary to the agent's assertion, our survey showed that the policies of the four largest companies were not identical. For instance, among forty-three participating policies providing $200,000 of term coverage for a 35-year-old man, one Metropolitan policy ranked first, Equitable's ranked third, Prudential's policy ranked fifteenth, and New York Life's was thirteenth from the bottom.

The buyer should keep in mind that some term policies are initially inexpensive and have very low cost indexes for the five-year period or even for the ten-year period, but then escalate in cost very rapidly if kept for twenty years or longer. A company selling this type of term policy may be using select and ultimate pricing schemes, which we describe on page 44. (The interest-adjusted net cost index unmasks that kind of pricing strategy because the ultimately higher premiums will be reflected in a higher index number.) Of course, the opposite can also be true: A policy may have a high initial premium but still can be a good deal if you keep it for ten or twenty years.

Remember, too, that if the size of the first-year premium is not a way to judge a policy's cost, neither is the length of the term. It's *how* the policies are priced over time that determines whether they are good or bad buys.

Some companies also have more than one term policy; one can be good, the other bad. That was the case with the Massachusetts Indemnity and Life policies, which are sold exclusively by the A. L. Williams organization. Its Modified Term policy ranked consistently near the bottom of our tables, while its Annual Renewable Term to 100 policy ranked consistently near the top.

THE A. L. WILLIAMS ORGANIZATION

The A. L. Williams organization is one of the new companies challenging the traditional orthodoxy of the life insurance industry. Founded in the late 1970s, the company sold about $71 billion of individual life insurance in 1986 compared with only about $51 billion sold by Prudential, one of the largest insurance companies in the world. The Williams organization achieved these sales by pushing term insurance to people who either owned small whole life insurance policies or lacked any life insurance at all. To Williams's credit, this selling strategy does give families more protection. The company says the average policy sold in 1986 had a face amount of $164,000, while the policies it replaced on the primary breadwinner had an average face amount of $34,000. Of course, Williams is not popular with the rest of the insurance industry, which treats the company as something of an outcast. Unfortunately, the policy most often sold was among the most costly term policies that we rated in our 1986 study. This was Massachusetts Indemnity's Mod-15, which, as we've noted, ranked consistently at or near the bottom of the Ratings.

Like agents for many other insurance companies, Williams agents wrongly focus on the premiums policyholders pay (in this case, monthly premiums), not on the policy's cost over time. As we've pointed out, that can be very misleading, because a policy with low premiums may actually be quite expensive over the years. Nevertheless, the A. L. Williams organization claims it has cut policyholders' insurance costs between 30 and 70 percent. That may be true if one simply compares a person's monthly outlay for the Mod-15 with the same person's monthly outlay for a whole life policy. But such comparisons say nothing about the real cost of the Williams term policy over time, or about how the cost of the Mod-15 compares with the cost of other term policies.

Nor has the Williams organization been candid about the true cost of the Mod-15. In its educational materials for its agents, the company declares that among eighty life insurance companies, Massachusetts Indemnity and Life had "the lowest average premium cost per thousand (dollars) of ordinary life insurance." The company says these figures come from the A. M. Best Company, which publishes life insurance statistics and evaluates companies. According to Andrew Gold, a senior manager at Best, the Williams organization was comparing apples and oranges. "We never describe those figures as cost per thousand, and that's where we feel it's misleading," he says. The Best list simply takes the total premium a company receives and divides it by the amount of insurance in force to arrive at an "average premium per thousand," which is not a measurement of the consumer's cost over a period of time. Further, the Best listing includes companies that sell all kinds of policies, including single-premium whole life, which is not comparable to term insurance.

Ironically, another policy in the Williams inventory was the least expensive term policy we looked at: Massachusetts Indemnity's Annual Renewable Term to 100 policy. But apparently the company didn't push it, and some agents told our readers this highly ranked policy was not available. The company says in its defense that it did set up a special telephone line to handle inquiries about this particular policy and actually issued about 2,600 policies to consumers.

Recently, the Williams organization discontinued the Mod-15 and has been selling a term policy called Common Sense term. An executive with the Williams organization told us that Common Sense term, which provides level premiums for twenty years, is "dramatically less expensive than the Mod-15." But when our reporter asked the company to supply a cost index for the policy, none was forthcoming.

The Williams Sales Pitch

The heart of the Williams sales pitch is the "theory of decreasing responsibility," which company chairman Arthur Williams explains in his book *Common Sense*. In essence, the theory states that you need a lot of coverage in your early years because your children are young, your debts are high, and any loss of income can be devastating. In your later years, you don't need much insurance because the children are grown, the mortgage is paid, and your debts are low. That has been our own theory for nearly fifty years.

But like many other insurance sellers, Williams's agents don't shrink from overstating their case, underrating the value of competitive products and sometimes pushing a mediocre-to-poor product themselves. In a sales presentation witnessed by our reporter, a Williams agent called whole life insurance a "rotten savings plan." "Aren't there tax benefits from whole life?" a prospective customer asked. The Williams agent flatly said no. But it's a well-known fact that the tax advantage of whole life has long been one of its virtues and a key selling point.

In *Common Sense*, Williams unequivocally tells his readers not to buy either whole life or universal life, and warns against buying life insurance as an investment. He correctly points out that dividend-paying policies usually have higher premiums than nondividend policies, but fails to note that the Federal Trade Commission (FTC) and others have found that over the last thirty years, dividend-paying policies have been better buys than those that don't pay any at all. Williams brushes aside the FTC's favorable comments on dividend-paying policies by saying that the agency was talking mainly about whole life, not term insurance. While it's true that dividends are a comparatively minor issue if you're buying term insurance, we think that Williams's arguments on this subject are self-serving and oversimplified.

Recruitment Techniques

If you meet one of the Williams organization's 145,000 agents, he or she will probably try to recruit you to *sell* insurance. "Every recruit is a potential sale and every sale is a potential recruit," says one Williams regional vice president. Art Williams likes to recruit what he calls "greenies," people who don't know much about life insurance and haven't been indoctrinated in the selling points for whole life insurance. A Williams agent tries to recruit other salespeople because the objective is to gather a network of other people to work for you. Once you reach a certain level in the company, you begin to earn part of the commissions sold by people under you in addition to the commissions you earn on the policies you yourself sell.

Art Williams maintains that the commission structure in his company is really not much different from that of traditional companies that pay overrides to their agencies and commissions to their agents. "The only difference between us and the others is that we believe in part-timers and they believe in full-timers," he said.

The bottom line is that it costs money to recruit, train, and compensate a sales force. Traditional companies push those policies that put plenty of money at the company's disposal and allow the company to pay fat commissions to their salespeople. How does A. L. Williams compete with that? Perhaps by pricing a term product so high that it, too, can generate large commissions. Either way, it's usually not the consumer who benefits.

RECOMMENDATIONS

Comparison shopping is crucial if you want to find an inexpensive term insurance policy. To help you in your search for one, we have devised worksheet 3, Term Insurance Checklist, which allows you to compare four different policies using Metropolitan's One-Year Term with Premium Adjustment policy as our example. There is also space for you to compare five-year interest-adjusted net cost indexes, even though you may not be able to obtain them. (In most states regulators require companies to furnish only the ten-year and twenty-year indexes.) You might, however, try to persuade a company or agent to figure that index for you.

In addition to the Checklist on page 58, we offer some additional points for you to keep in mind:

1. Always ask to see the interest-adjusted net cost index for the term policies you are considering. (Agents in thirty-eight states are now required to furnish the indexes on request). Use the index to compare one term policy with another. If the agent refuses to give you the index number or tells you it's too technical for you to understand, go elsewhere. Term insurance is almost a commodity product, like grain; the basic difference is price. Therefore, price should be the major consideration in buying it.

2. Look for a policy that offers good value whether you hold it for five, ten, or twenty years. You can't predict your insurance needs that far into the future but if you're buying term insurance because you have very young children, you'll probably need the coverage for at least twenty years. If you think you will need insurance for a longer period of time, beware of policies with low premiums in the early years but escalate in cost over time.

3. Unless you're certain you have only a short-term need for coverage, select a term policy that is renewable at least to age 65. This is important because some companies are bringing out new generations of term policies that are quite inexpensive but run for only ten or fifteen years and are not renewable after that.

4. If you find a policy that is particularly inexpensive at all durations, you may have to insist that the agent sell it to you. As we've pointed out, some agents for National Life of Vermont were told not to sell the policy that we ranked so highly, and some of our readers reported they had trouble buying the inexpensive, highly rated policy from Massachusetts Indemnity and Life.

5. Don't be put off if an agent disparages term as "temporary" insurance you'd want only to cover a mortgage or a business loan. Term insurance can be renewed well into old age. In any case, term premiums are lowest during the time when your children are young and you need a lot of protection; if the insurance itself is "temporary," so too, in all likelihood, is your need for much of it.

6. If an agent offers you an indeterminate premium policy, you can use the interest-adjusted net cost index to compare the policy with a fixed premium policy. Don't be frightened by the maximum premiums the company is allowed to charge. But if you're worried about the

possibility that the company will raise premiums to the maximum, don't buy an indeterminate premium policy.

7. On the whole, we recommend you buy the policy, not the company. Many agents will try to convince you that if you buy from their "quality" company, you'll be getting a good deal. That may or may not be the case. We do recommend, however, that you check on the financial stability of any company you choose to do business with. (See Chapter 11, "Choosing a Company.")

CONVERTIBILITY

In addition to price, convertibility is the major difference among term policies.

A convertibility clause allows you to convert your term policy to a cash value type of insurance such as whole life or universal life. The conversion privilege is especially important if you find you need life insurance after age 65, because some term policies can't be renewed after that age. If you think you'll need insurance later in life, whether for estate tax reasons or because you've married a person much younger than yourself and you expect to have dependents when you're past retirement age, you will need a policy with a good conversion clause.

There are probably very few people who will want to convert their term policies to whole life. But we recommend that you make sure any term policy you buy is convertible, at least until you reach 60. (Most companies allow you to convert without furnishing medical evidence that you're still in good health.)

Before buying a term policy, ask these questions:

1. For how long is the policy convertible? In general, the longer the period during which conversions are allowed, the more expensive the conversion privilege is likely to be. That cost, however, is not expressed separately; it's buried in the policy's overall cost.

In our 1986 study, for example, the two policies from National Life of Vermont have very different policy conversion provisions. The Yearly Renewable Term-15, which ranks among the top policies in the Ratings, allows a policyholder to convert only during the first two years. The company's Yearly Renewable Term-100, which ranks somewhat lower, allows policyholders to convert until they reach 85. Obviously the latter policy is more desirable if you think you'll need insurance after retirement.

2. What is the policy convertible to? Some are convertible to a garden-variety whole life policy, others to universal life, others to both. The more options available, the more flexibility you will have if you decide to convert sometime in the future. Your contract should indicate what kind of policy you can convert to, although some companies may allow you to convert to another kind of policy even if your contract doesn't specifically say so.

3. Do you get any credits or discounts on the premium when you do convert from a term policy? Such credits are rarely, if ever, guaranteed in your policy, and just because a company offers a good deal if you convert today doesn't mean it will offer a similar one if you want to convert fifteen years later. If you currently own a term policy, be wary if a company offers an unusually large enticement; a year of free insurance, for example, to convert to a whole life policy seems attractive, but in the long run you might be buying a very expensive policy.

4. Does the convertibility clause allow an original-age or an attained-age conversion? *Original age* means the rates for the new policy are based on your age when the term policy was first issued. *Attained age* means the company charges rates for the new policy based on your current age. If the company allows an original-age conversion, the cost to convert may be the amount of cash value under the new policy plus a small percentage (3 percent) to cover administrative expenses. The cost is intended to put the policyholder in the same financial position as if he had had the new policy from the original date. If you convert on an original-age basis, your premiums will be lower, but you may have to pay a large chunk of money to the insurance company. If you convert under an attained-age arrangement, your premiums will be higher, of course, but you won't have to pay a lump sum to the company.

REVERTIBLE POLICIES

A number of years ago when a special tax provision (since repealed) made term life insurance more attractive to sell, many companies devised a gimmick to sell more of it. They made their term policies revertible, using the select and ultimate pricing schemes described on page 44. When such a revertible policy comes up for renewal, the policyholder must take a medical exam. A favorable verdict from the doctor qualifies the policyholder for a rate lower than the renewal rate that is normally charged.

Suppose you bought a revertible policy when you were 40 and you passed the medical exam when the policy came up for renewal five years later. Your new premium would be based on the rate charged to newly examined 45-year-olds. There was only one catch. If you didn't pass the medical exam, you had no choice but to pay the regular premium at steeply increasing rates. After all, it's not an ideal time to go shopping for life insurance when you've just flunked a physical. So revertible term came to be called Las Vegas term; if you bought such a policy, you gambled that your health would remain stable over the years. Today, many companies have stopped selling revertible policies, but the policies haven't vanished completely. If you come across one, should you buy it?

In our 1986 survey, we evaluated several revertible policies, and calculated the interest-adjusted net cost indexes under two assumptions: (1) that the policyholder remained healthy, and (2) that he or she fell ill and could not renew at the lower rates. The results? A few of the policies looked good even if the policyholder got sick. Other policies, however, performed poorly in the long run. They were very inexpensive if the policyholder stayed well, but became very expensive if the policyholder had a serious illness.

To make an intelligent decision about these policies, you have to look at the cost indexes under both assumptions, which will be difficult to do because the company and the agent probably won't supply such a cost index calculated under the assumption you'll get sick. You can, of course, use our limited survey of these policies as a guide. But, in our opinion, most people should avoid revertible policies; they're a calculated gamble that might not work out.

MAIL-ORDER TERM INSURANCE

"High-level protection at affordable rates." "No cancellation for poor health." "Monthly rates will never go up." "No physical exam normally required." Mail-order term policies offer an easy way to buy life insurance. You simply select the amount of coverage you want, answer a few questions about your health, and return a form to the insurance company via the nearest mailbox.

You can easily buy mail-order term policies through trade and professional organizations or through financial institutions that pitch them to their members or credit card customers. Or you may have received such offers in your mail because a number of companies are now experimenting with direct mail-order term policies. Should you take these mail-order policies seriously?

To see how mail-order policies compare in cost with individual policies, we calculated the interest-adjusted net cost indexes for four of them: an American International Life policy sold to Citibank Visa card customers, a Fireman's Fund policy sold to American Express and Chase Manhattan Bank Visa cardholders, a Consumers United Insurance Company policy sold to members of the National Organization for Women, and a Home Life policy sold to members of the Association of MBA Executives.

The merits of these mail-order policies appeared to depend mainly on the buyer's age. While the mail-order policies were generally as good as the best individual policies for 25-year-olds, they were costlier than many individual policies for the older age groups. So a 25-year-old man or woman who wants $50,000 of coverage couldn't go wrong buying a mail-order policy from any of the companies in our sample. These policies (all nonparticipating) were as inexpensive as our top-rated nonparticipating policies. But 45-year-olds could do better elsewhere. For example, the Fireman's Fund policy for a 45-year-old man buying $50,000 of coverage has a ten-year cost index high enough to put the policy close to the bottom of the list. The American International Life policy for a 45-year-old woman buying $50,000 of coverage also ranks near the bottom.

Because most companies offering mail-order policies don't go to great lengths to review your physical condition and health habits, companies must charge rates that are high enough to cover the additional losses that inevitably result when some of these people die. Another drawback is that many of these policies offer only small amounts of coverage—$50,000, $75,000, or perhaps as much as $100,000. Whether the company would issue more insurance depends on the person's age and how much he or she wanted to buy.

If you decide to buy one of these policies, check out the sellers' sales claims. "Even if your health fails or you're in a terrible accident, your insurance is guaranteed to continue," assures a letter from American Express pitching the Fireman's Fund policy.

While it may be true that these policies won't be canceled, such statements imply that other types of term life insurance policies may be canceled if your health deteriorates. Not so. As long as you don't misstate something important on your application, individual policies in force for two years can't be canceled except for nonpayment of premiums.

Some of the mail-order policies, however, might be canceled if the company terminates the master contract with the bank or trade association. (Remember, these are group policies.) If that happens, the insurance company probably will let you convert to an individual term or to a whole life policy. If you quit the association that offered the insurance or you take your credit card business to another bank, do you lose your coverage? In most cases, no. But that's a point worth asking about before you buy a mail-order term policy.

Beware of companies that tout specific rate guarantees. While such guarantees might be comforting, they don't necessarily mean that the policy is inexpensive. A company offering such guarantees might have overpriced its policy at the outset. Watch out, too, for meaningless price claims such as, "You pay only 63 cents daily for $100,000 of life insurance." The true cost of the mail-order policy is reflected in the policy's interest-adjusted net cost index, not in the number of pennies it costs per day.

EMPLOYER-PROVIDED TERM INSURANCE

Your employer may offer you group term insurance as a fringe benefit. Usually the amount of coverage is a multiple of your salary—one or two times your salary is the most common, although occasionally a generous employer may offer more. A majority of employers pay the entire bill for the insurance, but occasionally the employee must share the cost.

How should this coverage fit into your life insurance program and how do the costs compare with the individually purchased policies?

If you know you won't stay with your present employer for long, don't count on the group policy as the centerpiece of your insurance program. You'll lose your coverage when you leave, and you may have to convert to an individual policy, which may be far more expensive than one you can find if you shopped the market yourself. If your days at your present job are numbered, think of any group term coverage simply as a bonus, and buy an individual policy that adequately covers your present insurance needs. If you plan to stay with your current employer, by all means consider the group term insurance as a vital part of your insurance program. But if the needs analysis on page 13 shows that you need more coverage than your employer provides, buy the additional coverage.

Your employer may offer group term insurance coverage through a *cafeteria plan* rather than as a standard fringe benefit. Under a typical cafeteria plan, the employer allocates a certain amount of money to each employee to pay the cost of fringe benefits. The employee then chooses from a menu of available benefits which ones he or she would like to have. The choices that are allowed by the current tax law include group term life insurance, disability income insurance, health insurance, 401(k) plan contributions, and cash. The employee is not taxed on the amount of money available to purchase these fringe benefits, but he or she must include as income the value of any taxable benefits selected and the amount of any cash payments received.

If you have a cafeteria plan and you must decide whether to purchase group term life insurance or take a cash payment and use the money to buy an individual policy on your own, the interest-adjusted net cost indexes can help. You can use them to compare the cost of your employer's policy with some of the individual policies currently on the market. As always, you must compare the same kind of insurance, such as term with term. The policy with the lowest index is the least expensive.

In addition, you must keep in mind that the cost of the first $50,000 of group term coverage is not reportable as taxable income. Because of the different tax treatment given to different amounts of coverage, you will need to make a separate cost comparison for the first $50,000 of coverage and for the coverage over and above the $50,000. When considering coverage of $50,000 or less, you must factor into the analysis the difference in the income tax treatment of both group term insurance and the cash payment you can take to pay for an individual policy. Because the purchase of $50,000 of group term insurance does not result in any taxable income to the employee, the index for the individual insurance must be adjusted to determine the equivalent pre-tax index.

To make that adjustment, first obtain the interest-adjusted net cost indexes for your employer's policy and for the individual policy you're thinking of buying. For example, we'll assume that the index for the

WORKSHEET 3. TERM CHECKLIST

	Example[a]	Policy 1	Policy 2	Policy 3	Policy 4
Company	Metropolitan	___	___	___	___
Policy name	YRT with premium adjustment	___	___	___	___
Amount of insurance	$100,000	___	___	___	___
First-year premium	$128	___	___	___	___
Subsequent premiums					
5th year	$142 current	___	___	___	___
	$298 guaranteed	___	___	___	___
10th year	$205 current	___	___	___	___
	$438 guaranteed	___	___	___	___
15th year	$368 current	___	___	___	___
	$648 guaranteed	___	___	___	___
20th year	$590 current	___	___	___	___
	$1,007 guaranteed	___	___	___	___
Interest-adjusted net cost index					
5-year	1.33 current	___	___	___	___
	2.34 guaranteed	___	___	___	___
10-year	1.51 current	___	___	___	___
	2.95 guaranteed	___	___	___	___
20-year	2.39 current	___	___	___	___
	4.41 guaranteed	___	___	___	___
Dividends expected?	No—policy has indeterminate premium	___	___	___	___
Illustrated dividends					
5th year	None	___	___	___	___
10th year	None	___	___	___	___
15th year	None	___	___	___	___
20th year	None	___	___	___	___
Policy renewable to:	Age 70, New York Age 99, other states	___	___	___	___
Is policy revertible?	No	___	___	___	___
Convertibility					
How long:	Age 60; or if over age 55, 5 years from issue date	___	___	___	___

	Example[a]	Policy 1	Policy 2	Policy 3	Policy 4
To what:	Whole life, but company has been allowing conversion to universal life	___	___	___	___
Attained age or original age:	Attained age	___	___	___	___
Rating classification (if substandard, what table is used?)	Preferred nonsmoker	___	___	___	___

[a] Example based on a $100,000 policy for a 35-year-old man.

employer's policy is $3 and the index for the individual policy is $2.50. To make a valid comparison between the cost of the first $50,000 of group term insurance and the cost of the first $50,000 of individual insurance, make the following calculation: Divide the index for the individual policy by 1 minus your tax bracket. If your tax bracket is 28 percent, the pre-tax interest-adjusted net cost index for the individual policy is:

$$\frac{\$2.50}{(1 - .28)} = \$3.47.$$

In this case, the equivalent pre-tax index ($3.47) is greater than the index for group term insurance ($3), so you would be better off using the money in the cafeteria plan to purchase the group term coverage.

If you need more than $50,000 of coverage, you can compare the interest-adjusted net cost indexes for the excess over $50,000 for the group term policy and for the individual policy without considering the question of income taxes. While such a comparison is useful, it may not be precise because the cost the employee must include in taxable income under the group term plan is based on a government table that will undoubtedly be different from the actual cost of the insurance. But the difference between the imputed cost for income tax purposes and the actual cost will probably not be great enough to distort the results of the comparison.

SAVINGS BANK LIFE INSURANCE

The term insurance policies available from many savings banks have consistently ranked high in our life insurance surveys. That's not surprising because state legislatures in New York, Massachusetts, and Connecticut have empowered savings banks to provide low-cost insurance for low and moderate income families. Savings bank life insurance (SBLI) was the brainchild of Louis Brandeis, a Boston lawyer who later became a U.S. Supreme Court justice. Brandeis believed savings banks could provide better protection at a lower cost by offering policies directly to the public, and eliminating the middleman or insurance agent. In 1908, savings bank life insurance was born.

Over the years, however, the insurance industry has successfully lobbied to keep savings bank life insurance from spreading into other states and to prevent savings banks in New York, Massachusetts, and Connecticut from selling insurance in large amounts.

But a recent change in Massachusetts law permits consumers who live or work in that state to buy as much as $250,000 of coverage from an individual policy offered by a savings bank. Recent changes in Connecticut law allow the consumer to buy up to $100,000 of individual coverage and up to $200,000 of group coverage, provided he or she has an account at a savings bank in the state. In New York, savings banks can offer only $50,000 of individual coverage. But a recent loophole in the state law now allows savings banks to offer consumers much larger amounts of group term insurance. Anyone who lives or works in New York can now buy up to $250,000 of group insurance provided he or she has an account at a savings bank in the state.

We strongly advise anyone who lives or works in these states to seriously consider filling his or her insurance needs with this low-cost type of term insurance.

5

Whole Life Insurance

Insurance agents like to say that owning a whole life policy is like owning a home: You have something to show for your investment. With a home you have equity; with a whole life policy you have "cash value," the magical words that have sold billions of dollars worth of whole life policies over the years. "There's money if you live and money if you die," was how one New York Life agent put it.

Until 1980, whole life was the kind of insurance most people bought, even though the amount of coverage most families could afford with this type of insurance often left them severely underinsured.

In the last few years, however, traditional whole life policies have lost some of their luster. In 1970 they accounted for 61 percent of all insurance sold; in 1986 they accounted for only 35 percent. Universal life instead has become the new bread-and-butter policy for many companies. Nevertheless, whole life policies are still a staple for several large, well-known insurance firms, and whole life may even regain its past prominence if interest rates decline and new, more modern whole life policies catch on.

Insurance companies and their agents generally prefer to sell cash value policies, including whole life, because these policies offer companies a chance for greater profit and agents a chance for larger commissions. Over the years, companies have devised forceful arguments for selling whole life policies—arguments we don't find very convincing.

For example, you may hear from an agent that the premiums for a whole life policy will never increase. That's not the whole story. You pay extra in the early years of the policy so that the premium stays level later on in the future. You may also hear that whole life is a "permanent" form of insurance. Permanence is not necessarily a virtue as far as life insurance is concerned, and the assertion is not even true. Many life insurance policies, including whole life, lapse. In 1985, 21 percent of all policies in force for less than two years lapsed; 10 percent of those in force for more than two years also lapsed. And, as we pointed out in chapter 1, most people don't need life insurance after retirement, although an agent may try hard to convince them they do. For people who will need insurance later in life, many term policies are renewable to older ages or can be converted to a cash value form of insurance.

You will probably also hear that whole life is a good investment. "Whole life teaches thrift," one agent told us. "Sure, there is one person out of one hundred who can and will faithfully invest the difference [between a term and a whole life premium], but I haven't met one yet." Of course, nothing obligates you to save the difference, and it's wrong to think you have to make the effort. Adequate coverage is the most important factor, and we believe that the only way most people can afford such coverage is to buy term insurance. (For more on whole life as an investment, see page 82.)

Whole life insurance does have a few virtues, but for the most part its drawbacks loom larger for the average insurance buyer.

WHAT IS WHOLE LIFE INSURANCE?

A whole life policy has three essential elements:

1. The premium—the amount you pay each year to keep the policy in force.
2. The death benefit—the amount guaranteed to your beneficiaries should you die.

3. The cash value—the amount you would receive if you cashed in your policy.

Some policies have a fourth element—dividends.

The traditional whole life policy delivers a set death benefit for a premium that stays constant from the day you buy the policy. The policy is designed to cover you for your whole life—hence the name. A whole life policy need not be renewed periodically to remain in force; you merely have to pay your premium every year. As we point out in chapter 4, the cost of the protection with a term policy increases as you get older because your chances of dying are greater. The same is true for whole life, though the level premium disguises that fact. How? The premium for a whole life policy far exceeds the actual cost of the protection in the early years of the policy, at a time when you're younger and your chances of dying are few. Moreover, in the early years of the policy's life, a portion of your premium not needed to pay for the death protection goes toward your cash value, which can be considered as a kind of savings account.

In effect, you overpay in the early years of the policy so that you can underpay in the later years. As time passes, more and more of the death benefit consists of your cash value. So the amount of money the insurance company is risking on your life—the net amount at risk—decreases, even though the face amount of the policy never changes.

Premiums

True, traditional whole life premiums rarely rise. But they start out high—much higher than the initial premiums for term insurance. A 35-year-old man pays between $2,000 and $3,000 a year for a $200,000 whole life policy from most of the companies in our 1986 survey. He pays about $250 for one of the top-rated term policies. Although his term premiums will increase each year, they won't equal the whole life premium until many years later, when his insurance needs most likely will have declined.

Some companies do market whole life policies with lower premiums in the first few years. Some of these policies are called "modified premium" and some are known as "graded premium" whole life. *Modified premium policies* have lower premiums in the first three or five years, then higher premiums that remain level for the rest of the policy-holder's life. These policies pay no dividends in the early years and build smaller cash values than regular whole life policies. Graded premium policies have premiums that start out low and gradually rise over the years. At some point, usually after ten or twenty years, graded premium policies begin to accumulate cash values.

The idea behind these policies is to make them look like term insurance and attract those buyers who would otherwise choose term. Some of them mimic term insurance so well that you may even think you have a term policy. One of our readers did. When she examined her policy, the fine print revealed that she had purchased "increasing premium whole life to age 74." She was astonished to learn that she would pay over $2,000 in premiums in just the first six years of the policy.

Cash Values

Although the cash value you accumulate in a whole life policy can be viewed as a kind of savings account, there are significant differences between a policy's cash value and a bank account. First, you can't take your money out without giving up the insurance protection, nor can you make partial withdrawals. Withdrawing money from a whole life policy is an all-or-nothing proposition. You can, however, *borrow* against the cash value at an interest rate specified in the policy. If you die while such a loan is outstanding, the amount you owe (plus interest) is deducted from the death benefit paid to your survivors. Similarly, if you cash in or "surrender" your policy and take the cash value, the amount of any outstanding loan is deducted from the sum the insurance company owes you.

A second difference between a whole life policy's cash value and a savings account is the tax treatment. We discuss the tax advantages of whole life on page 80.

MAJOR TYPES OF WHOLE LIFE POLICIES

Today, companies sell two basic types of whole life policies—those with a guaranteed cost and those that depend on the company's investment, mortality, and expense picture.

Guaranteed Cost Policies

These policies have a guaranteed premium, a guaranteed cash value, and they pay no dividends or excess interest—the policyholder knows exactly what the policy will cost over time. Guaranteed cost policies are the traditional nonparticipating policies sold most often by stock companies, which are organized for the benefit of their stockholders.

Nonguaranteed Cost Policies

These policies do not necessarily have fixed premiums, fixed cash values, or fixed death benefits; they have a built-in mechanism that enables policyholders to share in any excess interest. Thus, at the time of purchase policyholders do not know exactly what their policies will cost them over the years, because the elements of the policy that determine cost can change depending on the insurance company's investment and operating experience. Nonguaranteed cost policies include traditional participating (dividend-paying) policies sold by mutual companies, organized to provide insurance "at cost" to their policyholders, as well as such newcomers as current assumption whole life, sold by both stock and mutual companies. These policies usually pay no dividends.

The following section discusses the various aspects of nonguaranteed cost policies.

DIVIDEND-PAYING POLICIES

Traditional participating whole life, a type of nonguaranteed cost policy, has fixed premiums, fixed death benefits, and fixed cash values, but not fixed costs. The company's higher investment earnings, favorable mortality experience, and/or lower expenses (lower than those assumed when setting the premium) are returned as dividends. These dividends reduce the cost of the policy either by lowering the premium or by increasing benefits for the policyholder.

Dividends are paid at the company's discretion and are never guaranteed. Paid annually, they are expressed as dollars per $1,000 of coverage. For example, if you had a $100,000 policy and the company declared a dividend of $2 for your policy, you would receive $200.

Some whole life policies pay a *terminal* dividend, often a large one, if the policy is surrendered after twenty years or if the policyholder dies, although some companies may pay fewer dividends in general in the years before termination.

Dividend Options

You can take your dividend in cash, use it to reduce your next premium, leave it with the company to accumulate with interest, or use it to buy more insurance with no additional expense charges (paid-up additions). Dividends are also paid on the paid-up insurance, so these amounts can compound over the years. Although one-third of all dividends are used to buy more insurance, the amount you can buy each year may be small because you are buying paid-up additions, not premium-paying additions. For instance, a Seattle woman's total dividend accumulation for the year came to $1,135, which would buy only $1,505 worth of additional insurance. If the woman needed a lot more coverage, the $1,500 is a mere drop in the proverbial bucket. It may be years before dividends are large enough to buy the coverage you need—if you need more, buy it now.

Companies sometimes offer a *fifth dividend* option, meaning that you can use part of your dividend to buy one-year term insurance in an amount equal to the cash value of the policy. The balance of the dividend must be left with the company to earn interest.

You can also use your dividends to make your annual premiums "vanish" after a number of years. How? If your policy offers a *vanishing premium* option, you can pay the scheduled premiums for five or perhaps seven years. After that, the company assumes it has paid you sufficient dividends so that those dividends, plus the accumulated total cash value, are enough to pay the balance of your premiums. In other words, you may never have to pay another dime for your policy.

Sounds good, but there's nothing magical about vanishing premiums. The insurance company, in order to give you hefty dividends tomorrow, may charge you hefty premiums today. Also, even though a company's current dividend scale may seem adequate to pay all your future premiums, dividends actually paid in the future may turn out to be lower than those illustrated today. If that is the case, you'll have to continue paying the premiums for several more years just to keep your insurance in force—and you may already have paid large premiums for the privilege of having the vanishing premium option.

How Investment Earnings Affect Dividends

In the mid-1980s, investment earnings were the key component of the total dividends a company paid. The company translates its investment earnings into a dividend interest rate it figures into the dividend "formula." In fact, some agents sell whole life by touting the company's current dividend rate, although a dividend rate may not be the same thing as a rate of return on your policy—at times it's higher, other times lower. An agent may also tell you that the company pays investment earnings to policyholders using the portfolio method or the investment year method.

About five years ago almost all companies used the *portfolio method*. Now only about one-third do. Under this method, a company uses an interest rate in its dividend formula that is based on the earnings of all of the company's invested assets, including new premiums and premiums invested years before. In effect, the company allocates to each policy its proportionate share of the average earnings on all of these assets. As a result, when interest rates rise, the portfolio rate will usually lag behind current rates, and you may receive a smaller dividend for a few years. The opposite will happen when current interest rates fall. In that case, companies using the portfolio method are able to pay out a higher rate for a longer period and dividends will also be larger for a while.

Under the *investment year method,* a company separates the earnings on its new and existing investments made during the various periods and allocates to each policy some portion of the earnings from the new investments made each investment period as well as some portion of the earnings from investments made in previous years. The size of your dividend will depend in part on how much the company earned this year after investing the premiums you paid this year and on how much it earned on each of your premiums made in previous years. In times of rising rates, a company using the investment year method will usually credit higher rates to the current premiums (less expenses) you have paid. For example, the twentieth-year dividend shown for a newly issued policy will be higher than the twentieth-year dividend actually paid on your existing policy. In times of falling rates, the opposite would be true.

Which method is best? If a policyholder keeps a policy for life, riding out several interest rate cycles, it won't matter very much. The policies will perform about the same. But the method a company uses to determine its dividends can make a big difference in the sales illustration an agent shows you and can influence you to choose one company over another.

The dividend pie is divided among all policyholders, but everyone doesn't get the same-sized slice. Each slice represents every policyholder's contribution to the company. The policyholder's age, the kind of policy owned, and the length of time the policy has been in force also count in determining the size of the dividend. Some companies pay lower dividends to those policyholders who are substandard risks. For instance, in 1986 the illustrated tenth-year dividend on a $100,000 Guardian Life policy issued to a 35-year-old male nonsmoker was $1,014. If the man was a substandard Table 4 risk (see chapter 3), the illustrated dividend was only $952.

Some companies have allocated dividends fairly, while others have not. Existing policyholders, for example, may have been hurt when companies switched from the portfolio method to the investment year method in calculating dividends. Current interest rates were higher than the portfolio rates, and new policyholders were shown and paid higher dividends than those paid to policyholders who bought their policies long ago.

As we'll see, borrowing on your policy can also affect the size of your dividend.

Borrowing Against Your Policy's Cash Value

The borrowing privilege of a whole life policy has been one of its big selling points over the years, especially since the state regulators allowed the insurance companies to charge low rates for policy loans and, until 1987, the interest paid on policy loans was tax-deductible.

In the 1960s and 1970s, the policy loan rate was typically 5 or 6 percent. In the late 1970s when interest rates soared into the double digits, many policyholders borrowed against their accumulated cash values at 6 percent and reinvested the money in money market funds or bank certificates of deposit at rates of 13 to 15 percent, thus realizing a tidy low-risk profit. (Those who borrowed generally received the same dividends as those who did not borrow against their policies.)

Insurance companies, seeing their money flow into other financial institutions, got state regulators to increase the maximum loan rate to 8 percent, or the then-current market rate. Eventually the laws were changed, and today newly issued policies offer either an 8-percent fixed loan rate or a variable rate tied to the Moody's long-term bond index. Some companies offered existing policyholders the right to amend their contracts, accept the higher loan rates, and receive higher dividends. Those who chose to keep their 5- or 6-percent fixed loan rates usually received lower dividends. (Those who switched received higher dividends whether or not they borrowed against their policies.)

Many companies also instituted a practice called *direct recognition* for newly issued policies. Under direct recognition, a part of your dividend reflects the interest rates the company earns on the policy loan and on the portion of your cash values you have not borrowed against. The dividend interest rate paid on the borrowed portion of your cash values reflects your policy loan rate. Dividends will be higher if you don't borrow against your policy, or if you have a variable loan rate that is higher than the rate the company pays on the nonborrowed portion of your cash values. Some companies offer direct recognition to existing policyholders without changing the loan rate for the policy; others offer both direct recognition and a change in the policy loan rate.

Here's a simple example of how direct recognition affected one policyholder who owned a thirty-year-old, $10,000 policy issued by Sun Life of Canada. Under the company's direct recognition program, he would have received a $313.70 dividend if he had had no outstanding loans. But the man had borrowed some $5,300 against the policy's cash value, so his dividend amounted to only $107.20—roughly two-thirds less. If he had repaid the loan, he would have received a higher dividend.

Insurance companies maintain that direct recognition is a fairer way of handing out dividends because policyholders who don't borrow no longer subsidize those who do and are paid dividends reflecting their contributions to the company. But there are those who resent the constant pressure to amend their insurance contracts and accept variable loan rates and direct recognition. "This is a thinly disguised method to circumvent the original contract," one reader complained to us.

What should you do if your company asks you to switch? If you have a low fixed-rate loan provision in your contract and you plan to borrow heavily in the future, it probably doesn't pay to switch. But bear in mind that you are trading off a cheaper loan for smaller dividends. If you don't plan to borrow regularly, go ahead and accept direct recognition—you'll receive larger dividends. But try to do so without accepting a variable loan rate, because the higher interest you may pay is not tax-deductible.

What should you do if you've already borrowed on the policy and the company wants you to switch? If you have an outstanding loan but don't plan to borrow any more, it usually pays to accept direct recognition. If you plan to borrow again or have already borrowed the maximum from your policy, direct recognition probably isn't for you. You'll be money ahead with a lower loan rate. If you have the money, repay your loan and opt for direct recognition. You'll get larger dividends.

If you have accepted direct recognition, have outstanding policy loans, and are allowing your dividends to accumulate with interest, consider exchanging the dividends for a reduction in your loan balance or buying paid-up additions. You'll immediately lower your interest costs and receive larger dividends later. But first make sure the company isn't already doing that for you. One reader told us that although his policy agreement specified that dividends were to be paid in cash, his company had automatically used the dividends to reduce his loan balance. A company usually doesn't do that unless you request it. But if your policy dates back many years, you may have given the company the right to apply dividends to your loan balance and forgotten that you did so.

Remember, too, borrowing from your policy reduces the amount of insurance proceeds that would go to your family after your death, because the insurer will deduct the loan amount from the policy's death benefit and pay your family the difference. One man who bought a $10,000 policy in 1961 had a death benefit in 1986 of only $1,258. Over the years, unpaid loans and unpaid interest had eaten away at his family's protection, and he had apparently ignored warnings from the insurance company that his loan balance was approaching the danger level. (He could, of course, pay off the loans and interest due, and restore the death benefit.)

The Dividend Game

As we've noted, the size of a dividend depends almost entirely on the company's expenses, mortality experience, and investment earnings. Over the past few decades, steadily rising interest rates, plus the fact that people are living longer, have enabled most companies to return higher dividends to their policyholders than they had originally illustrated—in some cases, far more. For example, if a 35-year-old man had bought a $100,000 whole life policy from Northwestern Mutual in 1965, the agent would have shown him figures indicating that the total dividend would be $1,233 on a $100,000 policy. In 1985, Northwestern Mutual actually paid a total dividend of $3,740 on a $100,000 policy, assuming that the policyholder accepted the company's direct recognition offer and no policy loans existed between the 1984 and 1985 anniversaries.

Insurance buyers today have good reason to doubt whether companies will be able to deliver the high dividends agents still promote in their sales pitches. Interest rates have fallen from their peak of a few years ago, which means companies are earning less on their investments and these lower earnings must be reflected in future dividends. Recently, a growing number of companies have begun to use "predictions" for their illustrated dividends, sometimes frankly labeled as such, sometimes not. In some cases, these illustrated dividends are rosier than the company's current experience warrants. One company, for example, illustrated dividends that reflected lower expenses than it was currently achieving. The company hoped to stimulate enough sales to reduce its actual expenses, but it did state publicly that if the sales didn't materialize, dividends paid in the future would be lower than those illustrated.

The method companies use to determine the dividend interest rate— portfolio or investment year—also can dramatically affect the illustrations that agents show you. By switching to the investment year method, companies in the mid-1980s were able to illustrate much higher dividends to their customers because interest rates were very high. When interest rates began to fall, illustrations based on the investment year method no longer looked so attractive. As a result, companies using the portfolio method have had the edge because their portfolio average still reflects the sky-high rates earned on assets invested a number of years ago.

Keep in mind then that today's interest rates are not as important as the rates you expect the company to earn ten or twenty years from now, when your cash values will be much larger (cash values increase the longer you own the policy). Of course, no one can accurately predict future interest rates. We can only be sure that (1) under either the portfolio method or the investment year method that an agent currently illustrates, it's unlikely that high dividends will be paid over the next twenty or thirty years, and (2) dividends based on a portfolio rate will be more stable—if only because they will fluctuate less from year to year than dividends based on the investment year method.

CURRENT ASSUMPTION WHOLE LIFE

Current assumption whole life (sometimes called *interest-sensitive whole life*), another type of nonguaranteed cost whole life insurance, was born during the days of skyrocketing interest rates. Stock companies needed a product to compete with the par policies of mutual companies, which could pass along by way of dividends some of the gains from the prevailing high interest rates. Current assumption whole life policies filled this need.

With current assumption policies one or more of the elements affecting the cost—premium, death benefit, interest rate, cash value, and mortality and expense charges—are not guaranteed and are dependent on the insurance company's bottom line.

The Changing Cost Elements

Some of the current assumption whole life plans have "indeterminate premiums"—the premium is not fixed, but changes as interest rates change. The insurance company initially sets the premium to reflect a selected interest rate it expects to earn on its investments. This rate is called the *current rate*, which is guaranteed for one year or less. The rate is reviewed typically once a year and may be raised or lowered depending on current interest rates and/or the company's financial picture. The company in turn usually adjusts the policyholder's premium to reflect changes in these rates—a lower premium if rates have gone up and a higher one if rates have fallen. (A maximum premium amount is spelled out in the policy.)

A few companies may tie rate changes to an index such as the short-term Treasury bill rate, but most changes are made at the discretion of the companies themselves. (Insurance regulators limit the rate increase in a few states.)

Rather than paying a higher premium, some policyholders can accept a lower death benefit, which can be as much as 30 or 40 percent lower than the initial face amount if interest rates fall dramatically. But because companies are reluctant to automatically increase coverage for policyholders whose health may have deteriorated since they took out their policies, the death benefit never increases if interest rates go up.

Some current assumption whole life policies provide for fixed premiums but reflect changes in interest rates and mortality and expense charges in the policy's cash values. In other words, the company may credit higher or lower interest and make larger or smaller deductions for mortality charges. (Some policies may guarantee a minimum interest rate to be credited to cash values.)

Like traditional dividend-paying policies, current assumption whole life may also have vanishing premium options. Since there are no dividends with current assumption policies, whether or not the premium vanishes depends on the size of your present cash value and on how much interest the company pays on your future cash values. If high rates are credited, the cash value may be sufficient to pay up the policy after seven or eight years, but if rates are low, a policyholder may have to pay premiums for a longer period than the agent promised at the time of sale.

Loan Provisions

The loan provisions of current assumption whole life work the same way as traditional participating policies. These policies credit different rates to loaned and unloaned cash values. In other words, they follow the direct recognition described on page 69.

Regulatory Aspects

Current assumption whole life policies fall into a regulatory gray area. There are no requirements, for example, for fair and equitable treat-

ment of old policyholders as there are for companies selling participating whole life. (State regulators require that sellers of par policies
distribute dividends with some equity in mind. In a few states, regulators have actually forced companies to pay larger dividends to some
groups of policyholders. This is not a general practice, however.)

A task force of the American Academy of Actuaries has proposed
to the National Association of Insurance Commissioners (which issues
model regulations for states to adopt) that all illustrations and advertising for policies with nonguaranteed elements state exactly when and
under what circumstances those elements may change. Some companies are now disclosing these conditions to prospective buyers, but
many others are not.

HOW TO SHOP FOR A WHOLE LIFE POLICY

The best way to accurately judge the cost of a whole life policy is to
use the interest-adjusted net cost index and the interest-adjusted net
payment index.

Interest-Adjusted Net Cost Index

Devised almost two decades ago, the index is a major improvement
on the old net cost method of measuring a whole life policy's cost over
a period of years. Under the old method, you simply added up all the
premiums paid, subtracted the cash value and the dividends, and considered the result the actual cost of the policy. Using this calculation,
two policies might seem to have the same cost, when in fact if the
interest is considered (as in the interest-adjusted net cost index), one
is a much better buy than the other. The cost index for a whole life
policy is sometimes called the *surrender index*. Always look for a
surrender index that's as low as possible. Surrender indexes can even
be negative—the more negative the number, the less expensive the
policy. A negative cost index means that the accumulated dividends
plus the cash values exceed the accumulated premiums paid. (*Accumulated* means that the yearly figures are added and grow at compound
interest.) For further information on the index, see appendix B,
page 248.

Interest-Adjusted Net Payment Index

The payment index for a whole life policy does not reflect a policy's cash values, but rather measures the ongoing cost of holding onto the policy indefinitely (not cashing it in). It also measures the cost if you die while holding it. Again, the lower the number, the less expensive the policy.

When shopping for a whole life policy, keep these other points in mind:

1. *Duration.* Some policies are good or bad buys depending on how long you hold them. The Ratings show, for instance, that Mutual Benefit Life's Ordinary Life-1985 policy for a 25-year-old man buying $50,000 of coverage has a poor cost index if the man surrenders the policy at the end of five years, a mediocre index at the end of ten years, and a reasonably good index if he keeps the policy for twenty years.

Some policies have good payment indexes and bad cost indexes— they are no bargains if you live to cash in the policy, but good buys if you die while holding them. For example, Great West Life's Life 95 X-series for a 35-year-old woman buying $50,000 of coverage has a low $555 premium but skimpy cash values. (That's why it's important to look at both the net cost index and the net payment index when shopping for a whole life policy.)

2. *Policy Titles.* Our study showed that you can't judge a whole life policy by its name. You might think, for example, that Crown Life's Low Cost Life Preferred policy is something you shouldn't pass up. We think you should—it's neither low-cost nor preferred, and it ranked near the bottom or middle of the Ratings for nonparticipating policies.

3. *Par or Nonpar?* Even though our sample of nonpar policies in our 1986 study was small, it appears that par policies were, on the whole, better buys. That finding is consistent with a recent FTC report and with the marketing practices of most insurance companies. During recent years of high interest rates, companies have sold few nonpar policies because they were not competitive. Even stock companies, which traditionally issued nonpar policies, have preferred instead to sell universal life or current assumption whole life.

4. *Multiple Policy Offerings.* Some companies offer more than one whole life policy, targeting each for a specific group of potential policy-

holders. Prudential, for instance, sent us three policies: The Modified Life 5 and the Modified Life 3 have lower initial premiums than the Estate 25. In exchange for the lower initial premiums, a buyer gives up some dividends and cash value in the beginning, and cash values and dividends begin to build later than with the Estate 25 policy. As always, the interest-adjusted net cost and net payment indexes tell the story. As you can see from the Ratings, all three of the Prudential policies were fairly mediocre buys.

5. *Dividend History.* A number of companies have paid consistently high dividends over the years and are eager to promote this fact in their sales presentations, asserting that because no one can predict how large dividends will be in the future, past performance is the only guide. That may or may not be true. Certainly it doesn't hurt to look at the company's dividend history as reported in *Best's Review*, which can be found in most libraries. Note that Best's gives a company's dividend performance for one particular policy, face amount, and age, so the information may not predict what you'll actually receive because companies pay different dividends to different groups of policyholders.

RECOMMENDATIONS

Can you afford to cover your current insurance needs adequately with whole life insurance? After completing the needs analysis in chapter 2, we think the answer for most people will be no. The premiums are simply too high. A 35-year-old man, for instance, would pay between $2,000 and $3,000 for $200,000 of whole life coverage from most of the companies participating in our 1986 study. That's a good chunk of the yearly budget for most families. We recommend term insurance for most buyers, which is more affordable when you are young—when you need coverage the most.

If you *can* afford to protect your family adequately using either form of insurance, should you pick term or whole life? Let's consider the tax aspect first. Under current tax law, the accumulating cash values in a whole life policy are tax-deferred and partially tax-sheltered, so whole life might be a decent investment for people in a high-income bracket. But the Tax Reform Act of 1986 lowered everyone's marginal tax bracket, so whole life, as well as other tax shelters, might be far less appealing than before. Nevertheless, many financial publications and insurance agents push life insurance as one of the few remaining tax shelters. While those in the 15-percent tax bracket have little need for such shelters, people in the top tax bracket might consider whole life as an investment possibility while looking at other financial instruments as well (see "Whole Life as an Investment" on page 82).

Another reason to buy whole life is the possibility that you will need life insurance in your later years. For example, a man starting a family with a much younger woman can anticipate needing a life insurance policy well into his retirement years.

You can also think of whole life as a form of forced savings, especially if you have difficulty saving money systematically. But there are better ways to save, including payroll deduction plans at work, such as 401(k) plans. Also, the savings accumulation in the early years of a whole life policy is likely to be minimal. Our Ratings also show that most whole life policies are very poor investments if you plan to hold them for only a short time. We prefer more liquid investments that can be cashed in readily if you run into an unexpected need for funds. If you do decide to buy a whole life policy, use the checklist on page 78 and consider the following suggestions:

1. Don't judge a policy solely by its premium. A low or high premium is neither good nor bad. As we've pointed out, the interest-adjusted net cost indexes are the best measures of a policy's true cost. Look for policies that have both a low net payment index and a low net cost index. If the agent refuses to furnish them, go elsewhere.

2. Don't be confused by a *modified premium* policy—one in which the premium is low for a few years, then rises steeply. The initial low premium may be the bait designed to hook you on the company. A *vanishing premium* policy may also be a come-on. The idea of a fully paid-up policy in seven or eight years is appealing, but there's a real possibility those premiums won't vanish as quickly as the agent promised.

3. If you live or work in New York or Massachusetts, consider buying Savings Bank Life Insurance (SBLI) policies. Whole life policies as well as term policies are very good buys.

4. Despite current uncertainties over interest rates, we'd recommend choosing a participating policy over a nonparticipating one with a similar cost index. But pay close attention to the dividend illustration on a participating policy. Remember that dividends for future years are illustrations only and are not guaranteed.

5. Find out whether the company uses the portfolio method or the

WORKSHEET 4. WHOLE LIFE CHECKLIST

	Example[a]	Policy 1	Policy 2	Policy 3	Policy 4
Company	Northwestern Mutual	_____	_____	_____	_____
Policy name	Extra Ordinary Life	_____	_____	_____	_____
Amount of insurance	$100,000	_____	_____	_____	_____
Annual premium	$893	_____	_____	_____	_____
Interest-adjusted net cost index (surrender index)					
5-year	3.17	_____	_____	_____	_____
10-year	1.44	_____	_____	_____	_____
20-year	−2.44	_____	_____	_____	_____
Interested-adjusted net payment index					
5-year	8.93	_____	_____	_____	_____
10-year	8.93	_____	_____	_____	_____
20-year	8.92	_____	_____	_____	_____
Illustrated cash values[b]					
end of 5th year	$3,344	_____	_____	_____	_____
end of 10th year	$9,895	_____	_____	_____	_____
end of 15th year	$21,114	_____	_____	_____	_____
end of 20th year	$39,476	_____	_____	_____	_____
Dividends expected?	Yes	_____	_____	_____	_____
Illustrated dividends[b]					
end of 5th year	$215	_____	_____	_____	_____
end of 10th year	$624	_____	_____	_____	_____
end of 15th year	$1,318	_____	_____	_____	_____
end of 20th year	$2,353	_____	_____	_____	_____
Equivalent level dividend					
5th year	1.03	_____	_____	_____	_____
10th year	2.32	_____	_____	_____	_____
20th year	6.27	_____	_____	_____	_____
Cost index plus equivalent level dividend (worst-case scenario)					
5th year	4.20	_____	_____	_____	_____
10th year	3.76	_____	_____	_____	_____
20th year	3.83	_____	_____	_____	_____

	Example[a]	Policy 1	Policy 2	Policy 3	Policy 4
Direct recognition of loans in dividends	Yes	____	____	____	____
Method used to determine dividend interest rate					
Portfolio	Yes	____	____	____	____
Investment year		____	____	____	____
Other		____	____	____	____
Basis for dividend illustrations					
Current experience	Yes	____	____	____	____
Future experience		____	____	____	____
Other		____	____	____	____
How are dividends used?	Paid-up additions	____	____	____	____
Policy loan rate	8%, but can go lower	____	____	____	____
Rating classification (if substandard, what table is used?)	Standard nonsmoker	____	____	____	____

[a] Example based on $100,000 policy for 35-year-old man.
[b] Dividends and cash values are based on current scale and assume no borrowing.

investment year method in calculating its dividends. If interest rates are rising fast, and a company using the investment year method changes the rate every two or three years, you won't get the benefit of the rising rates as quickly. On the other hand, if interest rates are falling, dividends will stay higher for a longer period of time. In the last year or two, companies have changed their rates less frequently in order to continue illustrating higher dividends to their prospective customers.

6. If you want to know how big an impact the dividends have on the interest-adjusted net cost index, ask the agent for the *equivalent level dividend*. Adding that figure to the cost index gives you a worst-case scenario—the theoretical cost of the policy if no dividends are paid at all. Example: the interest-adjusted net cost index for five years is 3.17 and the equivalent level dividend is 1.03. The sum of those numbers—4.20—is a measure of the policy's cost without dividends. If you compare that number with similar figures for other policies, the lower the number, the better.

7. If you are considering a whole life policy mainly as an invest-

ment, check the rate-of-return estimates in the Ratings. Choose a policy that has a high yield at all durations, because you don't know when you'll want to cash it in. If you are interested in a policy we didn't rate, ask the agent to find out the *Linton yield* for you. (Linton yield is a method of calculating a rate of return for a cash value policy. See glossary.) Without this figure, your only clue will be the cost indexes, although a policy with a good cost index is likely to have a good Linton yield. (At least one company, Guardian Life, has begun to show estimated rates of return for its whole life policies.)

8. If you buy a whole life policy because you can easily borrow against the cash values, remember that outstanding loans at the time of your death will lower the death benefit paid to your survivors. Also, because the interest on policy loans is no longer tax-deductible, there's little advantage in using your whole life policy for leverage.

9. The interest-adjusted net cost index for a cash value policy such as whole life cannot be compared with that for a term policy. You can only use an index to compare term policies or one whole life policy with another, because the index doesn't take into account what the term policyholder can do with the money he or she saves by not paying the high initial premium required by whole life policies.

10. If an agent offers you a current assumption policy, you should know when the policy elements can change or you may be in for a big—and perhaps costly—surprise if your premium rises suddenly or your cash values dip dramatically. Ask the agent, for instance, if the company can change the premium, the mortality charge, and the interest rate. And, if so, how often? How is the new rate determined? How has the company treated old policyholders and what rates has the company credited to their cash values? Remember, actuaries base the price of the nonguaranteed elements of current assumption policies on projected future experience. If the mortality experience is worse than projected—for example, many more people die of AIDS—the cash values in your policy might grow very slowly.

TAX BENEFITS OF WHOLE LIFE

Whole life policies and other kinds of cash value insurance have enjoyed special tax advantages since the inception of the federal income tax in 1913. Over the years the insurance industry has lobbied long and hard (and successfully) to maintain the favorable tax status of life insurance policies. Let's take a look at how the tax privileges of whole life can affect your insurance policy.

Cash Values

Under current tax law, the interest credited within the cash value buildup in a whole life policy is tax-deferred. In other words, while the cash value in your policy generally increases each year, you don't have to pay taxes yearly on any of that increase. Whole life insurance is a tax-deferred investment up to the day you withdraw your money, and then only a portion of the cash value is taxed. You are taxed on the amount by which the cash value exceeds the sum of the premiums you paid over the years (minus any dividends). That's your "gain," on which you pay tax at ordinary income rates. That gain may not be trivial if you've owned a policy that paid consistently high dividends. For example, the expected gain on Northwestern Mutual's Extra Ordinary Life policy is some $12,000 if the policyholder surrenders it after 20 years. If the policyholder's marginal rate is 28 percent, some $4,000 of additional tax will have to be paid.

Sometimes you can make a "1035 exchange," which allows you to switch from one cash value policy to another and avoid paying taxes on your gain. In effect, you roll your cash value into the new policy, which continues to grow tax-deferred.

Death Benefits

Death benefits, whether from whole life or any other life insurance policy, are not subject to federal income tax or most state income taxes. The insurance proceeds, however, may count as part of your estate for tax purposes. Therefore, if your estate is greater than $600,000, your heirs may owe some federal estate tax.

Dividends

Life insurance dividends are not taxable, as are dividends from common stocks. While stock dividends represent a share in a company's profits, the Internal Revenue Service considers dividends from a life insurance policy to be refunds of a previous overcharge.

Loan Interest

When you borrow against part of the cash value of a life insurance policy, you pay interest on the loan. Under the new tax law, that interest is no longer deductible for individuals. In other words, the federal government no longer helps pay the cost of your borrowing, thus making the loan feature of whole life far less attractive than it once was.

WHOLE LIFE AS AN INVESTMENT

Historically, whole life insurance hasn't been a great investment. In 1979, the FTC found that the rates of return for dividend-paying policies averaged 1.9 percent over ten years and 4.6 percent over twenty years—a poor return at a time when market rates averaged between $6\frac{1}{2}$ and $7\frac{1}{2}$ percent. A 1985 FTC report found that whole life policies had improved somewhat, but their rates of return were still below the market rates on other investments.

Agents frequently tell buyers that there is no such thing as a rate of return on a whole life policy. Others say such a policy is a "package" of protection and savings and it's impossible to separate the two components in order to calculate an accurate rate of return. Actually, it is quite possible to separate the two components mathematically.

The rate-of-return figure most commonly calculated by actuaries is the Linton yield. The rate of return derived from the Linton yield depends on the assumption made about the cost of death protection— the lower the mortality charges used, the smaller the yield will appear to be. Higher mortality charges will result in a higher apparent yield. For our 1986 study, our consulting actuaries calculated Linton yields for each whole life policy at the end of five, ten, and twenty years, using the lowest mortality charges we had found in our study of term policies. Negative Linton yields at the end of five years reflect the fact that whole life policies in general have miserable rates of return if you hold them for this short period of time—expenses charged against the policy eat up much of your accumulated cash value. If you hold them for ten or twenty years, the rate of return for some policies is comparable with other investments.

Insurance regulators don't require companies to disclose rates of return for their whole life policies, and companies rarely give them out voluntarily. Nevertheless, agents often speak of a rate of return. Whether you can trust their figures is another story. A Prudential agent showed our reporter a Modified 5 whole life policy and asserted that the total return was in excess of "12 percent including dividends." But the agent was considerably off the mark. According to our calculations, the Linton yield for the Modified Life 5 for a 35-year-old woman buying $200,000 of coverage was about 5½ percent at ten years and about 9 percent at twenty years.

Since our last survey of life insurance in 1980, Linton yields have improved markedly. At that time a 2 to 6 percent yield was typical; a 7 to 10 percent return now isn't unusual if the policy is held for twenty years. It appears, then, that insurance companies have significantly improved their whole life policies.

But part of the improvement may be only temporary, since the high interest rates of the early 1980s have found their way into higher dividends on whole life policies, which in turn have found their way into the Linton yields. The yields for bonds, a typical investment vehicle for insurance companies, reflect current market conditions. Municipal bond yields in January 1982 peaked at 13.5 percent, while in January 1987 they were averaging about 6.6 percent. The high yields of 1982 eventually found their way into the dividends companies paid, and these dividends are reflected in our calculated Linton yields. If we should do the same calculations two years from now, the Linton yields might be much lower, reflecting the lower bond yields of 1987.

How do you determine whether a whole life policy is a good investment for you? Are you better off putting your money in a fully taxable investment rather than in a life insurance policy that is partially exempt from taxes? The answer depends on your marginal tax rate, the rate offered on a competing investment, and the rate of return on the insurance policy (a number you're not likely to find except from our cost survey).

How to Calculate Your After-Tax Return

Let's assume you're in the 28-percent tax bracket, and are offered a fully taxable investment returning 9.5 percent. You're also considering $200,000 of coverage from Northwestern Mutual's Extra Ordinary Life policy, which has a twenty-year Linton yield of 9.87 percent for a 35-year-old man.

To determine the after-tax return on the alternative investment, first subtract your marginal rate from 1 (1 − .28 = .72). That number is the percentage of your return that you actually can keep. Multiply that percentage by the return you'll receive from the taxable investment (.72 × 9.5 = 6.84). The result is your after-tax return, which can be compared with the return on the life insurance policy. In other words, the life insurance policy would have to return at least 6.84 percent to be a better deal than the taxable investment with a pretax return of 9.5 percent. As you can see, the Extra Ordinary Life policy does that. This is not exactly a perfect comparison, however, because the calculation assumes the life insurance policy is not taxable.

We carried the analysis further by asking Northwestern Mutual to tell us what portion of the cash value on its policy was taxable if a policyholder surrendered it at the end of twenty years. The total cash value is $46,278. Of that amount, the policyholder paid $33,320 in premiums, which is considered his investment in the product. His gain is $12,958, or about 28 percent.

To calculate a reasonable approximation of the after-tax yield on the life insurance policy, multiply your marginal tax rate by the percentage of the cash value that's taxable. In our example, the yield is .0784 (.28 × .28). In other words, because the effective tax rate on the gain is about 8 percent, you would keep 92 percent. Now multiply the percentage you keep by the policy's Linton yield, (9.87 × .92 = 9.08). This is your after-tax yield on the policy. Clearly, an after-tax return of about 9 percent on the whole life policy is better than the 6.84 percent after-tax return on the competing investment. Remember, though, that such an analysis assumes that current dividends will be paid forever. As we've pointed out, that's not likely to happen. In fact, it's a good bet that dividends and Linton yields will drop over the next twenty years.

To do a similar calculation for another policy, ask the agent for the policy's cash value after twenty years and what portion will be taxable. (You can also do this analysis with ten-year cash values.) With that number and the Linton yield from our study, you should be able to compare investments. Unfortunately, if you're considering a policy not in our study, it's almost impossible to get the information necessary to make a proper comparison among possible investments.

SINGLE-PREMIUM WHOLE LIFE

Single-premium whole life is more of an investment than life insurance protection, and is sold to people who have a good chunk of money to invest—usually $5,000 or more. Appealing to buyers as "spendable wealth," single-premium whole life magnifies all the tax advantages of whole life and is sold to investors as a tax shelter.

Here's how it works. You make a one-time payment to the insurance company. That payment buys a specific amount of insurance protection and forms the basis for your cash values. The company then agrees to credit interest to your money. Some companies quote that interest rate as a gross rate, others as a net rate. A *gross rate* means that the company will deduct policy fees and mortality and expense charges from your premium before interest is applied to the remainder. A *net rate* means that these expenses come out of the "spread"—the difference between what the insurance company earns on its own investments and what it credits to your account. If a company earns 11 percent on its investments, for example, and pays you an interest rate of 8.5 percent, it has a 2.5 percent spread out of which to pay these expenses.

The current rate a company credits may be guaranteed for a specific period—usually one year, but sometimes for as long as five years. Companies also guarantee to credit at least a minimum interest rate to your cash values, usually 4 to 6 percent. Again, the guaranteed rate may be quoted on a gross or a net basis. If the company quotes these rates on a gross basis, you won't actually earn those rates, but will receive something less.

Cancellation Penalties

Once you deposit money into a single-premium whole life policy, it can be costly to take it out. You may be liable for taxes on the interest your single premium earned, and most companies hit you with a surrender charge—usually 7 to 9 percent of the premium—if you cancel within the first few years. So if you had deposited $50,000 in a policy with a 7-percent surrender charge in the second year, the company would charge you $3,500 if you wanted to cancel the policy. These charges usually taper off and end by the tenth year.

Some policies take the sting out of these penalties by offering a bailout provision that, under certain conditions, waives the surrender charge. Some bailout clauses are triggered when the rate a company currently credits to your money is one to two percentage points less than the rate it initially credited. Bailout clauses may apply only for certain periods, however.

Loan Provisions

Perhaps the biggest attraction of single-premium whole life is its loan provision, which makes it possible to generate "tax-free" income by taking a loan against cash values. This feature makes it easy to sell single-premium life as an income-producing investment. Here's how it works: If you borrow against your policy, the insurance company still pays interest on your cash values, but uses two different interest rates. The portion of the cash value that serves as collateral for the loan is called the *loaned cash value* and receives a lower rate than the balance, which is your *unloaned cash value*. Companies also charge an interest rate on the policy loan. The difference between this policy loan rate and the rate on loaned cash values is called the *net cost of borrowing*. If, for example, a company charges an 8-percent rate on the loan and credits 5 percent on your loaned cash values, the net cost of borrowing is 3 percent.

There's another dimension to the mechanics of borrowing on single-premium whole life policies. If you borrow only against the interest portion of your cash values, the company charges the same rate on the policy loan as the rate it credits to loaned cash values, which makes the net cost of borrowing 0 percent. But if you borrow against the portion of the cash value that is considered principal—in other words, part of the single premium—the policy loan rate is higher than the rate credited to the loaned cash value.

Loans from life insurance policies are not taxable, so companies promote single-premium life as an ideal way to invest money, accumulate it tax-deferred, and borrow the earnings in order to produce a stream of tax-free income. Of course, policyholders must repay their loans if they want the full death benefit paid to their survivors. But for most buyers of single-premium policies, insurance protection is a secondary consideration.

As more companies advertise the tax advantages of these policies, some industry officials worry that Congress will consider single-premium whole life another tax loophole, and close it. If that happens, the major insurance companies are optimistic that Congress will continue to allow already existing loans to remain tax-favored.

Investment Advantages

How does single-premium life stack up as an investment compared with municipal bonds or tax-free money funds? It has several advantages: Your principal is stable; its value doesn't fluctuate the way it would in a bond or bond mutual fund. Nor do you have to worry that the insurance company will cancel the deal. Most bonds have call provisions that permit the issuer to call in the bond before it reaches maturity. There's no similar feature with single-premium life. If you invest instead in a tax-free money fund, your principal won't fluctuate, but at certain times the fund might credit your principal with far less than an insurance company does.

To accurately evaluate the merits of the insurance investment, you need to know how much you're paying in fees and charges. But like most whole life policies, the way these charges are bundled makes it difficult, if not impossible, to estimate. So, single-premium life is a bit of a gamble. If you buy it to generate tax-free income, you're also gambling that Congress will continue to allow these tax shelters. But if you're comfortable taking that risk, keep these points in mind:

1. Make sure the interest rate quoted is net of fees and charges, because you'll want to know what your money will earn after the insurance company takes its cut. Some agents quote a gross rate, some a net rate. Make sure any rates are comparable.

2. Make sure you understand the loan provisions and the rates a company charges and credits—both the policy loan rate and the rates credited to loaned and unloaned cash values for both interest and principal. If you buy the policy in order to borrow the tax-free earnings, choose a policy with the most favorable loan arrangements.

3. Find out how and when the company credits interest. Ask if the mortality charges come out of the spread, or has the company reserved the right to deduct mortality charges from the cash value? Are the mortality charges guaranteed? Companies offer plans with or without guaranteed mortality charges.

4. Single-premium life is not a very liquid investment. Before you sign up, consider whether you'll need to withdraw all of your money

within the next ten years. If you think you may, invest instead in a tax-free money market fund or a bank certificate of deposit with a short maturity. Your money may earn less, but at least you'll be able to withdraw it, if you need to, without paying a severe penalty. If you think you have a long-term savings need, also consider investing in a high-quality single-premium deferred annuity. Over a long period, some of these annuities will perform better than single-premium life policies. You can buy annuities from insurance agents, stockbrokers, and banks.

Other Recommendations

We do not recommend single-premium whole life for people who simply need insurance protection. Families who need a good deal of insurance protection should buy term, especially because single premium's tax advantages are not very meaningful to those in the 15-percent or even 28-percent tax bracket. Moreover, families with a large insurance need may not be able to afford the cost of the premium needed to buy adequate amounts of coverage from single-premium whole life.

6

Universal Life Insurance

Universal life is the life insurance industry's chameleon—agents like to say it adapts itself to almost any insurance need. Want to build cash values? A universal life policy can do that. Need term insurance? Universal life can act as a term policy. Strapped for cash to pay your premiums? Universal life lets you skip a payment or two.

Because of its versatility, universal life has eclipsed sales of whole life in recent years. It has fast become the industry's new bread-and-butter product, already accounting for nearly 40 percent of all life insurance sold.

Until universal life came along, the insurance industry had changed about as much as the Rock of Gibraltar, the familiar symbol of the Prudential Insurance Company. Year after year, the industry sold billions of dollars of whole life insurance, a product invented more than one hundred years ago, with a paltry rate of return to consumers of 2 to 6 percent. Universal life changed all that. For the first time, the insurance industry could sell a policy that paid rates competitive with other financial instruments, and sales pitches no longer emphasized insurance as death protection but insurance as a lucrative investment.

Universal life also gave many lesser-known companies a chance to shine. Some of the industry's household names, notably the big mutual companies like Prudential and Massachusetts Mutual, straggled belatedly into the universal life market. Today, some of these companies are still not keen about selling the product, and you may find their agents pushing instead old-fashioned whole life or the new variable life policies, which shift all the investment risk to policyholders. In our 1986 cost survey, the universal policies from some of the best-known companies proved the poorest buys for consumers.

HOW UNIVERSAL LIFE WORKS

With traditional whole life policies you never know for sure how much of your premium has gone to pay for company expenses, the cost of insurance protection, and the policy's savings component. And you never know what interest rate the company credits to your cash value. With universal life, you can see how all the elements of your policy work—the premium, the death benefit, and the cash value.

Premiums

The company credits your annual premium to your cash value account and deducts monthly from that account the cost of your insurance protection. The company may also deduct charges for its expenses. The balance is your cash value, which then accumulates with interest. Every policyholder receives an annual statement showing all transactions.

Cash Value

Money in the cash value account is readily available to you. You can borrow against it, withdraw the entire amount, or withdraw only part of it. The ability to make these partial withdrawals is a big advantage of universal life over whole life, although with a partial withdrawal your death benefit is reduced by the amount of the withdrawal and you can't restore the death benefit by repaying the amount withdrawn. You can put money back in your policy (subject to any expense charges) and the cash value will increase, but you may have to prove that your health is still good if you want to restore the death benefit.

Taxes

Like a whole life policy, a universal life policy provides a tax shelter of sorts. The interest earned on the cash value is not taxed as it accumulates. Only when you withdraw it, do you pay taxes on the portion that exceeds the sum of the premiums you have paid. But the taxation of a partial withdrawal also depends on how long you've held the policy. If you keep a universal life policy for fifteen years, the government won't tax a partial withdrawal unless you take out a sum equal to the amount you put into the policy. If you've held the policy for a shorter period, a withdrawal may be taxable depending on how much money you've put into the policy and how much you withdraw.

Coverage

Universal life coverage comes in two forms, called Option A and Option B. Under *Option A* your survivors receive the face amount of the policy, just as they do with term insurance or whole life insurance. Under *Option B* (for which you'll usually pay a higher premium), they'll receive both the face amount and your accumulated cash value. Suppose, for example, you buy a $100,000 universal life policy at age 42 and die ten years later, after the policy has built $11,500 in cash value. At your death, your survivors would receive the $100,000 face amount plus the $11,500 cash value.

Option A Versus Option B

Table 5 shows what happens to cash and cash surrender values and death benefits when a policyholder chooses Option A or Option B. Option A shows a level death benefit. Option B shows an increasing death benefit. A person can also choose Option B and pay the same premium he or she would pay under Option A, but the cash and cash surrender values would be lower than if the person had chosen Option A or had paid a higher premium.

To illustrate how this works, we have used the Challenger Max policy once offered by Life of Virginia. For the purposes of this example, we have assumed that the company credits a 7-percent interest rate throughout the life of the policy.

TABLE 5. UNIVERSAL LIFE—OPTION A VS. OPTION B

Option A—Level death benefit

Age	Annual premium	Cash value	Cash surrender value	Death benefit
40	$507	$2,326	$2,274	$100,000
45	507	5,279	5,279	100,000
50	507	8,870	8,870	100,000
55	507	12,993	12,993	100,000
65	507	22,542	22,542	100,000

Option B—Same premium as Option A

Age	Annual premium	Cash value	Cash surrender value	Death benefit
40	$507	$2,317	$2,266	$102,317
45	507	5,227	5,227	105,227
50	507	8,679	8,679	108,679
55	507	12,423	12,423	112,423
65	507	19,181	19,181	119,181

Option B—Larger premium than Option A

Age	Annual premium	Cash value	Cash surrender value	Death benefit
40	$839	$4,301	$4,194	$104,301
45	839	10,001	10,001	110,001
50	839	17,367	17,367	117,367
55	839	26,601	26,601	126,601
65	839	51,865	51,865	151,865

How Companies Price a Universal Life Policy

When actuaries price a universal life policy, they mix three ingredients: (1) the interest rate credited to the cash value; (2) the cost of the death benefit, often called the mortality charge or cost of insurance; and (3) the company's expenses. Naturally you'd want the interest rate to be as high as possible and the mortality charge and expenses to be as low as possible. But you won't often find all three elements highly favorable in a given policy. Companies usually try to find a formula that appeals to the consumer while generating profits for the company at the same time. The particular mix a company concocts determines whether a policy is a good or bad buy. Here's what you should know about the three main ingredients in a universal life policy:

1. *Interest Rate.* The interest rate credited to your cash value is the key element that sells the policy. If the company's investment experience has been good, it may credit high rates to its policyholders' cash values. A company's board of directors usually determines the rate, and may change it as often as once a month. Sometimes you may find a policy that pays a lower rate on the first $1,000 of your cash value, or you may find a company paying a slightly higher rate on very large cash values.

Each company guarantees it will credit your cash value with at least a minimum interest rate, typically 4 to 4½ percent. But over the past few years, companies have credited very high rates even though interest rates on other financial instruments fell dramatically.

The Life Insurance Marketing and Research Association has tracked this disparity. In January 1986, the median interest rate quoted for universal life policies was 10.2 percent, while the average rate for three-month Treasury bills was 7.04 percent. In November 1986 it was 9.2 percent, but the Treasury bill average had sunk to 5.35 percent. When we conducted our survey in 1986, interest rates for the policies we looked at ranged from 8¼ to 11 percent.

Companies that sell mostly whole life policies complain that their universal life competitors are offering much higher rates than their investment earnings justify. Because high interest rates are what sells universal life policies, no company wants to be the first to lower its rates. So far, companies have been able to keep rates high by reducing their profit margins, drawing on surplus accumulated from old policyholders, or by looking for more profit from their mortality charges. How long will the rate bonanza last? No one knows.

2. *Mortality Charge.* The mortality charge pays for your insurance protection, and a company counts on this charge to cover its death claims. It's also possible that a company can hit its policyholders with charges for administrative expenses hidden in the mortality charge, or raise the mortality charge as a way of compensating for its high interest rate. Each policy contains a table showing the maximum amount

the company charges you for its mortality costs. Legally, there's nothing to prevent companies from charging the maximum, but most companies were charging less when we did our study.

3. *Expense Charges.* The expense charges assessed against your policy normally do not change over the policy's life. Companies assess these charges as frontloads and/or backloads.

With a *frontloaded* policy, a company deducts anywhere from 5 to 9 percent of each premium for its expenses before it credits the premium to your cash value. It usually deducts the same amount from each premium, though a few companies take larger deductions in the first year and smaller ones in later years. With a *backloaded* policy, a company credits the entire premium to your account. But when you want to surrender your policy, or make partial withdrawals, it charges you a hefty sum for doing so. In our 1986 study we found that such surrender charges can be as high as 150 percent of the first-year premium, which means if you cash in the policy after a year or two, surrender charges might swallow your entire cash value.

Because the insurance company's expenses are greatest in the early years of the policy when selling costs and agents' commissions are high, the surrender charges gradually diminish for most backloaded policies, disappearing somewhere between the tenth and the fifteenth year. In a few policies, we found surrender charges rising after the first year and remaining high for a few years before gradually tapering off. With policies that have both frontloads and backloads, the loads are typically lower, and vanish more quickly than on policies with only one kind of load.

Initially, frontloaded policies were popular, but then agents complained that consumers were reluctant to buy policies that had high expense charges eating up their premiums. Now backloaded policies are in vogue—consumers don't see the charges until they withdraw part of their cash value or surrender their policies. But the charges are there nonetheless.

If you're interested in buying universal life, be aware that companies stress different ingredients of the pricing mix, depending on their marketing strategies. One company may try to impress consumers with its high interest rates, then offset the extra interest by imposing high charges for expenses and mortality costs, while another may stress its low expense charges and mortality costs, but offer a low interest rate on the cash value.

PICKING YOUR OWN PREMIUM

Unlike whole life premiums, universal life premiums are not cast in concrete. You can vary your premiums from time to time depending on your circumstances—a flexibility that makes universal life easy to sell as the only policy you'll ever need. "If I can show customers flexible insurance payments, they love it," says an agent for Union Central Life.

You can adapt a universal life policy to your changing family circumstances and can even pick the premium you want to pay. Or you can pay the *target* premium, which is the minimum premium designed to keep the policy in force for your entire life and still allow you to accumulate a rather substantial cash value. If you pay the target premiums year after year, your policy will behave much like a garden-variety whole life policy.

If you pay one-third to one-half less than the target premium, you'll accumulate some cash value and receive the same amount of insurance coverage you'd receive if you had paid the higher premiums. When you pay a lot less than the target premium, some policies behave like term insurance and build no cash values. Most companies don't like to sell universal life this way.

If you've paid the target premiums faithfully, you might be able to skip a payment or two in years when your budget is tight. And if you pay more than the target premium, perhaps by depositing a windfall you've inherited, you may never have to pay another cent on the policy. You can't just throw a million dollars into your policy, though. The tax code says that the amount you put in must bear some relationship to the amount of insurance you're buying. That rule (sometimes referred to as the "tax corridor") is intended to keep people from using a universal life policy as a tax-sheltered money market fund.

One of the benefits of owning a universal life policy is that you can easily increase your coverage without paying new policy fees and acquisition costs (although the company has the right to ask whether you have contracted some serious illness that may make you uninsurable). But if you buy a brand-new universal policy in order to get additional coverage, you would have to pay all these costs again. When you do increase your coverage, you can sometimes keep paying the same premium as before, although your cash value will then build more slowly.

There is nothing particularly magical about paying less than the target premium, skipping payments, or increasing coverage. Insurance is never free—you pay for the protection in one way or another.

For example, the cash value functions as a reservoir from which the company drains off the money to pay mortality and expense charges. If the cash value of your policy grows too slowly, either because your premium payments have been small or intermittent or because the company pays lower interest than you expected, the day will come when you'll have to come up with more money or your policy will lapse. One of our readers purchased a universal life policy in 1981, convinced that universal life was "the greatest thing since sliced bread." But as the interest rate credited to his account dropped lower and lower, he found out that when the rate hit 6 to 7 percent, the policy would run out of money. If he wanted to continue the insurance protection, he'd have to increase his annual premium of $1,200 to keep the $50,000 policy in force. "It did not take long," the reader said, "to figure out that universal life was simply expensive term insurance, and I dropped it like a hot potato."

THE CHAMELEON CAN BITE

Like a chameleon, a universal life policy can indeed fool you. These are some of the ways a universal life policy can turn out to be less attractive than it appeared:

1. A company can entice you with a sky-high interest rate today and switch to a more down-to-earth rate tomorrow, making your universal life policy a less-than-outstanding investment. Or an unscrupulous or incompetent agent can mislead you by showing cash value accumulations based on a higher rate than the company is currently paying.

2. Some companies quote their rates as simple interest; others quote a compound rate to make their policies more attractive. One company, for example, advertised its rate as 10.47 percent, which is the same as 10 percent interest compounded monthly. Many consumers who compared the 10.47 percent rate with another company's advertised nominal rate of 10 percent may not have realized that the two rates were identical.

3. A company can raise or lower its mortality charges, hiding other expenses in those charges. If, for example, inflation heats up again,

and a company's expenses are higher than expected, the company can recoup those costs by increasing its mortality charges. The annual statement that the company sends to the policyholder would reveal that the company had raised the mortality charge, but the policyholder may think advancing age had caused the increase. "The average guy on the street wouldn't know what happened," says a sales official at Connecticut Mutual.

4. The payment flexibility of universal life can lull you into a false sense that you're getting life insurance protection without really having to pay for it. Skipping payments or paying lower premiums is fine, but at some point you may have to pay higher premiums or add money to your account if you want to keep your insurance in force. The same thing can happen if an agent sells you a *vanishing premium* universal life policy. The premiums vanish only if interest rates stay high enough to generate large cash values that cover the cost of your insurance protection. If interest rates take a nosedive, the company will come calling for more money.

Vanishing-premium universal life policies have been as popular and as confusing as vanishing-premium whole life, described on page 66. One of our readers thought an agent had offered him a whole life policy, when in fact the agent was pushing a *dynamic vanishing-premium* universal life policy. The agent scrawled on the policy illustration that the reader could stop paying after the fifth year, yet a warning printed on the illustration said the premiums would vanish *only* if the company continued to deduct its current mortality charge and credit 11 percent interest. This was an unlikely assumption in early 1986.

TAILORING A UNIVERSAL LIFE POLICY

The biggest virtue of a universal life policy is its flexibility. A 30-year-old man buys a $100,000 universal life policy when his first child is born. He chooses to pay a low annual premium of $300 because he is just starting his career. The $300 will keep his insurance in force for awhile, but it is too low to build much cash value. In the third year he gets a $1,000 Christmas bonus, which he puts into the policy. That boosts his cash value to $1,488. In the fourth year he and his wife are expecting their second child, so he skips a premium payment and instead withdraws $500 to redo a bedroom. When the child is born he needs more insurance, so he doubles his coverage to $200,000. His $300 annual premium is far too low to maintain his insurance protection and generate cash value (which at this point is only $1,109), so the next year he doubles the premium to $600.

Because he wants to use his life insurance policy as a savings vehicle for his children's college educations, he must increase his premiums even more so that the policy will generate enough money to pay part of the cost. In the next few years, as his income goes up, he increases the annual premium gradually from $600 to $1,500. In the twelfth year he is able to pay a premium of $2,250.

By the time he's 47, his oldest child is ready for college and the policy's cash value now totals $22,172. He begins withdrawing money to pay college expenses, and reduces his coverage by $20,000 for each of the four years his children are in college. By the time his second child graduates, his coverage has dwindled to $40,000. The year after graduation, he gives each child $1,500 to start them on their own.

After that, he doesn't feel he needs his life insurance policy. Both he and his wife will have generous retirement pensions from their employers and his group term insurance policy through his employer will provide whatever insurance his wife would need until her retirement.

Table 6 shows the transactions this man makes through his policy. (The policy assumes very low expense loads.)

SPECIAL FEATURES

Universal life policies have a few special features you should know about if you choose to buy this breed of insurance coverage. Some of these features are unique to particular policies. In our study, for example, we found that the United Presidential 10/20 policy returned to the policyholder all the mortality charges paid after ten and twenty years, while Ohio National's Optimalife II called for an escalation of the mortality charges to the maximum if a policyholder's cash value dropped below a certain level.

Other features were common to several policies:

1. *Interest Rate Guarantees.* Nearly all the policies come with guarantees of 4 or 4½ percent. The Valley Forge Series II policy had one at 6 percent and also guaranteed that its current rate would never be less than the fifty-two-week Treasury bill rate, less one percent. Such

TABLE 6
FLEXIBILITY OF A UNIVERSAL LIFE POLICY

Age (years)	Amount of insurance	Premiums	Cash value	Withdrawal	Interest rate
30	$100,000	$ 300	$ 42	$ 0	8.00%
31	100,000	300	247	0	7.75
32	100,000	1,300	1,488	0	7.50
33	100,000	0	953	500	7.50
34	200,000	300	1,109	0	7.50
35	200,000	600	1,582	0	7.75
36	200,000	600	2,088	0	7.75
37	200,000	600	2,635	0	8.00
38	200,000	1,000	3,633	0	8.00
39	200,000	1,000	4,729	0	8.50
40	200,000	1,250	6,172	0	8.50
41	200,000	2,250	8,742	0	8.25
42	200,000	1,250	10,488	0	8.25
43	200,000	1,250	12,313	0	7.75
44	200,000	1,500	14,528	0	7.75
45	200,000	1,500	16,906	0	7.75
46	200,000	1,500	19,450	0	7.75
47	200,000	1,500	22,172	0	7.75
48	180,000	0	20,347	3,000	7.75
49	160,000	0	18,393	3,000	7.75
50	140,000	0	16,304	3,000	7.75
51	120,000	0	14,075	3,000	7.75
52	100,000	0	10,079	4,500	7.75
53	80,000	0	7,421	3,000	7.75
54	60,000	0	4,592	3,000	7.75
55	40,000	0	1,588	3,000	7.75
56	20,000	0	23	1,500	7.75
57	20,000	0	−56	0	7.75

guarantees aren't very important when interest rates are high, but assume a much greater significance when rates go down. If rates fall so low that companies start paying their guaranteed rates, a policy with a higher guarantee will have an edge.

2. *Policy Loan Provisions.* You can borrow against the cash value in your universal life policy at the set interest rate stated in your

policy. These can include an 8-percent fixed rate, a variable rate going no higher than 8 percent, or a variable rate tied to Moody's long-term bond index.

If you borrow, companies may credit the cash value you have not borrowed against with a higher rate than the cash value you have borrowed against. The policy loan rate and the rates credited to the cash values determine how favorable the loan provision is overall. Often the rate paid on the loaned cash value is the minimum guaranteed rate stated in the policy. But company practices vary. In our study, State Mutual's policy credited a 6-percent rate on loaned cash value, while Western-Southern's policy credited only 4 percent, the guaranteed rate. A company's current rate, based on the prevailing rates, is usually credited to the unloaned cash value.

3. *Guarantees Against Policy Lapse.* If you overuse the flexibility to set your own premium, your policy can run out of the money necessary to cover the cost of your insurance protection, and your coverage will lapse. Some companies guarantee they will not allow your coverage to lapse during the first two or three years of the policy as long as you pay a minimum premium. Occasionally you may find a company that extends such guarantees for as long as five years.

4. *Timing of Interest Credits.* Most companies credit interest on the day they receive your premium. But about one-third of the companies we studied chose to wait until the end of the month in which the premium was received. That's like a bank holding your payroll check and not crediting it to your checking account for several days.

5. *Excess Interest Penalties.* While many companies penalize you if you surrender a policy early, some deprive you of part of the interest credited to your cash value in the previous twelve months. That's called an excess interest penalty. *Excess interest* is the interest credited beyond the guaranteed rate. For example, your universal life policy has a cash value of $50,000 earning 8 percent, so your earnings would total $4,000 annually, disregarding compounding. But the company's guaranteed rate is only 4 percent, providing interest earnings of $2,000. If the company applied an excess interest penalty, you'd in effect be docked $2,000.

Century Life, Connecticut Mutual, First Colony, The Hartford, Life of Virginia, Metropolitan, Southwestern Life, and The Travelers all submitted policies that called for excess interest penalties in certain cases.

6. *Limits on Partial Withdrawals*. Some companies put restrictions on the amount of money you can take out of your policy. Connecticut Mutual, for example, allows no partial withdrawals in the first five years. When it does permit them, a policyholder can't withdraw more than 20 percent of the surrender value annually, and the minimum amount withdrawn must be at least $500. Other companies may have similar restrictions.

SHOPPING FOR A UNIVERSAL LIFE POLICY

It's virtually impossible for consumers to judge the cost of competing universal life policies on their own. While there is a standard cost comparison method for term and whole life (the interest-adjusted net cost index) that is accepted by both industry and regulators, there is no such widely accepted yardstick for universal life. True, regulators do require companies to disclose interest-adjusted net cost indexes for universal life policies, but such indexes are of dubious value because of universal life's flexible premiums. So, for our 1986 study we devised our own way to compare universal life policies, which you can adapt for your own purposes.

First, keep in mind that a major aim of our study was to find out which policies had the lowest expense and mortality charges, the ingredients of the pricing mix least likely to change. In order to do that, we projected each policy's cash and cash surrender value. The cash value is the fund from which your mortality charges and certain expense charges are paid. And, if you decide to cash in your policy, the cash value minus any backload charges becomes the surrender value.

We used each company's own expense and mortality charges, but a single interest rate for all—8 percent. As we've noted, the lower the expense and mortality charges, the higher your cash values are likely to be. For example, a 35-year-old man buying $100,000 of coverage from the top-ranked Woodmen of the World policy would accumulate some $12,625 in ten years. But if he bought the bottom-ranked Prudential policy, he'd accumulate only $9,556. We also accumulated cash and cash surrender values for each policy using the companies' own interest rates, which ranged from 8¼ to 11 percent in March 1986.

If you want to compare universal life policies, especially ones not in our Ratings, try the following procedure: Pick a current interest rate you consider reasonable, and ask several agents to show cash and cash surrender value accumulations, with a premium you select, for each year up to fifteen years. By asking each company for a projection using the same interest rate and the same premium, you can learn which policies have the lowest expense and mortality charges. (There's nothing to prevent a company from raising its mortality charges later on, but you can't predict such changes in advance.) Once you have determined which policies have the lowest charges and expenses, look at the interest rate. If two companies have similar expenses and charges and one pays a much higher rate—say one-and-one-half to two percentage points more—buy the policy with the higher rate. If interest rates are similar, other features such as policy-loan provisions or excess interest penalties might tip the balance in favor of one policy or the other. Remember, you want a policy that has both a good cash value and a good cash surrender value.

TOP-RATED UNIVERSAL LIFE POLICIES

The stars of our 1986 universal life study were policies sold by little-known companies. For example, Woodmen of the World, a fraternal organization, sells a policy that ranked at or near the top of every Ratings table. Central Life of Des Moines, Iowa; Alexander Hamilton Life of Farmington Hills, Michigan; and Security-Connecticut of Avon, Connecticut, also had outstanding policies. USAA Life, which markets directly to consumers, had a very good policy. Although USAA markets its auto and homeowners policies only to present or former military officers and their families, the company says it will sell its life insurance policies to anyone.

By contrast the policies offered by Prudential, Metropolitan Life, New York Life, and Equitable—the industry's big four companies—were mediocre at best.

The Ratings show that you can't judge a universal life policy only by its interest rate, even though many companies and agents want you to do just that. Sometimes a company with a low interest rate also has low expense and mortality charges, making it a better policy than one whose interest rate is a percentage point or two higher. Again, it's the mix of interest rate, expense charges, and mortality charges that determines whether a universal life policy is a good buy.

Southwestern Life's Vision Universal Life policy is a good example.

The policy for a 25-year-old man buying $60,000 of coverage ranks eighth in our Ratings, yet its 9.50-percent interest rate is lower than the interest rate for the twenty-three companies that rank below it. On the other hand, New York Life's Target Life II offered a flashy 11 percent interest rate, but its high expenses and mortality charges offset its unusually high interest rate, and the policy was a mediocre-to-poor buy.

Some companies have better cash values than surrender values, and vice versa. A frontloaded policy shows a lower cash value in the early years than a policy that recoups its expenses when you surrender it. A policy with only frontloads will have a surrender value equal to its cash value, while backloaded policies show a lower surrender value in the early years and may be bad buys if you have to cash them in soon after purchase.

For instance, Valley Forge's Series II policy for a 35-year-old man buying $100,000 of coverage, surrendered in the first five years, will be a poor buy because of its high surrender charges. These charges, however, terminate at the end of the tenth year.

By contrast, the policies of Kemper and Inter-State Assurance are somewhat better for those policyholders who need to cancel their coverage by the end of the fifth year. Both policies are frontloaded and have no surrender charges. Unfortunately, that is just about the only virtue of the Kemper policy, because high frontloads and high mortality charges result in low cash values and make it a poor buy overall. Inter-State's policy was somewhat better.

RECOMMENDATIONS

For most buyers, we still recommend term insurance as a simple, economical way to meet life insurance needs, even though universal life has remedied several of the drawbacks of the traditional whole life policy. Despite universal life's premium flexibility, many families will have trouble squeezing a universal life premium into the budget, especially if they buy enough insurance to provide an adequate death benefit.

In some ways, buying universal life is like buying term insurance and investing the rest of your premium money with the insurance company. How good is that investment? We calculated Linton yields (estimated rates of return) using each company's own interest rate and also using an 8-percent rate for each of the top and bottom five policies. For a 35-year-old man buying $100,000 of coverage, the Linton yields at the end of five years ranged from *minus* 10.15 percent to 10.79 percent. At the end of twenty years, the yields ranged from 6.26 percent to 11.13 percent. As an investment, then, the top-rated universal life policies appear to be as good or better than the whole life policies we rated. And the better universal life policies were not bad investments even if held for only a few years, while Linton yields at the end of five years for most of the whole life policies were negative. The Linton yields for the top universal life policies indicated that expenses don't consume as much of the premium as they do with whole life. Keep in mind, though, that the cash value buildup in a whole life policy is essentially guaranteed, while the company reserves the right to change the interest rate, which affects the cash value in a universal life policy.

Because the rate of return indicates what you are actually earning on your cash values and takes into consideration those expenses and charges that are paid from your cash value fund, the policy's rate of return is the number you need if you are considering universal life as an investment. Unfortunately, state regulators don't require insurance sellers to provide this information, and some companies are balking at proposals that would require them to disclose rates of return. One company executive put it this way: "No insurer is saying that if we credit 10 percent interest rates, we will provide a 10-percent return. We say we will credit 10 percent and that's all we say." Apparently it's up to the buyer to figure out the rest.

Before buying a universal life policy, use the checklist on page 105 and consider these points:

1. Don't focus solely on a high interest rate, which may be a come-on meant to entice you into buying a costly policy. Remember, too, that the further along in time a company projects your cash accumulations, the less believable are the projections.

2. Carefully note the differences between the cash value and the cash surrender value. These will be the same for some policies, but not for others, and some agents may highlight only the cash value. If you cash in the policy, it is the cash surrender value, not the cash value, that counts. If you keep the policy, the cash value is important because the company deducts the mortality costs and expenses from

WORKSHEET 5
UNIVERSAL LIFE CHECKLIST

	Example[a]	Policy 1	Policy 2	Policy 3	Policy 4
Company	Woodmen of the World	_____	_____	_____	_____
Policy name	Adjustable life	_____	_____	_____	_____
Amount of insurance	$100,000	_____	_____	_____	_____
Company's suggested target premium	$540	_____	_____	_____	_____
Premium you pick for comparison	$1,000	_____	_____	_____	_____
Company's current rate	9.40%[b]	_____	_____	_____	_____
Company's guaranteed rate	4.00%	_____	_____	_____	_____
Interest rate you pick for comparison	7.00%	_____	_____	_____	_____
Projected cash value with your interest rate and premium					
Year 1	$893	_____	_____	_____	_____
Year 2	$1,845	_____	_____	_____	_____
Year 3	$2,856	_____	_____	_____	_____
Year 4	$3,930	_____	_____	_____	_____
Year 5	$5,070	_____	_____	_____	_____
Year 10	$11,904	_____	_____	_____	_____
Year 15	$21,036	_____	_____	_____	_____
Projected surrender value with your interest rate and premium					
Year 1	$636	_____	_____	_____	_____
Year 2	$1,651	_____	_____	_____	_____
Year 3	$2,727	_____	_____	_____	_____
Year 4	$3,865	_____	_____	_____	_____
Year 5	$5,070	_____	_____	_____	_____
Year 10	$11,904	_____	_____	_____	_____
Year 15	$21,036	_____	_____	_____	_____
Policy loan rate	8% fixed	_____	_____	_____	_____

	Example[a]	Policy 1	Policy 2	Policy 3	Policy 4
Rate credited to loaned cash values	7.15%	_____	_____	_____	_____
Rate credited to unloaned cash values	9.40%	_____	_____	_____	_____
Excess interest penalties?	None	_____	_____	_____	_____
Limits on partial withdrawals	$250 minimum No limit on number	_____	_____	_____	_____
Frequency of rate changes	Twice a year	_____	_____	_____	_____
Timing of interest rate credits	Guaranteed rate credited monthly[c]	_____	_____	_____	_____
Special features	Current rate varies depending on size of cash values[d]	_____	_____	_____	_____
Rating classification (if substandard, what table is used?)	Standard nonsmoker	_____	_____	_____	_____

[a] Example based on $100,000 policy for a 35-year-old man.
[b] See special features.
[c] Difference between current and guaranteed rate credited annually on policy anniversary.
[d] Current rate credited if total unloaned cash value is $5,000 or more. If unloaned cash value is less, current rate is lower and varies according to how long policy has been in effect and the size of cash value.

that account. The higher the cash value, the easier it will be to skip payments later on.

3. Don't put too much value on the special features of universal life that some agents like to emphasize. A higher-than-usual guaranteed rate, for example, is nice but it's not much help if the policy is a poor one in other respects. Instead, use these special features as tie-breakers between two similar policies.

4. A universal life policy can't be left to gather dust in a drawer. The flexibility of its elements requires that you pay attention to all notices and statements from the insurance company so you will know if the policy is in danger of lapsing. If you're buying the policy for its flexibility, be sure you understand the trade-offs when you choose to pay lower premiums.

5. Keep in touch with your agent. It may be more important with universal life than with other types of policies. A good agent won't just sell you a universal life contract and then forget about you. He or she should contact you periodically to see whether the policy still meets your needs and whether you should consider any adjustments in premiums or in the amount of coverage.

7

Variable Life Insurance

Variable life policies are the insurance industry's answer to mutual funds. They offer consumers a chance to invest in the stock or bond market by wrapping their investments in a life insurance contract. "Life-insured investing" is how one company describes it.

Variable life first appeared in the early 1970s, more as the brainchild of insurance company actuaries than as a viable product intended for sale to the public. Because variable life policies are investments like stocks and bonds, they came under the scrutiny of the Securities and Exchange Commission (SEC), and quickly became entangled in the red tape of securities registration. That, plus the dismal performance of the stock market during the 1970s, sent variable life into hibernation.

Variable life is now slowly waking up. At the end of 1986 it accounted for about 2 percent of all insurance policies sold. That's minuscule compared with the industry's two big products—whole life and universal life—but some industry officials predict that by the end of the 1980s half of all new policies sold will be variable life.

Companies that have cleared the hurdles of SEC registration are now trying to pull away from the fiercely competitive universal life market and carve special sales niches for themselves with variable life. Says one company president: "We propose to improve our profitability picture by marketing variable products where we place the investment risk and the investment opportunity with the purchaser—with a markup of adequate basis points to cover our mortality risk and profit."

HOW VARIABLE LIFE WORKS

Premiums

When you buy a variable life policy, you agree to pay premiums for the life of the contract. Those premiums are usually fixed, but you can buy variable life with a single premium or with flexible premiums as well. If you buy *fixed-premium variable life*, the size of the premium is similar to a premium for a traditional whole life policy. For example, if a 35-year-old man bought a $200,000 variable life policy from the Equitable Life Assurance Society, he'd pay an annual premium of $2,434 compared with $2,504 for the company's traditional participating whole life policy.

Dividends and Expenses

Variable life policies are usually nonparticipating—that is, they pay no dividends.

Like traditional whole life, a portion of each variable life premium pays the company expenses, including agents' commissions, and a portion goes toward your cash value. From this accumulated cash value, the company pays the cost of your insurance protection. (As with all types of insurance, the cost of that protection increases as you get older.)

Cash Value and Death Benefit

While the cash value of a traditional whole life policy accumulates in the insurance company's general account and is invested in a variety of financial instruments ranging from short-term Treasury bills to long-term corporate bonds, the cash value of a variable life policy accumulates in separate accounts, each of which is usually invested in a single instrument. (The insurance company offers a menu of possible investments to the variable life policyholder—growth stocks, high-yield bonds, and money market funds, for instance.) The policyholder chooses the type of investment for his or her cash value account, and can usually divide the cash accumulation among two or more separate accounts.

Variable life policies also have a mechanism for sharing extra earnings *(excess interest)* with policyholders. In chapter 1 we point out that if an insurance company has high investment earnings, it may share those earnings with its policyholders. With participating whole life, companies share excess interest by paying higher dividends. With universal life, they simply credit higher rates to policyholders' cash value.

While the insurance company bears most of the investment risk with traditional cash value policies, policyholders bear the investment risk with variable life. If the investments perform well, the excess interest buys the policyholder more insurance and results in an increased cash value. In other words, the death benefit increases. If the investments do poorly, the death benefit decreases, although it never goes below the amount of coverage chosen at the time of purchase. Variable life policies, then, do not have a fixed death benefit but one that varies with the investment results of the particular fund a policyholder chooses for cash value accumulation.

Here's how the varying death benefit works: You choose a variable life policy that has a $50,000 death benefit and a $1,000 annual premium. Company actuaries figure that the $1,000 premium is large enough to cover expenses and allow for some profit, but they also figure the investments in your cash value fund must earn a minimum interest rate to cover costs and pay at least the $50,000 death benefit you initially selected. That rate is called the *assumed interest rate*, and is typically 4 or 4½ percent.

If the investments in your account continuously earn more than the assumed interest rate, the insurance coverage might increase to $53,000 in two or three years, or perhaps even double in ten or fifteen years. If the investment earnings fall below the assumed interest rate, coverage can decrease but will never be less than the initial $50,000 face amount. Suppose your coverage has increased at the end of the sixth year to $60,000, but that year the value of the stocks in your account tumbles, showing a −2 percent return. Then your coverage might drop to $58,000.

As we've noted, your cash value also varies with investment performance, increasing with good results and decreasing with poor ones. That's different from traditional whole life, in which the cash value gradually rises over the years according to a predetermined schedule spelled out in the policy.

Borrowing

You can borrow against your cash value with a variable life policy, but if you die while the loan is outstanding, the amount of the loan plus any unpaid interest is subtracted from the death benefit paid to your survivors. You can repay the loan plus interest and restore the initial death benefit, but borrowing can *permanently* affect the size of the variable death benefit. That is, if your cash value is reduced by a loan, the portion of that cash value that serves as collateral is "out of circulation" and misses a chance to grow as investment earnings grow. When this happens, the death benefit also grows at a slower pace. For example, a policyholder borrows about $2,000 against his $3,000 cash value at the end of the fifth policy year. At the end of the tenth year the cash value totals $4,657 and the death benefit is $50,926. If he had not borrowed, the cash value would have totaled $7,698 and the death benefit would have risen to $54,877. (This example assumes that the initial face amount is $50,500, and the company credits 8 percent each year.)

Companies limit the amount you can borrow, and these limitations vary from company to company. For example, Equitable allows policyholders to borrow on 90 percent of the cash value during the first ten years, and 100 percent after that. After the first year, John Hancock allows policyholders to borrow on 90 percent each year. But all the policies warn that if outstanding loans and unpaid interest exceed the cash value, the policy will lapse because there's no more money in the account to pay the ever-increasing cost of the insurance protection. Thus, if you use the policy as a source of easy loans and don't repay them, the day will come when you'll have no insurance protection at all.

Insurance companies, of course, charge interest if you borrow against your policy. The rate may be variable or fixed, typically at 4 to 5 percent. (Variable rates are usually linked to Moody's long-term bond index.) You can decide whether you want a fixed or variable loan rate when you first take out some policies; with others, you can switch from one type of rate to another during the life of the policy. When you borrow on your variable life policy, companies credit your accumulated cash values with different rates—the portion that serves as collateral for the loan receives a lower rate than the portion that doesn't. This difference between the rates credited to loaned cash values and to unloaned cash values is called the *net cost of borrowing*, and it ranges from .5 percent to 2 percent, depending on the company.

Taxes

Variable life policies receive the same tax treatment as any other kind of cash value policy: Interest credited to the accumulating cash value is tax-deferred until it is withdrawn. At that time, taxes may be due on the gain—the amount by which the cash value plus any dividends exceeds the sum of the premiums paid. Benefits paid to survivors are not taxed, and interest on policy loans is not deductible.

These days, insurance agents and financial planners are promoting the current tax treatment of variable life as a big plus compared with mutual funds. Under the new tax law, all interest, dividends, and realized gains from mutual funds are taxable.

VARIABLE UNIVERSAL POLICIES

Originally, companies sold variable life as a product that could keep policyholders' coverage current with inflation. If the underlying investments in the cash value account performed well, the death benefit would increase and thus provide greater purchasing power to offset any rise in inflation for a policyholder's beneficiaries. But, as inflation diminished, selling variable life as an inflation fighter didn't make much sense. Variable life is now sold primarily as an investment vehicle in which policyholders can personally manage the investments for their accumulating cash values. For this purpose, companies have introduced a second generation of variable life policies.

The new policies, borrowing their characteristics from both traditional variable and universal life, are called *variable universal*. Like variable life policies, they let policyholders select the underlying investments for their cash value accumulation. Like universal life, the policies have flexible premiums and a fixed death benefit—that is, the death benefit is fixed for a number of years until the cash values become so large that the death benefit must increase if the policy is still to be considered insurance for tax purposes. (The IRS requires a certain relationship between the size of the death benefit and the size of the cash values in order for a life insurance policy to receive favorable tax treatment. This relationship is called the *tax corridor* and is also discussed in chapter 6.)

You can borrow against cash values and also make partial withdrawals from a variable universal policy. But if you do, the face amount of the policy is permanently reduced by the amount of the withdrawal.

The cash values of variable universal fluctuate with the investment performance of the separate accounts you choose for your accumulation. If you invest in stocks, and they decrease in value, your cash values will drop too. If the value of your stocks rises, your cash values will also rise.

As with all investments, you must balance the potential reward against the risk. Each month, the insurance company deducts from your cash value the cost of insurance protection and other expense charges. If your cash values dip because the underlying stocks took a nosedive, you must either add more money to the account or risk losing your insurance protection.

A few companies that sell variable universal policies offer some protection against this possibility. They guarantee that your insurance will stay in force for a specific period if you agree to pay a certain minimum target premium in the first few years. During that period, the companies will guarantee to pay a death benefit even though your cash values may be insufficient to pay the cost of the insurance. Or companies may choose to limit the increase in mortality charges that may arise if the amount at risk for the company increases because of lower cash values. Companies offering this guarantee usually limit the charges to no more than you'd pay if your investments had earned the basic assumed interest rate of 4 or 4½ percent. With this guarantee, your coverage stays in force when your stock or bond portfolios are down, at least for a longer period of time.

Fees and Charges

Variable life policies, including variable universal, come with a laundry list of fees and charges that are spelled out in each policy's prospectus. Companies deduct some of these charges from your premiums and some from your cash values. The most common charges are front-end sales loads, surrender charges, administrative charges, cost of insurance (mortality charges), two kinds of risk charges, investment fees, and state premium taxes. (All life insurance policies are subject to premium taxes.) Let's look at each of these types of charges:

1. *Frontloads*. These are the charges the insurance company deducts from each premium to cover its sales expense, including sales commissions. Sales loads on a traditional whole life policy might eat up as much as 100 percent of the first-year premium. On a variable life policy, they consume only 20 to 30 percent because the SEC limits the amount a company can deduct for its sales expenses. Frontloads on variable life vary from company to company. For example, Monarch Life discloses that its sales load will not exceed 20 percent of the first-year premium and 4 percent of each subsequent premium. Equitable will deduct not more than 5 percent of each premium.

2. *Surrender Charges*. Usually expressed as a percentage of the annual premium, these are penalties charged if you cancel the policy in the first few years. These charges (called *backloads*) may be as high as 25 percent of your premium in the first year, gradually tapering off later on. Equitable, for example, takes 22.5 percent of your premium if you surrender at the end of the first policy year, 10 percent if you surrender at the end of the fifth year, and only 3 percent if you surrender at the end of the ninth year.

3. *Administrative Charges*. These may be deducted annually from the premium of a variable life policy and from either the premium or the cash value of a variable universal policy. First-year administrative charges often depend on the policy's face amount; the larger the policy, the higher the fee. Administrative fees, usually $35 to $75, cover such things as the company's cost of recordkeeping, billing, collecting premiums, processing claims, and reporting to policy owners.

4. *Death Benefit Risk Charges*. The company may deduct a portion of the premium to cover the cost of the death benefit guarantee. These charges, usually 1 to 3 percent of the premium, protect the company in case the policyholder dies when his or her investment experience is poor and the policyholder's earnings are too low to support the guaranteed death benefit the company has agreed to pay. In effect, the charges are a way for policyholders to foot the bill for the company's death benefit guarantees. (With variable universal, these charges may be deducted from the cash value.)

5. *State Premium Taxes*. These are also paid out of the premium. The amount of the tax varies from state to state, but generally averages about 2 to 2½ percent.

The charges deducted from a variable life premium are no small matter. Equitable states in the prospectus for its Champion variable life policy that if a 40-year-old man buys $57,041 of coverage with an annual premium of $1,000, about $300 covering a variety of charges will be deducted from his first-year premium. The company deducts about $130 from each subsequent premium.

The following charges are deducted from the cash value account:

1. *Cost of Insurance (Mortality Charges).* This is expressed as so many dollars per thousand dollars of coverage, and pays for the cost of your insurance protection. As with all life insurance policies, these charges per $1,000 of coverage increase with age.

2. *Charges for Mortality and Expense Risk.* These charges give the company an extra cushion in case the company has to pay more death benefits than it counted on when it set the premiums, or if its expenses turn out to be higher than expected. The charges are expressed as a percentage of your cash value, and usually range from .5 percent to .9 percent, depending on the company. These charges are sometimes called *asset charges*, and while they are expressed on an annual basis, they are deducted from your account daily.

3. *Investment or Advisory Fees.* These fees are deducted daily from your cash value account. They may range from .4 percent to 1 percent of the account value (on an annual basis) and cover management and operating expenses of the fund.

There may also be fees for switching money among the various accounts, and for making partial withdrawals on variable universal policies.

SHOPPING FOR A VARIABLE LIFE POLICY

The SEC requires companies to give customers a prospectus describing the fees, charges, and mechanics of their variable life policies. Unfortunately, the prospectuses are frequently laced with such technical jargon and complex terms that only company actuaries and SEC lawyers can understand them.

In the prospectuses, companies are supposed to show death benefits as well as cash and cash surrender values for their policies, while assuming that the underlying investments in the cash value account earn 0 percent and not more than 12 percent. But in most cases these illustrations are not very helpful. Policyholders don't actually earn the illustrated rates because the ones in the prospectus are *gross* rates and don't reflect the many expenses and fees that are deducted from a policyholder's account and/or premium. The cash and cash surrender values shown for those gross rates do, however, reflect all fees and charges. If you were able to calculate an actual rate of return based on these illustrated values, it would be substantially lower than the gross rates of return as indicated in the prospectus. Unfortunately, companies selling variable life are not required to disclose rates of return. Nor do they have to illustrate death benefits, or cash and cash surrender values for any particular age or face amount, which makes it difficult to compare policies.

The SEC does require companies selling variable life to show how much of the premium actually will be invested. But it's hard to compare policies with this information because, again, companies don't necessarily illustrate the same ages and face amounts.

Comparing Expense Charges

If you want a variable life policy, you should know how policies compare with each other on two major points—expense charges and investment performance. The prospectus won't help, because you need to know how the whole bundle of fees and charges interact and exactly what effect they will have on your cash and cash surrender values. We have never rated variable life policies, so we can't tell you which company's policy is best. We can only tell you how to make your own comparisons among policies. The method is similar to the one we devised for comparing universal life policies, and is reflected in worksheet 6 on page 119.

It works like this. If you're comparing traditional variable life (not variable universal), pick a current interest rate you think the company is likely to earn on its investments. Then pick a premium. Ask the sellers of other variable life policies to show you both cash and cash surrender values using the interest rate and the premium you give them. (Remember, the interest rate and the premium must be the same for all the policies.) The policies with the highest values will have the lowest combination of fees and charges. This method won't give a perfect comparison because the death benefits may not be the same, but it will give you a rough idea which companies charge the least. If the death benefits are reasonably comparable, this method will be even more accurate.

If you're offered a variable universal policy, you can use the same method we used for comparing regular universal life. In this case, you pick an interest rate, a premium, and a death benefit. (Remember, with variable universal the death benefit doesn't vary.) Have the agent show you the cash and cash surrender values using the numbers you select. Again, policies with the highest values will have the lowest combination of charges.

Comparing Investment Returns

Because variable life has a major investment component, competition naturally focuses on investment results. If you are interested in a variable life policy, you'll need to know the total return for each fund in which your cash values accumulate. Review the return for the past few years, if it's available. The company's annual or semiannual reports give these numbers; sales literature from an agent or broker may also list these returns. (If you have trouble finding the numbers, ask the agent or write to the company.) The figures reflect interest or dividends earned by the fund, capital gains and losses, and fund management fees, but *not* insurance company charges. Keep in mind that the performance of an investment account and the actual rate of return on any policy are *not* the same. Of course, current or past returns do not predict future investment performance. Just because a company's blue-chip common stock fund grossed 30 percent last year doesn't mean it will do so again.

Another selling point of variable life is the variety of funds a company offers. Policyholders can choose among blue-chip stocks, growth stocks, bonds, government securities, a combination of stocks and bonds, money market funds, and zero coupon bonds. Occasionally a company will offer more esoteric investments such as gold stocks, real estate, or call options. Some companies will also allow you to put your money in the company's general account, but in that case there's not much difference between a variable life policy and garden-variety whole life or universal life. With variable life, though, you do have the option of moving your money to a different account later on—perhaps to take advantage of a rising stock market, for example.

If you buy variable life because you want to control your own investments under the wrapper of a life insurance policy, you'll want a policy that lets you switch investments frequently. Most companies have made it easy for policyholders to manage their own accounts and practice market timing—they can move in and out of the stock, bond, or money markets as the rates go up and down. However, according to a survey by the *National Underwriter*, an insurance trade publication, the most popular investment option is a managed account in which the company offers a mix of investments, and a professional manager makes the investment decisions.

RECOMMENDATIONS

How good is variable life as an investment? Unfortunately we can't say because we didn't rate the policies and didn't figure rates of return the way we did for whole life and for some universal life policies. In theory, at least, variable life is supposed to be competitive with some mutual funds. What we *can* say is that it's costly to invest at all through an insurance company. An insurance company is, after all, selling life insurance, and it incurs expenses for sales and commissions and underwriting that may be greater than similar expenses at a mutual fund. You may well find cheaper ways to invest your money.

We can, however, offer some general advice.

1. Consider carefully whether you want to mix insurance protection with your investments. Generally, we think people should separate the two, because it's hard enough buying a life insurance policy without having to make an investment decision as well. Moreover, variable life policies entail risk, and we don't think that you should put your family's future protection in jeopardy. If you need a lot of insurance protection, you can't count on getting it from the rising death benefit on traditional variable life because it may be years before your death benefit is large enough to provide adequate coverage for your family.

2. Don't be swayed by variable life's tax advantages. Most families have a greater need for insurance protection than for tax breaks, especially under the new tax law. So unless you are in the highest tax bracket and anticipate a lot of investment income, tax advantages shouldn't be a major consideration.

3. If you want to buy a variable life policy as an investment, shop among the several companies offering them. By using the checklist on page 119 and the method we've outlined, you should find a policy with low fees and charges.

4. Don't be too impressed by the number of investment accounts a

WORKSHEET 6. VARIABLE LIFE CHECKLIST

	Example[a]	Policy 1	Policy 2	Policy 3	Policy 4
Company	Monarch Life	____	____	____	____
Policy name	DLI-100L	____	____	____	____
Initial face amount of insurance	$100,000	____	____	____	____
Policy premium	$1,433	____	____	____	____
Premium you pick for comparison	$1,433	____	____	____	____
Interest rate you pick for comparison	9%	____	____	____	____
Projected cash values with your interest rate and premium					
Year 1	$581	____	____	____	____
Year 2	$1,835	____	____	____	____
Year 3	$3,182	____	____	____	____
Year 4	$4,625	____	____	____	____
Year 5	$6,169	____	____	____	____
Year 10	$15,640	____	____	____	____
Year 15	$28,983	____	____	____	____
Projected surrender values with your interest rate and premium					
Year 1	$581	____	____	____	____
Year 2	$1,835	____	____	____	____
Year 3	$3,182	____	____	____	____
Year 4	$4,625	____	____	____	____
Year 5	$6,169	____	____	____	____
Year 10	$15,640	____	____	____	____
Year 15	$28,983	____	____	____	____
Projected death benefit with your interest rate and premium					
Year 1	$100,125	____	____	____	____
Year 2	$100,429	____	____	____	____
Year 3	$100,911	____	____	____	____
Year 4	$101,573	____	____	____	____
Year 5	$102,415	____	____	____	____

	Example[a]	Policy 1	Policy 2	Policy 3	Policy 4
Year 10	$109,452	_____	_____	_____	_____
Year 15	$121,956	_____	_____	_____	_____
Policy loan rate	4.75% fixed	_____	_____	_____	_____
Rate credited to loaned cash values	4%	_____	_____	_____	_____
Rate credited to unloaned cash values	9%	_____	_____	_____	_____
Dividends expected?	No	_____	_____	_____	_____
Investment choices	Money markets	_____	_____	_____	_____
	Government bonds	_____	_____	_____	_____
	Corporate bonds	_____	_____	_____	_____
	High income	_____	_____	_____	_____
	Blue-chip stocks	_____	_____	_____	_____
	Growth stocks	_____	_____	_____	_____
	Multiple strategies	_____	_____	_____	_____
	Zero-coupon bonds	_____	_____	_____	_____
One-year total return on funds[b]					
Money markets	6.71%	_____	_____	_____	_____
Government bonds	13.86%	_____	_____	_____	_____
Corporate bonds	15.66%	_____	_____	_____	_____
High income	Not applicable	_____	_____	_____	_____
Blue-chip stocks	18.31%	_____	_____	_____	_____
Growth stocks	21.93%	_____	_____	_____	_____
Multiple strategies	20.60%	_____	_____	_____	_____
Zero-coupon bonds	11.06% for short-term maturities 38.74% for long-term maturities	_____	_____	_____	_____
Three-year total return on funds[b]					
Money markets	27.97%	_____	_____	_____	_____
Government bonds	53%	_____	_____	_____	_____
Corporate bonds	62.46%	_____	_____	_____	_____
High income	Not applicable	_____	_____	_____	_____
Blue-chip stocks	59.12%	_____	_____	_____	_____
Growth stocks	69.69%	_____	_____	_____	_____
Multiple strategies	Not applicable	_____	_____	_____	_____
Zero-coupon bonds	Not applicable	_____	_____	_____	_____

	Example[a]	Policy 1	Policy 2	Policy 3	Policy 4
Is switching allowed?	Yes, five times a year without charge	———	———	———	———
Other charges	None	———	———	———	———
Rating classification (if substandard, what table is used?)	Standard	———	———	———	———

[a] Policy values given for a 35-year-old man.
[b] Total return reflects fund management fees but not mortality charges assessed by insurance company. Performance of an investment account and actual rate of return on the policy are not the same.

company offers unless you're really sure you want to manage your own investments and you plan to switch accounts frequently. We regard the variety of funds and the switching features as more icing than cake.

5. Look for policies that provide guarantees against loss of insurance protection when the policy's underlying investments perform poorly.

Companies selling variable life must offer policyholders the right to exchange the variable policy for one in which the cash values accumulate at a fixed interest rate. Annual premium variable policies usually can be exchanged within twenty-four months; single premium variable, within eighteen months.

SINGLE-PREMIUM VARIABLE LIFE

A single-premium variable policy works exactly like its parent, with one major exception. Policyholders pay one large premium, typically $25,000 to $50,000, when they take out the policy, and usually make no further payments. Some single-premium policies do allow policyholders to pay additional premiums for more coverage if they wish. In such a case the insurance company may ask policyholders to take a medical exam because more coverage means the company is liable for a larger death benefit.

The single-premium policy has a theoretical advantage over the annual premium version. More money goes to work for you faster. Because you initially deposit a large sum, you don't have to wait years to accumulate enough in your account to begin earning some big returns. If the investments you choose perform well, the accumulation grows faster and, of course, causes the death benefit to increase. If the investments do poorly, the death benefit decreases, but never below the initial face amount.

Companies selling single-premium variable must fix the relationship between the policy's initial face amount and the premium so that the IRS will consider the policy insurance and allow favorable tax treatment. Most companies set the policy's initial face amount at the minimum necessary for the policy to be considered life insurance, and this is the amount of coverage the company guarantees for a policyholder's life.

But, actuarially speaking, a specific single payment can also buy more insurance than the minimum coverage needed for compliance with the tax laws. So a customer usually can buy a maximum amount or any amount in between, although companies don't guarantee lifetime coverage if policyholders choose amounts greater than the minimum. For example, a 45-year-old man with $10,000 to invest can buy minimum coverage of $24,424 or maximum coverage of $116,395 from Monarch Life's Captn policy. The minimum coverage is, of course, guaranteed for life; the maximum for only fourteen years. When the guaranteed period ends, a policyholder may have to invest additional money in order to keep the insurance in force. This would also be necessary if the cash value account performed poorly.

Of course, insurance protection is not the major reason most people buy these policies. They are sold primarily as tax-deferred investments, and insurance provides the vehicle for the tax deferment.

Single-premium policies come with the same kinds of fees and charges as annual premium variable, although sales loads are likely to be lower because the company gets a larger premium up front. On some policies there are surrender charges in the early years, typically running between 5 and 9 percent of the premium.

There's one important point to keep in mind if you buy single-premium variable. For most of these policies, loans taken out against the cash value work like the loans for annual premium variable policies, not like the loans for single-premium whole life—there are usually no zero-cost loans.

The following table lists all the important features of the four major life insurance policies on the market today. Consult the specific chapter for more details and information.

TABLE 7. INSURANCE FEATURES AT A GLANCE

Type of insurance	Death benefit	Premiums	Dividends	Cash value
Term	Fixed	Start out low but increase every year or every few years on a preset schedule	Paid on some policies; usually small	None
Traditional whole life	Fixed	High but usually stay constant	Paid on some policies; may be large	Rises according to preset schedule shown in policy
Current assumption whole life	Usually fixed, but can vary under certain circumstances	High; can vary	Typically none	Can vary
Universal life	Can vary (within limits) at discretion of policyholder	Fairly high but can vary (within limits) at discretion of policyholder	Typically none	Grows at variable rate depending on several factors, including the interest rate paid on the cash value, which the company can change from time to time
Variable life	Can vary, but never dips below initial face amount	High; fixed	Typically none	Can vary depending on investments in underlying accounts

Table shows typical policy features; some unusual policies may vary.

8

Riders

Many insurance agents, given the chance, like to tack riders onto the policies they sell. Like options on a car, these extras add to the price and, naturally, put more commission into the sellers' pockets. At times, an agent may show you an illustration of a policy's values with the riders already included—make sure you don't unwittingly buy those you don't want. Frankly, we don't think you'll need most or any of these riders. The ones most frequently offered are accidental death, waiver of premium, cost of living, guaranteed insurability, term insurance, and spousal or family riders.

ACCIDENTAL-DEATH RIDER

If you choose the accidental-death rider (sometimes called *double indemnity*) and then die in an accident, the insurance company will pay your survivors double the face amount of the policy. Some riders pay triple if you die in an accident while you are a fare-paying passenger on a common carrier such as a bus or commercial airplane.

The accidental-death rider is usually available on all types of policies, but sometimes you can't buy it with annual renewable term insurance. If you buy the rider when you're young, the cost can be as little as 50 cents per $1,000 of coverage, and it increases with age. At Metropolitan Life, for example, a 35-year-old man buying a $100,000 whole life policy would pay $69 a year for his accidental-death rider. A 50-year-old man would pay $74.

Often the rider has strings attached, such as a rule that you must die within 90 days of the accident in order for your survivors to collect double. If your death is complicated—you suffer a heart attack two weeks after you're hit by a bus—the grounds for the insurance payoff become murky. Did your injuries or the heart attack cause your death? Sometimes a court must decide.

The accidental-death rider is no substitute for adequate coverage. If you think you need it, you probably don't carry enough insurance. If you are adequately insured, is the gamble of the accidental-death benefit worthwhile as an extra windfall for your heirs? We don't think so—insurance company statistics indicate that only about 6 percent of all policyholders are killed in accidents.

Airline flight insurance is a type of accidental-death policy. You can usually buy as much as $350,000 of such coverage from a salesperson at an airport booth before the flight, and you're covered during the time you're in the air. If the plane crashes and you're killed—and the odds against that happening are very high—the company pays the face amount to your survivors. Flight insurance is seemingly cheap—about 3.3 cents per $1,000 of coverage. True, if you took out a $100,000 policy, you'd pay a bit more than $3 for your coverage. But when you consider that companies pay out very little in actual claims, flight insurance is not cheap at all. A spokesman for Mutual of Omaha, one of the largest sellers of such policies, disagrees, maintaining: "If someone doesn't have adequate insurance, it's an opportunity to supplement their coverage."

We repeat, flight insurance, like the accidental-death rider, is a waste of money for most people. If you're adequately insured, bring your family a present from your trip instead of spending your money on a flight insurance policy. If you're not, see your insurance agent as soon as you get back.

WAIVER-OF-PREMIUM RIDER

This rider specifies that the premiums on your life insurance policy will be paid if you become disabled and can no longer work. In a sense, it functions as a miniature disability policy. But, unlike a regular disability insurance policy, which provides an income or pays the mortgage, the waiver-of-premium rider only pays your life insurance premiums.

For whole life policies, waiver-of-premium riders usually cost between 4 and 10 percent of the policy's premium, depending on your age. The younger you are, the cheaper the rider. For term policies, the waiver as a percentage of the original premium may be greater than for a whole life policy. This waiver-of-premium rider for term policies usually allows you to convert to a whole life policy if you become disabled, and the company views this conversion ability as an expensive privilege. Policyholders pay accordingly. For an annual renewable term policy, the cost of the waiver increases with each renewal. At Metropolitan, for instance, the cost of the waiver for a 45-year-old man buying a $100,000 policy is $56, but when he's 55 the price of the rider zooms up to $286.

For a universal life policy, the waiver-of-premium rider works differently. With term or whole life, the rider simply waives the entire premium; with universal life, it usually waives only the cost of insurance (mortality charge) that the company deducts monthly from your cash value account. For example, the annual target premium (minimum premium) for your universal life policy is $500. Each year, part of that premium (deducted in monthly installments) pays the mortality charges and the company's expenses, with the balance going toward your cash value. If your disability triggers the rider, the insurance company will pay only the portion of the $500 target premium that pays for the cost of your insurance protection. Of course, you can put more money into the policy if you want your cash values to build. But finding extra cash for your life insurance policy when you're already coping with a disability may be impossible.

Sometimes you might find waiver-of-premium riders for universal life policies that are particularly generous, although they are usually more expensive than the ones that waive only the monthly cost of insurance. These super waivers pay the insurance cost and add to your cash value as well. Some will pay the average of the premiums the policyholder paid over the last few years, while others pay a predetermined scheduled premium for the length of time the policyholder is disabled.

The mortality and expense charges for universal life policies vary considerably from company to company; the waiver-of-premium riders vary in price as well. The price, for all types of policies, often depends on a number of factors:

Definition of Total Disability

Some companies will waive premiums if policyholders can no longer perform work they have always done before or work they are "suited to by training or experience." Other clauses say that disabled policyholders must be unfit for *any* work before the company will waive their premiums. Of course, the more liberal the definition of total disability, the better for the consumer.

Waiting Periods

Most clauses say that you must wait six months from the time you're disabled before the company starts paying your premiums. Occasionally you might find a company that makes you wait only four months. Once you've waited the required time, the company usually makes the waiver retroactive and refunds all the premiums you paid during the waiting period.

Age for Eligibility

Most waiver-of-premium clauses take effect only if you're disabled before age 60—the later the cutoff age, the better. If the cutoff age is 60 or earlier, the company assumes that the disability will continue for the rest of your life. Sometimes a clause will specify that you can become disabled after age 60 but before age 65. In that case, the company will pay your premiums until you reach 65, and sometimes it will agree to pay them for at least two more years.

Conversion Privileges

Some waiver-of-premium riders attached to term policies allow policyholders to convert to whole life. Some companies allow you to convert while the waiver is in effect. Others won't, because the company doesn't want to get stuck paying the higher whole life premiums.

We recommend that most families buy disability income policies that will provide money for living expenses if the breadwinner becomes disabled. For families with little or no disability insurance, the waiver-of-premium rider may be worth considering, but it's still wiser to spend the money on a more adequate disability income policy.

If you do decide that you want the waiver, keep in mind two points:

1. *Cost.* Make the agent break out the exact price of the rider from the total premium cost and show you in dollars and cents how much it will cost each year. That way you can judge whether the benefit is worth the extra expense. Cost disclosure regulations require companies to supply the cost indexes of policies without riders, but see if the agent can get an index with the rider included. Remember, though, that some companies may have very generous riders, and the interest-adjusted net cost index, including the rider, will reflect that.

2. *Clauses.* You'll want the most liberally worded clauses you can find. At the end of the checklists in chapters 4, 5, 6, and 7, add the words "waiver-of-premium clauses," and note the provisions of the rider for each policy you're considering.

COST-OF-LIVING RIDER

Cost-of-living riders were more popular when the inflation rate hit double digits. The option is still available, and although some companies offer it with whole life policies, they are much more likely to push it with universal life. (It is generally not available with term policies.)

The rider offers you the right to buy additional coverage in proportion to the current cost of living, without having to prove you're still in good physical condition. For example, if the consumer price index rises 2 percent over the year, you can buy additional coverage equal to 2 percent of your policy's face amount. Companies limit the amount you can buy each year, sometimes to no more than 10 percent of your policy's face amount. So if the rate of inflation suddenly zooms up to 20 percent, no insurance company would let you increase your coverage by that percentage, at least not without taking a medical exam.

Most cost-of-living riders attached to whole life policies let you buy additional coverage in the form of one-year term insurance. A few riders may allow you to buy your additional coverage as slivers of whole life insurance, while some use dividends to buy a combination

PART III

Exploring
the Marketplace

9

Should You Switch Policies?

Once you've bought an insurance policy, should you consider it an unbreakable pact between you and the insurance company? "Replacement is a subject no one on this side of the heavenly gates has the answer to," says an executive of Union Central Life.

Replacement is a ticklish issue in the insurance industry because companies don't want to lose existing policies and agents don't want to lose renewal commissions. (Some companies and agents specialize in replacing policies, regardless of whether or not such replacement is in the consumer's interest.) And there's a fine line between replacing a policy and "twisting"—inducing a person to switch policies by using false or misleading data. Twisting is against the law. Replacement isn't.

For many years, conventional wisdom in the insurance industry dictated that replacement was bad for policyholders. After all, they had to pay new "loads" or expenses, including an agent's commission, each time they bought a new policy. And, of course, replacement was bad for the original issuing company—no company wants to lose policies that are already on the books. Over the years the insurance industry has succeeded in getting that conventional wisdom embodied into law.

The National Association of Insurance Commissioners (NAIC) regularly issues model regulations intended to serve as standards for insurance regulators in each state. Model regulations on replacement, issued in 1969 and again in 1979, required agents to provide policy owners with lengthy, detailed replacement forms and give them a warning that policy replacements were in general a bad idea.

In 1984 the NAIC issued a third regulation, which has been adopted by about twenty states so far. The new regulation discourages replacements a little less than before, but it still does not require the agent to give the consumer an updated interest-adjusted net cost index on the old policy, recalculated using the present as a starting point. Instead, the regulation only requires the old agent and company to supply the policyholder with some information on dividends, premiums, cash values, and death benefits, which is useful to some extent, but still doesn't tell policyholders enough about the continuing cost of the policy and makes it difficult indeed to compare an existing policy with a new one.

SEEKING AN UPDATED COST INDEX

If you have a high-cost policy, it may be time to replace it. Ask the new agent for the interest-adjusted net cost index on the policy he or she is proposing, so you can make a cost comparison between the new policy and the old one. Try to obtain a similar, updated index on your present policy from your current insurance company—the old index you may have received when you first took out the policy can no longer be compared with the index of a new policy. Remember, though, that indexes can be compared only between *similar* policies. You can't compare the index of a term policy with that of a whole life policy, for example. As always, the policy with the lower index is the better deal.

Insurance regulators don't require companies to furnish updated indexes, so you may have to coax the agent to get it for you. If he or she refuses, write to the company yourself and request it. (We have provided a sample letter in chapter 12 that you can adapt for this purpose.) Unfortunately, most companies aren't equipped to provide such information on a routine basis. Some will give you the index—especially if their numbers look good. Others won't.

If the old company refuses to supply the updated index, there's no easy way to compare the costs of the two policies unless you want to calculate the indexes yourself. We tell you how to do that in appendix B on page 248. If the anniversary date for your old policy is within the next six months, evaluate the policy as of the next anniversary date. If the anniversary date is more than six months away, use the policy values for last year.

SOME REPLACEMENT GUIDELINES

Before rushing to replace your policy, ask yourself these questions:

1. Does the new policy fully meet your insurance needs? If an agent wants to switch you from a term policy to a whole life or universal life policy simply because it builds cash value, make sure the new policy provides the same amount of coverage at a price you can afford. The cash values, which are likely to be small in the early years of your new policy, won't help your family much if you die unexpectedly and are severely underinsured.

2. Are you still insurable? If you've contracted a serious or chronic illness, a new insurance company will either reject you or charge you much higher rates. Obviously, policies owned by sick people are not good candidates for replacement.

3. Will the suicide and contestability clauses be in effect again? For most policies, yes. The *suicide clause* found in most policies states that a company won't pay a claim if you commit suicide within two years of taking out the policy. During the *contestability period*, also two years as a rule, the insurance company can refuse to pay a claim if you've misrepresented material facts on your insurance application. As we point out in chapter 3, if you've lied about something important, and the insurance company relied on that misstatement in granting you the coverage, it can deny all or part of your survivor's claim for death benefits.

4. Is the agent honest about what he's replacing? Make sure you understand clearly what the new agent intends to do about the replacement. Agents eager to sell a new policy often will try to persuade you to cancel your old policy and put the accumulated cash values into a new vanishing-premium or even a single-premium policy. Sometimes they may succeed in getting you to borrow on the cash values and use the money to buy a new policy. This arrangement may be good for the agent, but not necessarily for you. You might end up with two policies that don't meet your insurance needs, and you will have to repay the

loan on the cash values if you want the full death benefit restored on your old policy. What's more, the agent may have seriously misinformed you about the whole transaction. This happened to a *Consumer Reports* reader who owned a whole life policy and whose insurance agent wanted him to buy the company's vanishing-premium universal life policy that the agent claimed would be fully paid up in six years. Our reader wanted to surrender his whole life policy, but the agent told the policyholder that the cash value in the old policy totaled only $100, and the company would not permit him to take it out. A few months later the reader discovered, much to his dismay, that he really had $600 of cash value in the policy, and the agent had arranged for him to borrow against it in order to pay the premium on the new universal life policy.

5. What happens during the transition period? If you do switch, keep your family protected during the transition period between the two policies. You wouldn't want to be without coverage, even for a short time, so don't drop your old policy until the new one is fully approved and delivered.

MORE REPLACEMENT GUIDELINES

Here are some guidelines for switching policies in particular situations:

1. *If You Need More Coverage.* One of the most common replacement situations occurs when you want to replace a small policy with a larger one. Should you cancel the $50,000 policy for a $100,000 policy? Or should you keep the policy and simply buy another one for $50,000? "One way is to look at the interest-adjusted cost index for the $100,000 policy and compare it with an updated cost index for the $50,000 policy," advises Harold Skipper, professor of insurance at Georgia State University and an expert in insurance replacement. "If the updated index for the old $50,000 policy is better than the index for the $100,000 policy (or about the same), keep the $50,000 policy and buy another $50,000 worth of coverage. But if the index for the old policy is worse, buy the $100,000 policy and drop the old $50,000 policy." It's easier to keep track of one policy than two. And some companies will give you a price break when you're buying large amounts of insurance at one time.

2. *If You Own Term.* A decision about whether to replace a term policy with another term policy is relatively easy because there's no

cash value to consider, and dividends, if any, are probably small. If you do find a term policy that's a better buy than the one you have—measuring the cost over a ten- or twenty-year period, not just looking at the initial premium—there's usually little reason not to switch.

You may not want to change term policies every year, though. If a person has switched policies frequently, a company might refuse to give him or her new coverage. Companies prefer business that stays on the books.

But an agent may urge you to switch from term to whole life or universal life. If you still need lots of protection for your family, don't switch. If, for some reason, you do want cash value insurance, you usually can convert through your term policy's conversion clause. But try first to obtain an updated cost index for the whole life policy offered to you and compare it with the cost indexes for policies from other companies. If you want to switch to a universal life policy, use the method for comparing policies outlined in chapter 6.

3. *If You Own Whole Life.* If you have a nonparticipating whole life policy issued before 1978, you probably have costly insurance and can get a better rate of return either from a new whole life policy or from a universal life policy priced under more current interest rate assumptions. If you own a participating policy that has paid only the dividends illustrated when you bought it, the policy is also likely to be high in cost and you may want to replace it. Because such skimpy dividends may be an indication of how your company treats its old policyholders, you might also want to try another insurance company's products. But the actual decision to replace should still hinge on the cost indexes. If there is little difference between the updated cost index for the old policy and the cost indexes for the new policies you're considering, keep the old policy.

As a general rule, it's unwise to replace cash value policies frequently, because Linton yields (imputed rates of return) for most whole life policies are negative in the first few years. A person surrendering in the early years would receive little or nothing back.

Over the last few years, some companies have specialized in *exchange policies*—that is, offering to replace old whole life policies (usually the nonpar variety) for new current assumption whole life policies, which allow policyholders to share in the company's investment experience. Here's how exchange policies work: You assign the old policy to the new insurance company, which issues a new policy for the same face amount. The company uses the cash surrender value of the old policy to calculate the premiums you'll pay for the new policy—the larger the cash surrender value, the lower the new premiums. Since sellers of these policies tout the high interest rates usually credited as a compelling reason for policyholders to switch, these exchanges will be far less attractive if interest rates are down. Again, the cost indexes will reveal whether you should take these policies seriously or not. Exchange policies do have one very significant drawback. They carry high back-end loads or cash surrender charges, sometimes as much as 125 percent of the first-year premium. These charges gradually taper off, but on some policies they don't disappear completely for twenty years.

If you own a whole life policy, should you drop it for term insurance? Most agents, of course, won't recommend you do this, although one company, the A. L. Williams organization, has challenged the industry's orthodox approach, and specializes in replacing whole life policies with term insurance. (See chapter 4, "Term Insurance.") Certainly, if your whole life policy doesn't meet your needs and is expensive (as measured by the cost indexes), we see nothing wrong with dropping it and buying low-cost term insurance. You'll reduce your immediate insurance bill and you'll probably get far more coverage for the same amount of money.

If you have a *good* whole life policy—one that is low in cost as measured by the cost indexes and has paid generous dividends over the years—you may want to hang onto it and buy a term policy that will give you the additional coverage you need. Can you afford to carry both policies? If you have only a limited amount of funds to spend on life insurance, take the plan that provides the most protection for the premium you can afford.

4. *If You Own Universal Life.* A replacement decision involving universal life requires a different approach. If you're comparing similar universal life policies, or a universal life policy with a whole life policy, ask the agent to project some cash value accumulations for you. If you're comparing an old whole life policy with a new universal life policy, ask the agent selling the universal policy to give you a projection of your cash surrender value for specified time periods—five, ten, and fifteen years. The agent should use the same premium you're paying for the whole life policy, the same face amount, and the company's current interest rate. You must also inform the company or agent that

the whole life policy's cash surrender value will be paid into the universal life policy as an additional first-year premium.

Now have the agent who sold you the old whole life policy tell you what your cash surrender values will be at the same points in time, and what dividends you are likely to receive. In this case, whichever policy provides the most cash at surrender is probably the better deal. But keep in mind that whole life premiums and cash values are guaranteed, while both interest credits and mortality expenses can change over time for universal life policies.

You can do a similar comparison if you already have a universal life policy and a new agent tries to persuade you that his or her policy is better. Ask the agent to show you surrender values for the new universal life policy using the same premium and the same face amount as for the old policy. If the new policy generates a significantly higher cash value, then a switch may be appropriate.

However, comparisons of a universal life policy with a whole life policy, or with another universal life policy for that matter, are rough approximations at best. You don't know what the universal life companies will actually credit to the cash value over time, or what interest rates the whole life company will use to calculate future dividends.

Sometimes an agent may try to persuade you to switch because of some special additions to a policy, such as a cost-of-living rider or an interest rate guarantee. Extra features are always nice, but they hardly make a case for switching policies.

GETTING YOUR MONEY BACK

If you switch policies, does the company return any premiums you've paid for the year? Life insurance contracts are usually silent on this point. If you drop an auto or homeowners insurance policy before the policy year is over, the company has to follow a well-defined procedure for refunding any "unearned premium"—that is, a part of the premium for which the company did not provide coverage. Because there's no established procedure for life insurance policies, it's the company's decision to return any unearned premium. If you're dropping a term policy, some companies return nothing and others may return a portion of the annual premium you paid. If a company refuses to refund part of your premium, ask your state insurance department for help. (You can use the letter in chapter 12 as a model.) If you're canceling a cash value policy, you're entitled to any cash surrender value the policy may have built up. Remember, however, that in the early years of a policy, there may be no cash surrender value, or it may be very small.

Most policies contain Depression-era clauses that give the insurance company the right to delay paying your cash value for up to six months. If the delay is longer than sixty days, companies will generally pay interest on your money. Nevertheless, you may run into a company that is less than eager to return your cash surrender value. If the company delays payment for more than a reasonable length of time, ask your state insurance department to help recover your money.

10

How Life Insurance Is Sold

In the spring of 1986, a life insurance agent tried to sell a policy to a young married man with a year-old son. The man was a prime candidate for insurance, but the agent instead tried to sell him a $100,000 policy on the child's life. She suggested an "appreciable life, interest-sensitive investment product"—a universal life policy. The agent didn't fully explain the policy, but stressed that owning this insurance was like owning a good stock, and that the young man was fortunate indeed to have the opportunity to buy it. Furthermore, she told him that money would accumulate in the policy over the years in large amounts sufficient to pay for the child's future college expenses, and there was a very high chance that the child would be a multimillionaire by age 65. The agent gave the customer one page of a three-page computer illustration that showed the policy would have $6.5 million of cash value when the child reached his 65th birthday, and when the child turned 70, the cash value would total $12 million.

The agent arrived at these fantastic cash values by using an interest rate of 16 percent—a highly unrealistic rate in the spring of 1986 when rates were falling rapidly. And because the agent didn't provide a complete illustration, the young father didn't see the warnings and caveats about interest rates that the company doubtlessly noted on the other two pages. The proposed policy called for annual premiums of $792 for *only* four years. After that, the agent said, the man would never have to pay another cent. The agent actually was selling him a vanishing-premium policy, but didn't mention that if the company failed to credit the same interest rates she was projecting, he would have to pay additional premiums to keep the policy in force.

Unfortunately, this example reveals how most life insurance policies are sold today. The young man's experience is one that is all too familiar—the cash value policies pushed by many agents don't meet the needs of the average consumer, but agents, anxious to make higher commissions, try to convince buyers to purchase them anyway. Frequently, agents ask their customers to accept the cash value product on blind faith, and they carry with them a bible of sales pitches to help buyers see the light. These sales presentations are often clouded by assertions that are mistaken, half-true, misleading, or incomplete.

In 1986, one of our reporters went shopping for life insurance in New York City. She visited an independent agent who represented several insurance companies, as well as eight other company agents representing Massachusetts Mutual, New York Life, Penn Mutual, Prudential, State Farm, State Mutual, Union Central, and the United States Life Insurance Company.

Several of the agents initially discouraged our reporter from shopping around. "If you have faith in what I tell you, you will buy what I suggest" was how one put it. "There's not much to compare when you're dealing with simple policies," said another. "I will shop the market [for you]," offered an eager agent, quickly adding, "I don't want two or three other people doing the same thing. You'll just be confused by three agents all telling you they are the best."

The agents, on the whole, strongly promoted those policies that fit their companies' marketing strategies. That usually meant pitching some kind of cash value policy—either whole life or universal life. Of the nine agents our reporter visited, three pushed whole life and four pushed universal life. One recommended term and one offered a combination.

ERRONEOUS INFORMATION

The State Farm agent told our reporter that dividends for the company's term policy would amount to a whopping $88,000 over thirty years. "God, that sounds high to me," he then commented, almost in disbelief. (It was high. Dividends for some highly rated term policies for a woman our reporter's age buying $100,000 of insurance ranged from about $6,500 to $15,000 over a thirty-year period.) After rechecking his rate book, the agent stated that his figure *was* correct. He then told her that those dividends were guaranteed. (Companies never guarantee their dividends.) When the reporter asked how she would receive this windfall, the agent said, "They'd send a check for $88,000." (Dividends are usually paid gradually over a period of years.)

The independent agent, illustrating a universal life policy from The Travelers, said that the policy was currently paying 11 percent. But at that time, the company was paying only 10 percent—not a big difference, but it could mean about $2,400 over a twenty-year period on a $100,000 policy.

The Penn Mutual agent's advice on how to buy term insurance was just plain wrong. "You'd buy the one that's cheap today because it's going to go up anyway," he said. A low first-year premium does *not* guarantee that the policy will be cheap over the long run. A person following that advice could easily end up with a very expensive policy.

HALF-TRUTHS

The United States Life Insurance Company agent warned our reporter against buying term. "If you want insurance for more than four, five, or six years, you're just throwing your money out. You're not going to get anything back." That statement is misleading. Term policies don't build cash values, but the policyholder doesn't come away empty-handed. He or she has adequate coverage for the whole time the policy is in force, and the insurance company will pay a death claim if death occurs. Protection, after all, is why most people need life insurance. Those who want to invest money as well as buy insurance coverage can buy term insurance and invest the premium dollars saved in the early years, when term premiums are relatively low. As the years pass, that investment fund may well exceed the cash value that would have built up in a whole life or universal life policy.

The Massachusetts Mutual agent attacked term from a different perspective. "Term insurance becomes prohibitively expensive. Less than 2 percent of all term insurance results in a claim," he said, implying that people drop term policies when the premiums rise in the later years. (He neglected to mention that most life insurance policies rarely result in death claims.) Although the 2-percent figure comes from a study of questionable validity, the statistic has taken on a life of its own among insurance agents and you may frequently hear agents refer to it, labeling term insurance as "poor for providing death benefits." In fact, if a 25-year-old man bought term insurance, mortality tables show that he would have only about a 2-percent chance of dying by the time he was 40. Meanwhile, his family would have been adequately protected.

To imply that people drop their term policies solely because they become too expensive is also misleading. Most simply outgrow their need for insurance coverage. Others drop one term policy for another that's less expensive, or convert to whole life or universal life. One agent even wrote us and said that he "could not look the spouse of a client in the eye honestly and tell him or her that term insurance is best when there is a 98-percent chance that the surviving spouse will never see that death benefit."

The claim that term premiums become prohibitively expensive at older ages also implies that the cost of other kinds of insurance does not increase. But the cost of insurance protection always rises over the years, even with a cash value policy that has level premiums. Why? Because an increasing part of the death benefit each year is made up of the policyholder's *own* cash value. The amount of true insurance protection therefore decreases each year—and thus the consumer's cost per $1,000 of protection rises, even though the face amount never changes.

Though most agents on our reporter's shopping trip tried hard to discredit term insurance, they also belittled other products they weren't eager to sell. For instance, those agents who preferred to sell whole life policies made disparaging remarks about universal life. The New York Life agent warned our reporter that Congress was planning to tax the savings accumulation in universal life policies because companies had been offering such high rates, but denied that Congress was also planning to tax the savings accumulation in whole life policies as well (which was the case at the time).

The Prudential agent trying to sell our reporter whole life described it as "a stable type policy," implying that universal life was not. With a whole life policy, he said, the policy's key elements are all "guaranteed." True, interest rates in the general economy do affect the rates companies pay on universal life policies, but they also affect the assumptions companies use to figure dividends for whole life policies. The rate of investment return for most whole life policies today depends heavily on the dividends. Those are not guaranteed.

The Massachusetts Mutual agent didn't like universal life either. He told our reporter that universal life policies did not have guaranteed death benefits, but whole life policies did—not exactly a true statement. He meant to say that in some cases the cash accumulated in a universal life policy may be insufficient to pay the premiums and keep the insurance in force. If that happened, the customer would have to pay more in premiums. But as long as the policyholder pays the target premium, death benefits will be paid, as is the case for other types of life insurance policies.

SINS OF OMISSION

One of the agents presented our reporter with five sets of figures for a universal life policy. Although the first page of each presentation clearly indicated the data were not valid without page two, the contents of page two were never supplied. The reporter could only presume that the agent didn't want her to know about several important caveats the company felt compelled to make.

Another agent promoted the advantages of universal life over a bank certificate of deposit. Money saved in the life insurance policy was tax-free, he said; money saved in the bank was not. The agent forgot to mention that if our reporter wanted to withdraw money from the policy, she might have to pay ordinary income taxes on part of the total amount withdrawn, because the money accumulates tax-free only as long as it remains in the policy.

THE MISSING INDEX

Unfortunately, most life insurance buyers don't use the interest-adjusted net cost indexes to calculate the real cost of a policy, even though these indexes have been available since 1973. A study by the Life Insurance Marketing and Research Association and the American Council of Life Insurance found that in 1980 only 11 percent of all insurance buyers used the index to compare policies. Nearly 60 percent simply used the premiums for their comparisons, which, as our studies have shown, is absolutely the wrong way to accurately compare the costs of policies.

It is our view that the indexes are suffering from intentional neglect. Most of the industry doesn't want to use them, and many companies and agents aren't in favor of any cost disclosure at all. "We don't want people to feel the index is the major key that unlocks all the mystery," says an official of the American Council of Life Insurance.

"The index is still a little foreign to the agents," claims another insurance executive, although it's hard to see how the indexes could still be some exotic import fifteen years after the National Association of Insurance Commissioners issued its first regulation mandating their disclosure.

True, the NAIC regulation, now adopted by thirty-eight states, isn't exactly buyer-friendly. A compromise among companies, agents, and insurance regulators, the regulation states that companies and their agents must give the interest-adjusted net cost indexes for policies (as well as a buyer's guide explaining what the indexes mean) no later than the actual time of delivery of the policy—that is, *after* people have bought their policies. Clearly, if consumers got this essential information *before* they signed on the dotted line, some agents might lose a sale. And even though the regulation does give buyers a chance to change their minds within ten days and cancel their policy, few consumers are likely to second-guess their original buying decision. If the customer does want to know what the index is on a particular policy before buying, the regulation states that the agent must supply it—but only if the buyer *asks* for it.

But, our reporter found out that asking for it doesn't necessarily mean you'll get it, even in New York State, which requires agents to give out the index when the application is taken. Two agents, for example, flatly refused to give her the index, and another acted as if she had requested something from Mars. "I really don't know what they mean," confessed an agent for the United States Life Insurance Company. An independent agent appeared to know what the interest-adjusted index meant, but he was not about to divulge it. Instead, he told our reporter that buying insurance was like buying Lipton tea at one store and Lipton tea at another. "There's no difference," he insisted. "If something happens, they'll pay you. It's just a different person handling your insurance." In other words, he was claiming what many consumers unfortunately believe—there's no real difference among policies.

When our reporter insisted on seeing the index, he told her to ask the state insurance department. "They have a whole book of these," he said, growing annoyed with her persistence. (The New York Insurance Department currently has no such book.) Finally the agent said: "Suppose I said it was 3.2. What would it mean? The comparisons are irrelevant unless you've been in the life insurance business and know what to compare." Statements like these are enough to discourage all but the most dogged buyer.

The New York Life agent invited our reporter to sit by his computer while he produced price figures for whole life and term policies. The reporter saw the index numbers flash on the screen. Yet when the agent printed out the figures, the indexes weren't there. Our reporter asked if there was any way to compare his whole life policy with, say, Prudential's. "Yeah," replied the agent. "Call up a Prudential agent. I'd say they're within $5 of us."

The Prudential agent wasn't any too eager to compare policies either, but he was eager to demonstrate how whole life was a better buy than term. In attempting to make his case, he used the traditional net cost method of comparing policies.

Because this outmoded method doesn't consider the interest you could have earned on your money if you didn't use it to pay for your life insurance premiums, it's not a suitable way to compare similar policies, let alone the dissimilar ones the Prudential agent was showing. Among responsible segments of the industry, it has long since been superseded by the interest-adjusted net cost method.

Unhappily, current state regulations requiring disclosure of the indexes are not strong and are poorly enforced as well. For example, even though the New York Insurance Department has a reputation for being one of the toughest in the country, it has never found a single violation either by a company or by an agent for failing to disclose the cost index. Perhaps that would change if more consumers demanded the full disclosure of comparative indexes before they purchased life insurance policies.

A COUNTRYWIDE PROBLEM

The problems our reporter encountered are not peculiar to New York. The Consumer Federation of America (CFA), a coalition of consumer organizations, sent researchers to visit 200 life insurance agents in Massachusetts, Maryland, Virginia, Ohio, Wisconsin, Minnesota, Illinois, and New York. Posing as first-time buyers of life insurance, the researchers uncovered many of the same abuses as our reporter encountered on her shopping trip. For example, they found that only about half the agents were willing to discuss the particular policy the researcher asked about, only one-fifth were willing to provide the interest-adjusted net cost indexes, and almost two-thirds of the agents failed to give the researchers enough information for accurate policy comparisons. Agents frequently asked the CFA researchers if they were planning to shop around and compare policies. If they said yes, the agents refused to provide any further information.

CUTTING THROUGH THE SALES PITCH

It's easy to feel confused and overwhelmed when you set out to buy life insurance. Here are some tips to make the job easier:

1. Make sure the agent gives you *all* the relevant pages of the sales illustration. At the bottom of the page it will usually say, for example, "page 2 of 3 pages." That's your clue there may be more to the story than the agent is necessarily telling you. If you insist on seeing all the pages and the agent still shrugs them off as unimportant, head for the door. On the other hand, beware of the agent who overwhelms you with so much information that you get totally confused and intimidated.

2. See if riders have been included in the policy values the agent is illustrating. Many agents automatically include them, especially the accidental-death and waiver-of-premium riders. Look for the abbreviations ADB (accidental-death benefit) and WP (waiver of premium) in the upper corners or at the bottom of the illustration. If you don't want the riders, ask for new policy values without them.

3. Make sure the agent shows you both the cash value and the cash surrender value if he or she is illustrating either whole life or universal life. A favorite sales tactic is to show only the cash value, which may be considerably larger than the cash surrender value. If you cancel,

you'll receive only the cash surrender value. Remember, in the early years of many policies, there could be little, if any, cash surrender value, and you would walk away empty-handed.

Also, some policy illustrations may have headings that are unclear to you. The illustration the agent showed the young man we described at the beginning of this chapter had columns labeled "contract fund" and "cash value." The contract fund was really the policy's cash value, and the cash value represented the cash surrender value, but the name disguised those facts. You may sometimes also see the words "net value" and "accumulated value," both of which mean the same thing as cash surrender value and cash value, respectively. The moral: If you don't understand what something means, ask.

4. Agents sometimes quote unrealistic rates, so pay close attention to the interest rates used in the cash and cash surrender value projections. For example, the interest rates agents quote for universal life and current assumption whole life can be higher than those currently credited by the company. Some agents also use numbers that reflect assumed improvements in mortality rates over the years, but such improvements may not actually materialize. These practices are deceptive, and the industry is beginning to worry that such unrealistic illustrations are giving insurance companies a bad reputation with their prospective customers.

Our recommendation: Any agent showing you values based on a 13-percent interest rate when current market rates hover in the 6 or 7 percent range is suspect. Ask for more realistic assumptions or, failing that, find a more honest agent.

5. If you decide to buy a whole life policy, be sure you understand the basis for the dividends an agent illustrates for you. Some companies show their current dividend scales, which reflect their actual mortality, expense, and investment experience. Others show dividends that are based on what they *hope* their mortality, expense, and investment results will be.

6. Be wary of agents who use the deceptive traditional net cost method of comparison. If an agent underlines the total premiums you must pay on a policy, plus the total cash value, and then subtracts the two numbers and claims the policy will cost you nothing, leave. Life insurance is *not* free.

7. Be skeptical when an agent discusses price solely in terms of cost of insurance or mortality rates, which are expressed as dollars

per $1,000 of coverage. Such rates tell you nothing about the expense charges built into the policy. As we've noted before, those expenses are not inconsiderable, especially for whole life or universal life policies.

8. Be suspicious if an agent shows you a handwritten illustration—the numbers may come from the agent's head, not from the home office. In that case, write to the company's headquarters and ask for a company-generated illustration. Unfortunately, even if the agent produces a computer-generated illustration, it could be wrong. An agent often has the capacity to plug interest rates and mortality improvements into the computer and make the illustration reflect whatever he or she thinks will sell the policy.

Our advice: Don't rely completely on illustrations for a life insurance policy. Take any useful information they offer, and enter it on the checklists we have provided in chapters 4, 5, 6, and 7. Ask the agent for any other information you need to complete the checklists.

9. Don't be overly impressed by a string of initials after an agent's name. The most common one is Chartered Life Underwriter (CLU). That designation indicates that the agent has passed examinations in his subject and is presumed to be knowledgeable about life insurance products. While these initials may prove that an agent has a good understanding of life insurance, they are no guarantee that an agent is honest or will steer you to the best policy for your needs. Sadly, when our reporter did her insurance shopping, some of the most misleading statements were made by agents who were Chartered Life Underwriters.

As you can see, shopping for life insurance requires persistence. While some agents are genuinely helpful, many others go to great lengths to discourage comparison shopping on the part of the consumer. When CU's reporter asked one agent for some literature on understanding life insurance, the agent unenthusiastically handed her some booklets, saying: "When you have trouble falling asleep at night, read those. You'll be asleep in no time."

READING A POLICY ILLUSTRATION

On the following pages, we show three policy illustrations. In the first example, the State Farm graded-premium whole life policy, dividends are eventually used to pay future premiums (vanishing-premium policy). The first page of the illustration gives a good explanation of the cost indexes and presents them clearly and prominently so a prospective customer can't possibly miss them. The second page of the illustration delineates policy values, assuming that dividends will accumulate with interest. State Farm tells customers what the column headings mean and clearly lays out its disclaimer on dividends. In the upper right corner, note that the policy values include the waiver-of-premium rider. The illustration, however, shows a column of figures that indicates the net cost of the policy—the accumulated cash value minus premiums paid. As we've noted before, this is the traditional and now outmoded way of showing the cost of a policy, and has been replaced by the interest-adjusted net cost method now generally in use among responsible segments of the insurance industry. But apparently the net cost method of calculation is alive and well, and some companies still persist in showing these misleading cost figures to their prospective customers.

The United States Life universal life policy illustration is not nearly as helpful as the one from State Farm. The column headings—"net value" and "accumulated value"—are not explained. Presumably the terms are discussed on the explanation page, which, however, the agent failed to supply. Note the abbreviation "WP," for waiver-of-premium rider, at the bottom of the second page. The cost indexes are given, but they seem to appear almost as an afterthought. The company does warn customers, at the bottom of pages 1 and 2, to ask for all pages of the illustration.

The Guardian Life whole life policy illustration also advises consumers to look at all the pages and instructs them to "see attached sheets with important footnotes." These footnotes give the basis for the dividends illustrated in the policy. In this case, they reflect the company's actual 1987 mortality, expense, and investment experience and not what the company hopes to experience in the future. The footnotes also indicate that the policy has a "direct recognition of loans" provision. A big plus for this illustration is the disclosure of a rate of return, which tells buyers what their cash values actually earn. A minus, though, are the figures indicating the policy's net cost. They are not displayed as prominently as they are for State Farm's policy, but the figures are there nevertheless.

Guardian Life also states: "The cost of the above policy cannot be determined without taking into account the interest that would have been earned had the premiums been invested rather than paid to the insurer." That is exactly what the interest-adjusted net cost indexes are for. This language refers to the time value of money that the indexes take into account in order to get a true reading of a policy's cost. You'll see similar language in the illustrations for other policies. Unfortunately, many companies tend to bury this reference, don't adequately explain it and, even worse, don't place it in the appropriate section near the actual cost index figures. In the Guardian policy, the actual interest-adjusted net cost indexes are marked with a reference to footnote (2). But the footnote doesn't seem to exist.

STATE FARM

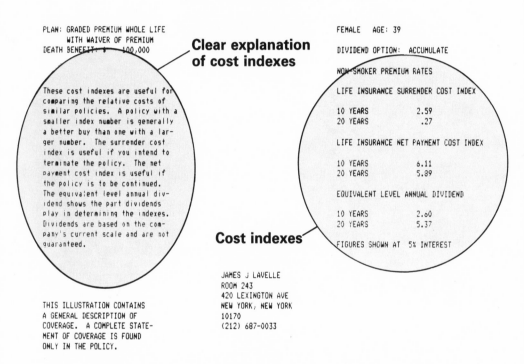

Indicates a vanishing-premium policy

Clear explanation of cost indexes

Cost indexes

PREMIUM OFFSET
ILLUSTRATION

PLAN: GRADED PREMIUM WHOLE LIFE
      WITH WAIVER OF PREMIUM
DEATH BENEFIT: $ 100,000

These cost indexes are useful for comparing the relative costs of similar policies. A policy with a smaller index number is generally a better buy than one with a larger number. The surrender cost index is useful if you intend to terminate the policy. The net payment cost index is useful if the policy is to be continued. The equivalent level annual dividend shows the part dividends play in determining the indexes. Dividends are based on the company's current scale and are not guaranteed.

FEMALE   AGE: 39

DIVIDEND OPTION: ACCUMULATE

NON-SMOKER PREMIUM RATES

LIFE INSURANCE SURRENDER COST INDEX

10 YEARS   2.59
20 YEARS   .27

LIFE INSURANCE NET PAYMENT COST INDEX

10 YEARS   6.11
20 YEARS   5.89

EQUIVALENT LEVEL ANNUAL DIVIDEND

10 YEARS   2.60
20 YEARS   5.37

FIGURES SHOWN AT 5% INTEREST

JAMES J LAVELLE
ROOM 243
420 LEXINGTON AVE
NEW YORK, NEW YORK
10170
(212) 687-0033

THIS ILLUSTRATION CONTAINS
A GENERAL DESCRIPTION OF
COVERAGE. A COMPLETE STATE-
MENT OF COVERAGE IS FOUND
ONLY IN THE POLICY.

PAGE 1   STATE FARM LIFE AND ACCIDENT ASSURANCE COMPANY   HOME OFFICE: BLOOMINGTON, ILLINOIS

Column headings

Waiver-of-premium rider

```
AMOUNT:   $100,000                                              PLAN: GRADED PREM (WHOLE LIFE, PREM
                           DIVIDEND OPTION: ACCUMULATED DIVIDENDS      INCR $  119.00 ANNUALLY FOR 10
NON-SMOKER PREMIUM RATES                                         YRS) WITH WAIVER OF PREMIUM
   INITIAL ANNUAL PREM. $417.00 ULTIMATE ANNUAL PREMIUM TO AGE 60: $1,607.00 THEN $1,543.00
```

END OF POL YEAR	ANNUAL OUTLAY	TOTAL CASH AVAILABLE*	TOTAL CASH AVAILABLE MINUS TOTAL OUTLAY*	TOTAL DEATH BENEFIT	PRIOR YR. ANN. DIV. + INT ON ACCUM.DIV.*	VALUE OF ACCUMULATED DIVIDENDS SURRENDERED*	ACCUMULATED DIVIDENDS AND DMS*	GUAR CASH VALUE
1	417	0	-417	100,000	0	0	0	0
2	536	117	-836	100,117	0	0	117	0
3	655	298	-1,310	100,298	117	0	298	0
4	774	541	-1,841	100,541	181	0	541	0
5	893	1,297	-1,978	100,856	243	0	856	441
6	1,012	2,246	-2,041	101,254	315	0	1,254	992
7	1,131	3,424	-1,994	101,765	398	0	1,765	1,659
8	1,250	4,849	-1,819	102,400	511	0	2,400	2,449

Traditional net cost of policy

Basis for dividends   **Terminal dividend**

```
* Figures include dividends which are illustrated according to the current dividend scale and are not guaranteed.
  Dividends are based upon the mortality and expense experience of the Company and reflect investment earnings on new
  investments. Where indicated, dividends include a DMS dividend, available at death, maturity or surrender of the
  policy after the 10th year.

  CURRENT PURCHASE RATE = RATE CURRENTLY BEING PAID, NOT GUARANTEED FOR PAYMENTS BEGINNING IN THE FUTURE.
  TOTAL CASH AVAILABLE = GUARANTEED CASH VALUE + ACCUMULATED DIVIDENDS + DMS DIVIDEND.
  TOTAL DIFFERENCE = TOTAL CASH AVAILABLE LESS TOTAL PREMIUMS.
  TOTAL DEATH BENEFIT = AMOUNT (GUARANTEED DEATH BENEFIT) + ACCUMULATED DIVIDENDS + DMS DIVIDEND.
PAGE 2                     STATE FARM LIFE AND ACCIDENT ASSURANCE COMPANY    HOME OFFICE: BLOOMINGTON, ILLINOIS
```

Explanation of column headings

Basis for interest rate used in dividends

UNITED STATES LIFE

PLAN: MEDALIST V   (INCREASING)   **Column headings**

| | | CURRENT RATE | | | ILLUSTRATIVE RATE | | |
| | | --------OF 10.00%-------- | | | --------OF 8.00%-------- | | |
YR	ANNUAL OUTLAY	NET VALUE	ACCUM VALUE	DEATH BENEFIT	NET VALUE	ACCUM VALUE	DEATH BENEFIT
1	844	0	717	100,717	0	703	100,703
2	844	42	1,497	101,497	0	1,452	101,452
3	844	888	2,344	102,344	795	2,251	102,251
4	844	1,807	3,262	103,262	1,645	3,100	103,100
5	844	2,803	4,258	104,258	2,548	4,004	104,004
6	844	3,879	5,335	105,335	3,505	4,960	104,960
7	844	5,046	6,501	106,501	4,521	5,976	105,976
8	844	6,306	7,761	107,761	5,595	7,051	107,051
9	844	7,670	9,125	109,125	6,733	8,189	108,189
10	844	9,139	10,595	110,595	7,932	9,388	109,388
11	844	11,017	12,181	112,181	9,488	10,653	110,653
12	844	13,013	13,887	113,887	11,106	11,980	111,980
13	844	15,143	15,725	115,725	12,794	13,376	113,376
14	844	17,410	17,701	117,701	14,546	14,837	114,837
15	844	19,822	19,822	119,822	16,364	16,364	116,364
16	844	22,090	22,090	122,090	17,948	17,948	117,948
17	844	24,516	24,516	124,516	19,591	19,591	119,591
18	844	27,111	27,111	127,111	21,293	21,293	121,293
19	844	29,888	29,888	129,888	23,053	23,053	123,053
20	844	32,858	32,858	132,858	24,872	24,872	124,872
21	844	36,365	36,365	136,365	27,072	27,072	127,072
22	844	40,176	40,176	140,176	29,402	29,402	129,402
23	844	44,317	44,317	144,317	31,869	31,869	131,869
24	844	48,818	48,818	148,818	34,478	34,478	134,478
25	844	53,708	53,708	153,708	37,236	37,236	137,236
26	844	59,018	59,018	159,018	40,147	40,147	140,147
27	844	64,806	64,806	164,806	43,237	43,237	143,237
28	844	71,107	71,107	171,107	46,509	46,509	146,509
29	844	77,957	77,957	177,957	49,963	49,963	149,963
30	844	85,390	85,390	185,390	53,592	53,592	153,592

TOTAL AT AGE

60	16,881	32,858	32,858	132,858	24,872	24,872	124,872
65	21,102	53,708	53,708	153,708	37,236	37,236	137,236
70	25,322	85,390	85,390	185,390	53,592	53,592	153,592
100	50,644	852,296	852,296	952,296	25,463	25,463	125,463

MATURITY AGE 100
REL 2.0   THIS PROPOSAL NOT VALID WITHOUT PAGE – 2

Company's warning

Column headings

```
- - - - - - - - -- PROJECTED VALUES BASED ON - - - - - - - - -
       GUARANTEED RATE                              GUARANTEED RATE
       -------OF 4.50%-------                       -------OF 4.50%--------
      ANNUAL     NET    ACCUM    DEATH         ANNUAL     NET    ACCUM    DEATH
 YR   OUTLAY   VALUE    VALUE  BENEFIT    YR   OUTLAY   VALUE    VALUE  BENEFIT

  1     844       0      518   100518     21     844    1887     1887   101887
  2     844       0     1037   101037     22     844    1073     1073   101073
  3     844      96     1552   101552     23     844      57       57   100057
  4     844     603     2058   102058     24     844       *        *        *
  5     844    1098     2553   102553

  6     844    1577     3032   103032
  7     844    2036     3492   103492
  8     844    2470     3926   103926
  9     844    2873     4328   104328
 10     844    3234     4690   104690

 11     844    3836     5001   105001
 12     844    4375     5248   105248
 13     844    4835     5417   105417
 14     844    5199     5490   105490
 15     844    5446     5446   105446

 16     844    5258     5258   105258
 17     844    4901     4901   104901
 18     844    4347     4347   104347
 19     844    3566     3566   103566
 20     844    2520     2520   102520

TOTAL AT AGE
 60   16881    2520     2520   102520
 64   20258       *        *        *
      UNLESS PLANNED PREMIUM IS INCREASED, POLICY WILL TERM. IN YR. * 24

BENEFITS/RIDERS: WP

PREM CLASS: STD.

COST INDICES, BASED ON  5% INT ADJ RATE:  SCI=SURRENDER COST; NPI=NET PAYMENT
                            10 YEAR    20 YEAR    AGE 65        NY        844.07
CURRENT           : SCI -     1.33      -1.35      -2.36
RATE - 10.00% :__NPI -        7.95       7.25       7.07        NLP       58.28
GUARANT           : SCI -     5.55       6.42       N/A
RATE -  4.50% :  NPI -        7.93       7.12       N/A
EQUIV LEV NON GUAR ELEMENT    4.22       7.77       N/A        AMPP      844.07

REL 2.0        THIS PROPOSAL NOT VALID WITHOUT EXPLANATION PAGE   "MEDALIST V"
```

Waiver-of-premium rider

Cost indexes

Another warning

GUARDIAN LIFE

250,000 WHOLE LIFE PREF NON-SMOKER
DIVIDENDS TO LOWER THE PREMIUM

Company's warning

**Traditional
net cost of policy**

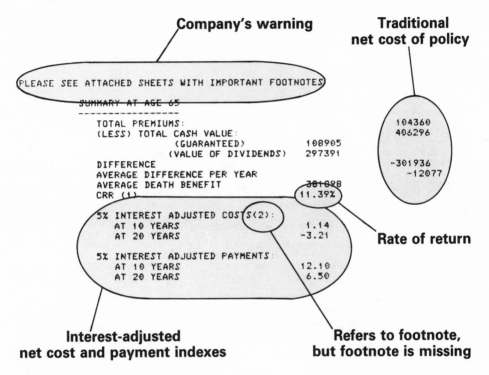

PLEASE SEE ATTACHED SHEETS WITH IMPORTANT FOOTNOTES

SUMMARY AT AGE 65
―――――――――――――――

TOTAL PREMIUMS:
(LESS) TOTAL CASH VALUE:
      (GUARANTEED)   108905
      (VALUE OF DIVIDENDS) 297391
DIFFERENCE
AVERAGE DIFFERENCE PER YEAR
AVERAGE DEATH BENEFIT   381828
CRR (1)   11.39%

5% INTEREST ADJUSTED COSTS(2):
    AT 10 YEARS   1.14
    AT 20 YEARS   -3.21

5% INTEREST ADJUSTED PAYMENTS:
    AT 10 YEARS   12.10
    AT 20 YEARS   6.50

104360
406296

-301936
-12077

Rate of return

**Interest-adjusted
net cost and payment indexes**

**Refers to footnote,
but footnote is missing**

Basis for dividend projections

```
      **  GUARDIAN  LIFEPLAN  ILLUSTRATIONS  **

                      PREPARED ON 03/24/87     PAGE 3
```

GUARANTEED CASH VALUES AS SHOWN ON THIS ILLUSTRATION ARE ONLY AVAILABLE IF ALL
PREMIUMS HAVE BEEN PAID.
FIGURES DEPENDING ON DIVIDENDS ARE NEITHER ESTIMATED NOR GUARANTEED. BUT ARE
BASED ON THE 1987 DIVIDEND SCALE.
THE 1987 DIVIDEND SCALE REFLECTS CURRENT COMPANY CLAIMS. EXPENSE, AND INVESTMENT
EXPERIENCE (APPLICABLE TO ALL POLICIES) AND TAXES UNDER CURRENT LAWS. ACTUAL
FUTURE DIVIDENDS MAY BE HIGHER OR LOWER THAN THOSE ILLUSTRATED DEPENDING ON THE
COMPANY'S ACTUAL FUTURE EXPERIENCE.
THE COST OF THE ABOVE POLICY OVER A PERIOD OF YEARS CANNOT BE DETERMINED WITHOUT
TAKING INTO ACCOUNT THE INTEREST THAT WOULD HAVE BEEN EARNED HAD THE PREMIUMS
BEEN INVESTED RATHER THAN PAID TO THE INSURER.
NET DEATH BENEFIT ON ALL PERMANENT PLANS MEANS THE FACE AMOUNT PLUS RIDERS. IF
ANY, PLUS THE END OF YEAR DIVIDEND LESS POLICY LOANS. A FULL DIVIDEND IS NOT
GENERALLY PAID UPON DEATH DURING THE POLICY YEAR. OTHER VARIABLES ARE
POSSIBLE. YOUR AGENT WILL DEFINE THE RULES UPON REQUEST.
THE POLICY LOAN INTEREST RATE SHOWN ON YOUR ILLUSTRATION IS PAYABLE IN ADVANCE
AT A DISCOUNT RATE EQUIVALENT TO AN ANNUAL RATE OF 8.00% DIVIDENDS ARE AFFECTED
BY POLICY LOANS. UNDER CURRENT ECONOMIC CONDITIONS. IN ANY GIVEN POLICY YEAR THE
GREATER THE AMOUNT OF LOAN. THE SMALLER THE DIVIDEND. (THIS DOES NOT APPLY TO
ECONOMIX TERM, WHICH HAS NO LOAN VALUE.)
(1) THE COMPARATIVE RATE OF RETURN SHOWN REPRESENTS THE RATE, NOT CONSIDERING
THE EFFECT OF TAXES, WHICH THE POLICYHOLDER WOULD HAVE TO EARN ON AN ADJUSTED
SERIES OF OUTLAYS TO ACCUMULATE TO THE TOTAL CASH VALUE AT THE END OF THE PERIOD.
THE ADJUSTED SERIES OF OUTLAYS EQUALS THE ACTUAL OUTLAY IN EACH YEAR LESS THE
COST OF INSURANCE PROTECTION FOR THAT YEAR. WHICH IS BASED ON THE 1980 CSO BASIC
TABLE (K).

LIFEPLAN ILLUSTRATIONS - OUTLAY OPTION - L
```

**Refers to rate of return**

**Footnote (2) missing—refers to
interest-adjusted net cost indexes**

**Direct recognition
applicable in this policy**

**Refers to importance of cost indexes**
```

11

Choosing a Company

In the look-alike world of financial services, one stands out. The one who has never missed a dividend. The one with a solid foundation—over $40 billion in assets. The one with the long record—at least 120 years of financial success.
—advertisement for The Travelers Companies

Apparently the better-mousetrap theory still works. In their first year of business most companies are lucky to survive. At Integrity we broke a record. Our first year in business has proven that when you design better products, the world will invariably beat a path to your door.
—advertisement for Integrity Life Insurance Company

These two ads for life insurance companies recently appeared in financial magazines. They reflect the range of companies found among the 600 or 700 life insurance companies that sell virtually all policies to the public.*

There are the well-established companies like The Travelers that stress their vast assets and choose to emphasize the success of the past, and there are the newcomers like Integrity Life that promote newer products and bank on their future success. Of course, because life insurance companies take your money today and promise to provide

*There are actually 2,200 life insurance companies in the United States, but many of these are corporate shells set up by agents for tax purposes.

protection tomorrow, trust and reliability always form the basis of their advertising. Traditionally too, all life insurance companies prefer to promote the image of quality rather than the individual policies they sell.

We have always advised consumers to buy by policy, not by company. Nevertheless, you should give some thought to the company that eventually sells you a policy. After all, you want the company to be alive and well when the time comes for you to collect your accumulated cash values, or your survivors to receive their death benefit.

You may find an ideal, low-cost policy from a company that has been around for years, such as The Travelers, or you may find one from a newcomer such as Integrity Life. In 1985 the number of companies selling life insurance reached an all-time high, and many of the newcomers brought competitive new products to an industry that had become tired and resistant to change. More competition, however, has resulted in reduced company profit margins that could lead eventually to financial instability for some in the years ahead.

How do you evaluate the stability and reliability of a company—the old and the new, the large and the small, the stodgy and the innovative? In this chapter, we offer some suggestions.

BEST'S RATINGS

For eighty-eight years, ratings from the A. M. Best Company have been the alpha and omega of the insurance industry. In fact, the ratings that Best awards companies are so crucial that insurance company officials sometimes travel to Best's headquarters in Oldwick, New Jersey, to plead their case for a higher rating. Each year Best publishes its ratings in *Best's Insurance Reports*, a thick volume found in most libraries.

Best assigns a rating to 60 percent of the life insurance companies it examines. These ratings are A + (superior), A (excellent), B + (very good), B (good), C + (fairly good), and C (fair). The remaining companies are rated NA (not assigned), usually because the company so noted is either inactive, too small, has too little experience, disputes the rating Best gives, is in receivership, or has provided incomplete financial information. A "c" (contingent) modifier beside a rating means that a company's performance has declined, but not enough to warrant a lower rating. An "e" modifier means that a rating is assigned to the parent company; the subsidiary can qualify for its own rating after five years.

In determining the ratings, Best looks at company profitability, leverage (use of debt), liquidity, adequacy of reserves (the amount of money a company has set aside to pay claims), and company management. It also examines a company's lapse rates, the quality of its investments, and the return on those investments. If an examination reveals any extraordinary situation with a company's investments, such as a very large capital gain or an unusual distribution of maturities, Best notes that as well. All the information comes from the companies themselves and from the official documents and statements companies must file with state regulators.

The actual formulas used in the ratings are secret, but lately Best has been more open about its rating system. For example, insurance officials know that Best looks at a company's exposure to *adjusted surplus*. Surplus is an insurance company's net worth (assets minus liabilities). The adjusted surplus is a measure of a company's exposure to both investment and claims risk. Companies rich in surplus—usually the largest ones—generally receive the highest ratings, although the biggest companies don't always offer the highest-rated policies (as noted in our 1986 study).

In 1986, Best awarded 254 companies an A+ rating, 254 companies an A rating, and 145 companies a B+ rating. We recommend that you buy from a company rated A or A+, and you should be able to find a good, low-cost policy from among one of these 519 companies. But bear in mind that these ratings are not an absolute guarantee of financial stability—a high rating doesn't mean that a company won't fail, and a low one doesn't mean that it will. "Companies tend to go from near-perfect ratings to insolvent more often than they go from a low rating to insolvent," says Roger Day, past president of the National Association of Insurance Commissioners (NAIC) and former insurance commissioner for the state of Utah.

While life insurance companies rarely go out of business, some highly publicized insolvencies and near-insolvencies did occur in the early 1980s in the Baldwin-United group and the Charter group. At the time they became insolvent in 1982, the two Baldwin companies had A ratings from Best. Charter Security Life Insurance Company of New York had an A+ rating as recently as 1981. As Charter slid into financial difficulty, Best lowered the company's rating to a B+.

It's important to know whether you're buying a policy from a parent company or its subsidiary. Many companies conduct business through their subsidiary companies, and sometimes don't make it clear which company will issue your policy. Some companies and their agents promote the name of the well-known parent company, but your policy may be issued by the lesser-known (and perhaps less financially sound) subsidiary.

If you're buying a policy from a lower-rated subsidiary, you may feel more secure if the parent is rated A or A+, but, again, a top-rated parent is no absolute guarantee of its offspring's financial strength. Sometimes a new parent company injects needed cash into its subsidiary, so from a safety standpoint you won't go wrong buying one of the subsidiary's policies. On the other hand, the parent company may be ready to sell the subsidiary because it's losing money. If you're unsure about buying from a subsidiary company, write to the parent and ask whether the subsidiary is a new acquisition or whether a sale is pending.

While Best's ratings do offer some guidance about a company's financial strength, they have limitations. For example, a company's Best's rating won't tell you whether the company will have excess interest to share with its policyholders. If there's excess interest, it means that if you own a term policy with an indeterminate premium, the company won't have to raise the premium to the maximum level specified in the policy. Or, if you have participating whole life, the company pays high dividends regularly. Similarly, if you have universal life, you would prefer a company that credits high interest rates and assesses low charges.

An A+ rating from Best doesn't guarantee that any of these things will happen, but it gives you a clue to the company's financial strength, and that assessment will ultimately determine whether a company has excess interest to share with its policyholders.

The fact that a company is large and rich enough to heavily promote its size and ratings should not necessarily count in your buying decision. One of our subscribers switched to a term policy that received a high rating in our 1986 study. Prudential, his former company, sent him a list of queries about his new company, including such questions as: "Does your insurance company: (1) Have an A+ rating from A. M. Best? (2) Have over $500 billion of total life insurance in force? (3) Have the size to manage investment risks often associated with expected superior returns that policyholders participate in through dividends?"

Naturally, Prudential could answer yes to every single question, but our subscriber had correctly noted that the questionnaire had no references to the interest-adjusted net cost indexes he had used to evaluate and buy his new term policy.

The fact that Prudential pays dividends and has a force of 24,000 agents and 1,600 offices was irrelevant to our reader. So was the fact that Prudential had an A + rating, because the reader's new company probably had an A or A + rating too.

STANDARD & POOR'S RATINGS

Standard & Poor's, best known for its ratings of corporate and municipal bonds, also rates insurance companies, *if* they request it. In early 1987, thirty-four companies paid the $15,000 Standard & Poor's charges for such a rating.

The S&P rating is an estimate of a company's ability to pay claims and perform according to the terms of its policies. The ratings are:

1. AAA (extremely strong capacity to meet contractual policy obligations).
2. AA (very strong capacity).
3. A (strong capacity).
4. B (adequate capacity).
5. BB (uncertain or weak capacity).
6. CCC (weakest or an uncertain capacity).
7. D (in default).

A plus or a minus indicates further modification of the rating. In 1987, all but two of the companies had AAA ratings; the other two had A + ratings.

Standard & Poor's also assesses a company's future performance—how and what its balance sheet will look like. S&P claims that its ratings are more heavily influenced by the judgments of its analysts and by qualitative factors such as the quality of the company's management than by any mathematical formulas.

The S&P ratings don't address the solvency of subsidiary companies. "Consumers shouldn't infer anything about a subsidiary from its parent," says a senior official at Standard & Poor's. "Most subsidiaries are not as strong as their parent even when they have the same name. Subsidiaries get bought and sold, have a higher risk business, and have less capital in them."

Because few companies have S&P ratings, and the ones that do tend to be the biggest companies, the ratings are of marginal use to the average consumer. But as more and more companies acquire an S&P claims-paying rating, the ratings may well develop into significant signposts for life insurance shoppers. Keep in mind, though, that the top ratings issued by Best and by Standard & Poor's are not identical in meaning or weight.

THE GUARANTY ASSOCIATIONS

What happens when an insurance company does go under? What protections exist for the policyholders? Will death benefits be paid? Will policyholders be able to cash in their policies and walk away with their accumulated cash surrender value?

If an insurance company gets into serious financial trouble, regulators (or sometimes the insurance company itself) may arrange for a stronger company to assume the policies of the failing carrier. In that case, the policyholder's coverage simply continues with the new company.

But sometimes state regulators call on the *guaranty associations* to protect policyholders. Thirty-nine states have these guaranty associations, which provide that existing life insurance companies will make good on the promises of an insolvent company. (See appendix F.) When a court liquidates a life insurance company, the guaranty associations go into operation. All life insurance companies writing policies in the state where the insolvent company is based are assessed fees according to how much business they do in that state. These fees are then pooled and become the basis for paying the claims made by policyholders against the insolvent company. The associations usually pay the full face amount of any death benefit owed to survivors of policyholders from the insolvent company, but many associations limit the amount of the death benefit to between $500,000 and $1 million. Nor will the association give full cash values to policyholders who want to cash in their policies. They limit the payouts to between $100,000 and $500,000. Most associations also limit the interest rate paid to policyholders who hold interest-sensitive policies such as universal life.

The guaranty associations typically don't cover variable life policies because the separate accounts for variable life policies are not considered obligations of the insurance company's general account. You would have to make a claim against the separate account if your insurance company became insolvent.

Under the old laws governing the guaranty associations, policyholders could collect from the guaranty association in the state where the insolvent insurance company was chartered. Under the new laws, policyholders collect from the guaranty association in the state where they live. Unfortunately, if policyholders happen to live in one of the eleven states that do not have an association, they are out of luck.

Incidentally, it is illegal for an insurance company or an agent to mention the existence of the guaranty association as a part of a sales presentation. But if prospective buyers ask about the association, the agents can answer their questions.

12

When You Need Help

When you set out to buy life insurance, you tend to put your trust in an agent. You rely on the agent to help you choose a good policy, to advise you when to increase or decrease your coverage, and to lend a helping hand when you need to file a claim. Certainly, many agents perform these services competently and reliably. But, as we've noted, that trust can also be misplaced. Too many agents' primary concern is to sell you a policy that maximizes their income. Your primary concern is to buy a policy that protects your family adequately at a price you can afford. Unfortunately, these aims often conflict.

At times you may have to go elsewhere for help, perhaps to the insurance company, outside investigative agencies, or to your state insurance department.

In this chapter we offer sample letters you can adapt when you need help in obtaining the cost indexes, canceling a policy, obtaining reports from investigative agencies, or filing a death claim. Use the wording we have provided in these letters but fill in the names, dates, and circumstances that apply to your own situation.

FINDING THE INDEXES

You need the interest-adjusted net cost indexes in order to compare a term policy with another term policy and a whole life policy with another whole life. But you may have to get the cost indexes yourself. The following letters can help. If an agent tells you he can't furnish the index, send him the following letter (if you live in one of the thirty-eight states that require agents to provide the index).

Letter to agent requesting interest-adjusted net cost indexes:

Dear ———:

As provided by the insurance regulations of [*your state*], this letter confirms my verbal request of [*date*] that you furnish me the ten- and twenty-year interest-adjusted net cost indexes (surrender indexes) and the interest-adjusted net payment indexes for the following policy:

"Wonderlife" whole life policy, $100,000 face amount, without riders, for a 40-year-old man eligible for your nonsmoker rate. [*Give specific information for your policy.*]

If possible, I would also like to see five-year cost indexes for this policy.

I will appreciate your prompt cooperation, and will inform you of my decision about the policy we discussed after I have reviewed the indexes you provide.

Sincerely,
[*Your name*]

If this letter brings no response, send the following letter to the insurance company's customer service department. Include a copy of the letter you sent to the agent.

Letter to insurance company requesting cost indexes:

Dear ———:

I request that, as provided by the insurance regulation of [*your state*], the Goodlife Insurance Company [*name of company*] furnish me the ten- and twenty-year interest-adjusted net cost indexes (surrender indexes) and the interest-adjusted net payment indexes for the following policy:

"Wonderlife" whole life policy, $100,000 face amount, without riders, for a 40-year-old man eligible for your nonsmoker rate. [*Give specific information for your policy.*]

If possible, I would also like to have five-year cost indexes for these policies.

On [*date*], I requested that your agent [*agent's name*] furnish me this information, but he has failed to do so. (Copy of my letter to him is attached.)

I hope the company will promptly furnish me information I still need to decide about the policy I discussed with your agent. I will appreciate your immediate assistance.

Sincerely,
[*Your name*]

If the company refuses to provide the indexes, it's time to write to the insurance department in your state. You can send this letter to the department's customer service bureau. Remember, though, you can send this letter only if you live in one of the thirty-eight states that has cost disclosure regulations. Be sure to include copies of the letters you sent to the agent and the company.

Letter to state insurance department requesting help getting cost indexes:

Dear ———:

I am informing you that, contrary to the insurance regulations of [*your state*], Mr. John Evader [*agent's name*], an agent for the Goodlife Insurance Company [*name of company*], and the Goodlife Insurance Company [*name of company*] have both failed to provide me the ten- and twenty-year interest-adjusted net cost indexes and net payment indexes I requested for the company's "Wonderlife" whole life policy.

I requested the information from the agent on [*date*] and from the company on [*date*] by letter (copies attached). As of this date, I have received no response.

I hope you can look into this matter promptly and take the

appropriate steps to enforce compliance with your insurance regulations. I appreciate any help you can give me.

Sincerely,
[*Your name*]

REPLACING A POLICY

When you switch policies, you should get updated cost information about your old policy. Without it, you can't make a fair appraisal of the cost of the old policy with the new. In order to get this information, send the following letter to the original issuing company.

Letter requesting updated cost index:

Dear ———:

An agent for another company has recommended that I replace my existing $100,000 "Wonderlife" policy [*name of policy*], number [*give policy number*]. I purchased this policy five years [*number of years*] ago when I was 35 years old [*age when you bought policy*].

To determine whether it would be advantageous to buy the proposed replacement policy, please furnish me the updated interest-adjusted net cost indexes and net payment indexes for the above identified policy. I would like five-, ten-, and twenty-year indexes calculated from my current policy year beginning January 30, 1988. [*Give your policy's anniversary date.*] I have enclosed a description of the method I'd like you to use in making this calculation.

I will appreciate your prompt response to this request, and I will assume that your failure to respond indicates that it would indeed be advantageous for me to buy the replacement policy.

Sincerely,
[*Your name*]

NOTE: If you want a realistically updated cost index, you need to know how it was calculated. There are no regulatory standards for calculating indexes on existing policies, so companies may use different methods. We suggest you supply the company with the method we outlined in appendix B on page 248. Then you will know exactly how the company has arrived at its figures for the new index.

CANCELING A POLICY

The cost disclosure regulations give you the right to cancel your policy within ten days after you receive it. Whatever the reason for your decision to terminate, you may want to send the following letter to the insurance company invoking your right to cancel. We suggest you send such a letter by certified or registered mail.

Letter canceling policy within ten days of delivery:

Dear ———:

As provided by the cost disclosure regulations of [*your state*], I am notifying you that I wish to cancel my $100,000 "Wonderlife" whole life policy [*name of policy*] issued on [*date*]. The policy number is [*give policy number*].

I received the policy and a "Buyer's Guide" on [*date*], and I am canceling within the ten-day period provided by the regulations. I would like you to refund the $650 [*give premium amount*] I paid on [*date*].

I will appreciate your prompt refund of my premium payment.

Sincerely,

[*Your name*]

FAILURE TO RETURN PREMIUM

The company may delay returning your premium after you cancel the policy. In that case, you can send the following letter to your state insurance department. (Even if you have canceled after the ten-day "free look" period, you can still ask the state insurance department to help you get a portion of your premium returned to you. Use the following letter, but omit the reference to the ten-day cancellation period.)

Letter to insurance department complaining of company's failure to return premium:

Dear ———:

I am informing you that the Goodlife Insurance Company [*give company name*] has failed to refund the $650 [*give premium amount*] I paid for a $100,000 "Wonderlife" whole life policy [*give policy*], number [*give policy number*]. I canceled the policy on [*date*] within the ten-day cancellation period provided by the insurance regulations of this state. (Copy of my cancellation letter is enclosed.)

I would like you to look into this matter to ensure that the company promptly complies with its obligation to refund my premium as provided by the insurance regulations of this state.

Thank you for any assistance you can give me.

Sincerely,

[*Your name*]

REQUESTING INFORMATION FROM OUTSIDE AGENCIES

Sometimes you may be turned down for an insurance policy because of information based on a report made by an independent investigative firm such as Equifax Services in Atlanta or the Medical Information Bureau in Boston. (In a few states, the insurance company must tell the consumer why it is denying coverage, even if the basis for denial is not an investigative report.)

If a company rejects you, you can send the following letter to the insurance company to find out why.

Letter to insurance company asking reason for rejection:

Dear ———:

Your agent [*name of agent*] informed me on [*date*] that my application for your "Wonderlife" whole life policy ($100,000 face amount) has been rejected. However, he gave me no reason for the rejection.

Because this action is so unexpected, I think it is likely my rejection is based on incomplete or inaccurate information you may have received from a credit reporting agency and/or the Medical Information Bureau.

I therefore request that, as provided by the Fair Credit Reporting Act, you give me the name and address of any reporting agency that furnished a report on me.

I will appreciate your prompt cooperation in this matter.

Sincerely,

[*Your name*]

You can use the following letters to ask outside reporting agencies for information that an insurance company may have used to deny you coverage.

Letter requesting information contained in an investigative report:

Equifax Services
Director of Consumer Affairs
P.O. Box 4081
Atlanta, GA 30302

Dear ———:

I was notified by the Goodlife Insurance Company [*name of company*] on [*date*] that my application for insurance was denied [or that the premium for insurance I had requested was increased] at least in part because of information contained in a consumer investigative report you furnished to the insurer.

I therefore request that you disclose to me by telephone interview, as provided by the Fair Credit Reporting Act, the nature and substance of all information you have about me in your files, the sources of that information, and the identity of recipients of your reports furnished within the last six months.

I am providing the following information to help identify me and my file: my full name is: _____; I live at: _____; my Social Security number is: _____. Because I am requesting a disclosure by telephone, please tell me when I can call and with whom I must talk to obtain the disclosures I have requested.

I will appreciate your prompt cooperation in this matter.

Sincerely,
[*Your name*]

Letter requesting information from Medical Information Bureau:

Medical Information Bureau
P.O. Box 105
Essex Station
Boston, MA 02112

Dear ———:

The Goodlife Insurance Company [*name of company*] informed me on [*date*] that it had rejected my application for a $100,000

"Wonderlife" whole life policy, in part because of my poor health. Rejection on these grounds was unexpected because I believe I am in good health. I think the company may have based its decision at least in part on inaccurate medical information you may have furnished to the insurer.

I therefore request that you furnish medical information you may have on me to my personal physician [*name of doctor*] at [*address and telephone number*]. I am also asking that you give to me directly any information of a nonmedical nature that you may have furnished to the Goodlife Insurance Company.

To help identify me, my full name is: _____; I live at: _____; my home telephone number is: _____; my Social Security number is: _____.

Should you require further identification, please contact me at your earliest convenience. I will appreciate your prompt cooperation in this matter.

Sincerely,
[*Your name*]

FILING A DEATH CLAIM

If you are the beneficiary of a life insurance policy and need to file a claim, first try phoning your insurance agent or, if you have no agent, the local office of the insurance company that issued the policy. The agent or the local office may send you a claim form asking for details of the policyholder's death. The company may also ask for a certified copy of the death certificate and a copy of the policy.

Here is a letter you can use to confirm your telephone call to the insurance company.

Letter to company confirming telephone call about a death claim:

Dear ———:

This is to confirm that on [*date*] I notified [*name of agent*] or [*person you spoke to at local office*] that as the beneficiary of the "Wonderlife" whole life policy number [*give policy number*], I am requesting all benefits now due and payable as a result of the death of John Doe [*name of insured*], my husband [*or other relationship*] on [*date*].

You indicated that the company would send claim forms and instructions so that my claim can be paid promptly. I will appreciate your immediate cooperation in this matter.

> Sincerely,
> [*Your name*]
> Policy beneficiary

You may have to write to the insurance company directly about a death claim if you've moved and don't have an insurance agent, or if the company has no office in your town. Write to the address on your latest communication from the company. Send a copy of the death certificate, a copy of the policy, a statement of the cause of death and, in the case of accidental death, documentation such as a police report. Be sure you, as the beneficiary, sign the letter. Again, we recommend you send this letter by certified or registered mail.

Letter to insurance company reporting a death claim:

Dear ———:

As part of my request for payment of all benefits now due and payable to me as the beneficiary of the "Wonderlife" whole life policy [*give policy name*], policy number [*give number*], insuring the life of John Doe [*name of insured*], I enclose the following documents:

Completed company claim form

Copy of insurance policy

Certified death certificate

Copy of police accident report or other official report confirming death was by accident [if applicable]

Please notify me if you need other information to complete this claim. I will appreciate your immediate payment.

> Sincerely,
> [*Your name*]
> Policy beneficiary

PART IV

Appendixes

Appendix A
The Ratings Charts
GUIDE TO THE RATINGS

The data for the policies rated on the following pages was gathered in late 1985 and published in 1986. Since then, many companies have revised their policies. Nevertheless, we present these Ratings because they serve as a guide to the insurance marketplace and because no such compilation of policy ratings can be found anywhere else. If you're interested in a particular company's policy that ranked highly in our study, check to see if the company is offering an updated version of the same policy. If it is, use the interest-adjusted net cost indexes to evaluate the new term and/or whole life policies, and use the method outlined on page 101 to evaluate universal life. Use the directory we have provided in appendix G (page 263) to locate the companies.

What follows is an explanation of how we determined the rankings for the three kinds of insurance policies featured in our study.

Term Policies

For each of the term policies in our study we calculated the interest-adjusted net cost index for five, ten, and twenty years, using the 5-percent rate as specified in the National Association of Insurance Commissioners (NAIC) regulation. Policies that were among the least expensive at a given duration are designated in the Ratings by a ●, those that were among the most expensive are designated by a ●, and policies that were somewhat less costly than average are designated by a ◕. Those that were average are shown with a ○ and those that were somewhat more costly than average are shown with a ◑.

To determine the Ratings order, we considered a policy's cost grouping at each of the three durations. If two policies did equally well, we used the ten-year index to break ties. If there were further ties, the first-year premium was the tiebreaker.

All of the policies reflect nonsmoker rates. In some cases, companies sent us preferred rates, which require a person to be a nonsmoker and meet other qualifications as well. Policies with preferred rates are marked with an asterisk. A few companies sent us nonsmoker rates for both preferred and standard classes. The Ratings show both. The policies in our term study include the waiver-of-premium rider because it was once common for insurance companies to automatically attach this rider to their policies. Companies have now eliminated this practice. Therefore, the cost indexes you find in the marketplace today will not include the waiver-of-premium rider.

For nonparticipating policies at the $200,000 amount, we show only the top forty and the bottom six. We list summary information for all the policies, however, in the alphabetically arranged tables beginning on page 182. Policies are ranked according to the rates for men, with the female rates listed alongside the male rates. As you can see by scanning the Ratings, women generally pay less because the average woman lives about seven years longer than the average man.

Whole Life Policies

For each of the whole life policies in our study, we calculated the interest-adjusted net cost index at five, ten, and twenty years. This index measures the cost of the policy if you surrender it after these durations (also called the *surrender index*).

We also calculated a ten-year interest-adjusted net payment index for each of the rated policies. The payment index does not reflect the policies' cash values, but measures instead the ongoing cost of holding your policy and not cashing it in, plus the cost of a policy if you die while still holding it.

Because you don't know when you will die, both indexes are important in evaluating a whole life policy. In the Ratings, we rank each policy from ◐ (better) to ● (worse) on each of four measures—net cost at five, ten, and twenty years, and net payment at ten years. We ranked the policies according to their total score. If there was a tie, we used the twenty-year interest-adjusted net cost index as the tie-breaker. First-year premiums broke further ties. Linton yields were not used to determine the Ratings order, though high-rated policies generally have good Linton yields.

All the policies reflect nonsmoker rates. They do not include the waiver-of-premium rider. Policies for preferred risks are marked with an asterisk.

Universal Life Policies

In our study of universal life policies, we calculated the cash values and cash surrender values for each policy, basing the accumulations on an average annual premium of $1,000. But for 45-year-old buyers purchasing $100,000 of coverage, we assumed an annual premium of $1,500 because some companies required minimum premiums exceeding $1,000.

A major aim of our study was to find out which policies had the lowest expense and mortality charges, which are the ingredients of the pricing mix we consider least likely to change. To do that, we projected each policy's cash value and cash surrender value using each company's own expense and mortality factors, but with a single interest rate for all—8 percent. The first group of symbols in the Ratings tables shows which companies performed best using this measure. (The five symbols used are the same.)

To give companies credit for the rates they were currently paying (ranging from 8¼ to 11 percent), we also projected the cash value and cash surrender value for each policy using the company's own interest rate as of March 1, 1986. We did those calculations for seven time periods: one, two, three, four, five, ten, and twenty years. In the Ratings, the first five are combined into a five-year average.

The Ratings give equal weight to the cash value and the cash surrender value because you probably don't know when you'll want to cash in the policy. The cash value is the fund from which your mortality charges and certain expense charges are paid. If you decide to cash in your policy, the cash value—minus any surrender charges—becomes the cash surrender value.

We gave equal weight to the five-year and ten-year values, less weight to the twenty-year values. We judge the twenty-year figures to be less believable; we don't expect either the companies' interest rates or their mortality charges to remain constant for such a long time. The Ratings show only twenty-year cash values; the twenty-year cash surrender values are virtually identical. After we had weighted all the totals at each interest rate, we averaged the two results to determine the final ranking. A company's ten-year cash value accumulated at 8 percent broke the ties, if any.

We figured the accumulated cash values under each policy's Option A and Option B and found virtually no change in the Ratings order. Our Ratings show only Option A. Aetna's Aeconoflex policy, however, ranked somewhat higher under Option A than under Option B.

Ratings

(as published in *Consumer Reports*, June 1986)

Term insurance

Listed in order of estimated overall cost, based on 5-year, 10-year, and 20-year cost estimates, weighted equally. Policies marked with an asterisk are available to "preferred risks" only. Revertible policies will have an RH or RU following the policy name. RH indicates the estimated cost of such a policy when the buyer remains healthy; RU indicates the estimated cost if the buyer's health worsens midway through the period analyzed. All rates shown are for nonsmokers; smokers' rates are generally higher.

$50,000 · Age 25 · Nonparticipating

COMPANY NAME	POLICY NAME	Male First-year premium	Male 10-year cost index	Male Relative cost 5-year	Male 10-year	Male 20-year	Female First-year premium	Female 10-year cost index	Female Relative cost 5-year	Female 10-year	Female 20-year
Massachusetts Indemnity & Life	Annual Renewable Term 100	$ 58	1.49	●	●	●	$ 58	1.49	●	●	●
First Colony	CA95*	90	1.79	●	●	●	92	1.84	●	●	●
Federal Kemper	T95	90	1.80	●	●	●	90	1.80	●	●	●
Washington National	Annual Renewable Term 90	87	1.81	●	●	●	87	1.74	●	●	●
Old Line Life	LT-10 [RH]	94	1.87	●	●	●	94	1.87	●	●	●
Old Line Life	LT-10 [RU]	94	1.87	●	●	●	94	1.87	●	●	●
American Agency Life	Ten Year Renewable & Convertible Term*	101	2.02	●	●	●	100	2.00	◐	◐	●
American Agency Life	5 Year Renewable & Convertible Term*	99	2.03	●	●	●	97	1.95	◐	◐	●

United Investors	Vitalife Annual Renewable Term	101	2.06							88	1.81
Northwestern National	LT-10 [RH]	104	2.09							104	2.08
Northwestern National	LT-10 [RU]	104	2.09							104	2.08
Great Southern	Termpacer	83	2.14							82	2.03
First Colony	Select 20 [RH]	89	2.20							91	2.21
Sun Life of Canada	Nova Yearly Renewable Term	107	2.25							109	2.20
First Colony	CA99*	107	2.27							107	2.26
Liberty National	Annually Renewable Term	113	2.32							106	2.16
Life of Virginia	Yearly Renewable Term	108	2.34							101	2.18
Manufacturers Life	Select 10	103	2.36							103	2.36
First Colony	Select 20 [RU]	89	2.20							91	2.21
IDS	Yearly Renewable Term	121	2.50							112	2.37
United Investors	Adjustable Annual Renewable Term	126	2.53							113	2.29
State Mutual	Yearly Renewable Flexterm Level Term	120	2.50							109	2.26
Alexander Hamilton	5 Year Level Term	125	2.59							118	2.42
Continental Assurance Co.	Adjustable Prem. Annual Renewable Term	124	2.62							125	2.54
Guardsman	Yearly Renewable & Convertible Term	128	2.69							125	2.64
Travelers	5 Year Level Term	141	2.86							144	2.91
Fort Dearborn	Annual Renewable Term	141	2.87							135	2.75
Farmers New World	5 Year Renewable & Convertible Term	139	2.90							121	2.50
Crown Life	Select Yearly Renewable Term	126	3.06							130	3.10
Crown Life	Yearly Renewable Term	151	3.06							153	3.07
ITT Life	5 Year Renewable & Convertible Term	140	3.10							133	2.90
United Life & Accident	Yearly Renewable Term	149	3.11							147	3.04
Crown Life	5 Year Renewable Term	165	3.34							157	3.18
Massachusetts Indemnity & Life	Modified Term	367	3.62							329	3.34

$50,000 Age 25 Participating

		Male					Female				
		First-year premium (10-year premium)	10-year cost index	Relative cost 5-year	10-year	20-year	First-year premium (10-year premium)	10-year cost index	Relative cost 5-year	10-year	20-year
COMPANY NAME	POLICY NAME										
New York Savings Bank	5 Year Renewable & Convertible Term	$69	1.47	●	●	●	$62	1.29	●	●	●
Metropolitan	One Year Term with Premium Adjustment	74	1.54	●	●	●	74	1.49	●	●	●
Northwestern Mutual	10 Year Term—Increasing Premium	82	1.67	●	●	●	76	1.56	●	●	●
Massachusetts Savings Bank	Yearly Renewable Term	84	1.68	●	●	●	84	1.68	●	●	●
Teachers Ins. & Annuity Assoc.	5 Year Renewable Term	83	1.69	●	●	●	83	1.69	●	●	●
Union Central	Annual Renewable Term to 100	70	1.70	●	●	●	70	1.70	●	●	●
National Life of Vermont	Yearly Renewable Term—15	81	1.83	●	●	—	81	1.83	●	●	—
Northwestern Mutual	Term to Age 70—Increasing Premium	93	1.89	●	●	●	86	1.75	●	●	●
Massachusetts Savings Bank	5 Year Renewable Term	103	1.89	◐	○	○	103	1.89	●	●	●
Phoenix Mutual	Annual Renewable Term to Age 70	78	1.92	●	●	●	79	1.92	●	●	●
Union Labor	Annual Renewable Term	78	1.94	●	●	●	78	1.94	●	●	●
Aid Association for Lutherans	Yearly Renewable Term	105	2.09	◐	◐	◐	86	1.76	●	●	●
National Life of Vermont	Yearly Renewable Term—100	93	2.06	◐	◐	○	79	1.74	●	●	●
New York Life	Increasing Premium Term to Age 70	89	2.07	◐	○	○	92	2.11	◐	◐	◐
General American	Yearly Renewable Term to 95*	88	2.16	◐	○	○	84	2.37	◐	○	○
Home Life	Yearly Renewable Term to 75	94	2.17	◐	○	○	94	2.17	◐	○	○
Western & Southern Life	Annual Renewable & Convertible Term	111	2.24	○	○	◐	106	2.12	○	○	◐
Massachusetts Mutual	5 Year Renewable Term	137	2.26	◐	◐	●	138	2.15	◐	◐	●
Minnesota Mutual	Adjustable III	176	2.32	◐	○	●	136	1.97	○	○	●
General American	Yearly Renewable Term to 70*	110	2.18	○	○	○	102	1.96	○	○	◐
Union Labor	5 Year Level Term	118	2.19	○	○	○	118	2.19	○	○	◐
Mutual Benefit Life	Yearly Renewable Term	92	2.24	◐	○	◐	91	2.08	◐	○	◐

New England Mutual	**Yearly Renewable Term to Age 95 [RH]**	109	2.31	○	○	○	105	2.23	○ ○
General American	Yearly Renewable Term to 95	93	2.33	◐	○	◐	87	1.96	◑ ◐
General American	Yearly Renewable Term to 70	117	2.33	○	○	○	106	2.11	◐ ○
Aetna	Flexi-Term	115	2.34	○	○	○	112	2.28	○ ○
Connecticut Mutual	Yearly Renewable Term	118	2.36	○	○	○	103	2.07	○ ◐
Mutual of New York	Yearly Renewable Term	107	2.41	○	○	○	106	2.37	◐ ◐
New England Mutual	**Yearly Renewable Term to Age 95 [RU]**	109	2.59	○	◑	◐	105	2.45	○ ○
New England Mutual	5 Year Renewable & Convertible Term	135	2.50	◐	◐	◐	132	2.38	● ◐
Massachusetts Mutual	Yearly Renewable Term	125	2.51	◐	◐	◐	125	2.49	◐ ◐
Minnesota Mutual	Convertible Annual Renewable Term	127	2.69	◐	◐	◐	118	2.49	◐ ◐
Connecticut Mutual	Yearly Renewable Term—7	122	—	—	—	—	122	—	— —
Southern Farm Bureau	5 Year Renewable Term	155	2.72	●	◐	◐	139	2.43	● ◐
Metropolitan	5 Year Renewable & Convertible Term	169	2.62	●	◐	◐	160	2.48	● ◐
Guardian Life	Yearly Renewable Term—Scheduled*	141	2.82	●	●	◐	129	2.57	● ◐
Western & Southern Life	5 Year Renewable & Convertible Term	161	3.22	●	●	●	156	3.12	● ●
Guardian Life	Yearly Renewable Term—Maximum*	141	3.31	●	●	●	129	3.00	● ●
John Hancock Mutual	Yearly Renewable Term	174	3.60	●	●	●	166	3.43	● ●
Guardian Life	Yearly Renewable Term—Scheduled	181	3.67	●	●	●	169	3.42	● ●
Guardian Life	Yearly Renewable Term—Maximum	181	4.16	●	●	●	169	3.85	● ●

$50,000 Age 35 Nonparticipating

COMPANY NAME	POLICY NAME	Male First-year premium	Male 10-year cost index	Female First-year premium	Female 10-year cost index
Massachusetts Indemnity & Life	Annual Renewable Term 100	$ 64	2.11	$ 64	2.11
Old Line Life	LT-10 [RH]	110	2.25	98	1.98
First Colony	CA95*	114	2.28	101	2.01
Federal Kemper	T95	115	2.30	105	2.10
Northwestern National	LT-10 [RH]	117	2.37	110	2.21
Northwestern National	LT-10 [RU]	117	2.37	110	2.21
United Investors	Vitalife Annual Renewable Term	107	2.54	100	2.28
Washington National	Annual Renewable Term 90	101	2.59	89	1.99
Great Southern	Termpacer	87	2.64	85	2.36
First Colony	Select 20 [RH]	93	3.00	96	2.72
Manufacturers Life	Select 10	110	3.17	107	2.60
Old Line Life	LT-10 [RU]	110	2.76	98	2.28
American Agency Life	5 Year Renewable & Convertible Term*	123	2.81	105	2.26
Life of Virginia	Yearly Renewable Term	115	2.92	108	2.69
First Colony	CA99*	125	2.97	122	2.78
IDS	Yearly Renewable Term	130	2.98	129	2.95
United Investors	Adjustable Annual Renewable Term	130	2.99	122	2.74
Liberty National	Annually Renewable Term	123	3.03	116	2.69
Sun Life of Canada	Nova Yearly Renewable Term	130	3.14	119	2.91
American Agency Life	Ten Year Renewable & Convertible Term*	139	2.79	109	2.17
First Colony	Select 20 [RU]	93	3.00	96	2.72
Travelers	5 Year Level Term	155	3.42	153	3.30

State Mutual	Yearly Renewable Flexterm Level Term	135	3.42	○	○	120	2.92	○	○
Continental Assurance Co.	Adjustable Prem. Annual Renewable Term	142	3.45	○	○	136	2.98	○	◐
Fort Dearborn	Annual Renewable Term	156	3.48	○	○	152	3.34	◐	◐
Alexander Hamilton	5 Year Level Term	152	3.53	○	○	139	3.19	○	◑
Crown Life	Select Yearly Renewable Term	128	3.58	○	◑	133	3.53	◑	●
Crown Life	Yearly Renewable Term	158	3.73	◑	◑	156	3.39	◑	●
Guardsman	Yearly Renewable & Convertible Term	148	3.86	◑	◑	142	3.13	○	○
United Life & Accident	Yearly Renewable Term	170	4.13	●	◑	161	3.67	●	●
Crown Life	5 Year Renewable Term	187	4.19	●	●	178	3.88	●	●
Farmers New World	5 Year Renewable & Convertible Term	182	4.11	●	●	152	3.40	◑	◑
ITT Life	5 Year Renewable & Convertible Term	191	4.86	●	●	163	3.94	◑	●
Massachusetts Indemnity & Life	Modified Term	429	4.93	●	●	384	4.52	●	●

$50,000 Age 35 Participating

COMPANY NAME	POLICY NAME	Male First-year premium	Male 10-year cost index	Male Relative cost 5-year	Male Relative cost 10-year	Male Relative cost 20-year	Female First-year premium	Female 10-year cost index	Female Relative cost 5-year	Female Relative cost 10-year	Female Relative cost 20-year
Massachusetts Savings Bank	5 Year Renewable Term	$121	1.96	●	●	●	$121	1.96	●	●	●
Metropolitan	One Year Term With Premium Adjustment	86	1.97	●	●	●	82	1.80	●	●	●
Massachusetts Savings Bank	Yearly Renewable Term	84	1.98	●	●	●	84	1.98	●	●	●
New York Savings Bank	5 Year Renewable & Convertible Term	84	2.10	●	●	●	81	1.97	●	●	●
Northwestern Mutual	10 Year Term—Increasing Premium	88	2.13	●	●	●	82	1.93	●	●	●
Union Central	Annual Renewable Term to 100	73	2.22	●	●	●	71	1.91	●	●	○
Teachers Ins. & Annuity Assoc.	5 Year Renewable Term	102	2.38	●	◐	◑	102	2.38	●	◐	—
National Life of Vermont	Yearly Renewable Term—15	85	2.44	●	◑	—	85	2.44	●	◑	◑
Northwestern Mutual	Term to Age 70—Increasing Premium	100	2.46	◑	◑	◑	93	2.23	●	◑	◑
Phoenix Mutual	Annual Renewable Term to Age 70	88	2.52	◑	◑	◑	86	2.31	●	◑	◑
Union Labor	Annual Renewable Term	88	2.55	◑	◑	◑	88	2.55	◑	◑	◑
Massachusetts Mutual	5 Year Renewable Term	165	2.54	○	◑	◑	164	2.49	◑	◑	◑
Western & Southern Life	Annual Renewable & Convertible Term	114	2.56	○	◑	◑	108	2.37	◑	◑	◑
General American	Yearly Renewable Term to 95*	94	2.79	◑	○	○	89	2.40	◑	◑	◑
National Life of Vermont	Yearly Renewable Term to 100	98	2.80	◑	○	○	87	2.38	●	◑	◑
Aid Association for Lutherans	Yearly Renewable Term	117	2.81	○	○	○	102	2.41	○	◑	◑
Home Life	Yearly Renewable Term to 75	105	2.84	○	○	○	105	2.84	○	○	○
Connecticut Mutual	Yearly Renewable Term	119	2.84	○	○	○	106	2.43	◑	◑	◑
Minnesota Mutual	Adjustable III	229	2.88	●	◑	◑	198	2.39	◑	●	●
New York Life	Increasing Premium Term to Age 70	92	2.90	○	○	○	96	2.59	◑	○	◑
Aetna	Flexi-Term	126	2.90	○	○	○	122	2.55	○	○	◑
General American	Yearly Renewable Term to 70*	127	2.92	○	○	○	118	2.46	○	○	◑

New England Mutual	Yearly Renewable Term to Age 95 [RH]	113	2.98	111	2.62
Massachusetts Mutual	Yearly Renewable Term	140	3.04	139	2.97
General American	Yearly Renewable Term to 95	100	3.09	92	2.60
General American	Yearly Renewable Term to 70	135	3.12	123	2.60
Mutual of New York	Yearly Renewable Term	108	3.15	107	2.73
Minnesota Mutual	Convertible Annual Renewable Term	134	3.20	125	2.83
Union Labor	5 Year Level Term	151	3.21	151	3.21
Guardian Life	Yearly Renewable Term—Scheduled*	144	3.22	131	2.88
Mutual Benefit Life	Yearly Renewable Term	102	3.30	102	2.84
Connecticut Mutual	Annual Renewable Term—7	126	—	126	—
New England Mutual	Yearly Renewable Term to Age 95 [RU]	113	3.47	111	2.96
Guardian Life	Yearly Renewable Term—Maximum*	144	4.24	131	3.77
Metropolitan	5 Year Renewable & Convertible Term	228	3.49	208	3.18
Southern Farm Bureau	5 Year Renewable Term	190	3.57	179	3.31
New England Mutual	5 Year Renewable & Convertible Term	186	3.80	161	3.09
Western & Southern Life	5 year Renewable & Convertible Term	185	4.11	179	3.68
John Hancock Mutual	Yearly Renewable Term	202	4.42	187	3.89
Guardian Life	Yearly Renewable Term—Scheduled	193	4.46	180	4.13
Guardian Life	Yearly Renewable Term—Maximum	193	5.49	180	5.01

$50,000 — Age 45 — Nonparticipating

COMPANY NAME	POLICY NAME	Male First-year premium	Male 10-year premium	Female First-year premium	Female 10-year premium
First Colony	CA95*	4.45	$223	3.37	$169
Northwestern National	LT-10 [RH]	4.60	221	3.65	176
Northwestern National	LT-10 [RU]	4.60	221	3.65	176
Old Line Life	LT-10 [RH]	4.60	221	3.64	176
Massachusetts Indemnity & Life	Annual Renewable Term 100	4.66	107	4.66	107
United Investors	Vitalife Annual Renewable Term	5.20	178	3.95	137
Federal Kemper	T95	4.66	233	3.88	194
Life of Virginia	Yearly Renewable Term	5.42	165	4.96	153
Great Southern	Termpacer	5.07	117	3.72	99
United Investors	Adjustable Annual Renewable Term	5.66	200	4.40	159
First Colony	CA99*	5.78	207	5.43	185
First Colony	Select 20 [RH]	6.21	137	5.51	131
Manufacturers Life	Select 10	6.30	170	4.64	148
American Agency Life	Ten Year Renewable & Convertible Term*	5.59	279	3.86	193
Washington National	Annual Renewable Term 90	5.87	194	3.84	130
American Agency Life	5 Year Renewable & Convertible Term*	5.92	238	3.92	163
Crown Life	Select Yearly Renewable Term	6.25	172	5.60	159
Travelers	5 Year Level Term	5.99	253	5.35	231
IDS	Yearly Renewable Term	6.28	198	5.50	196
Union Labor	5 Year Level Term	6.35	287	6.35	287
First Colony	Select 20 [RU]	6.21	137	5.51	131
Liberty National	Annually Renewable Term	6.41	221	5.02	181

Relative cost columns (5-year cost index, 10-year, 20-year) for both Male and Female are indicated graphically.

Sun Life of Canada	Nova Yearly Renewable Term	227	6.68	205	5.76
Continental Assurance Co.	Adjustable Prem. Annual Renewable Term	236	6.88	185	4.86
Fort Dearborn	Annual Renewable Term	281	6.95	261	6.08
State Mutual	Yearly Renewable Flexterm Level Term	243	7.26	203	6.03
Alexander Hamilton	5 Year Level Term	302	7.50	264	6.64
Old Line Life	LT-10 (RU)	221	6.55	176	5.05
Crown Life	Yearly Renewable Term	262	7.35	222	6.13
Massachusetts Indemnity & Life	Modified Term	511	8.10	445	7.71
United Life & Accident	Yearly Renewable Term	287	8.20	245	6.90
Crown Life	5 Year Renewable Term	327	7.98	294	7.03
Guardsman	Yearly Renewable & Convertible Term	293	8.47	210	6.02
Farmers New World	5 Year Renewable & Convertible Term	350	9.17	279	7.24
ITT Life	5 Year Renewable & Convertible Term	392	10.40	302	7.90

$50,000 Age 45 Participating

		Male					Female	
COMPANY NAME	POLICY NAME	First-year premium	10-year cost index	Relative cost (5-yr / 10-yr / 20-yr)	First-year premium	10-year cost index	Relative cost (5-yr / 10-yr / 20-yr)	
Massachusetts Savings Bank	Yearly Renewable Term	$149	3.32		$149	3.32	
Massachusetts Savings Bank	5 Year Renewable Term	232	3.49		232	3.49	
National Life of Vermont	Yearly Renewable Term—15	118	4.16		118	4.16	
Union Central	Annual Renewable Term to 100	118	4.21		93	3.44	
Northwestern Mutual	10 Year Term—Increasing Premium	153	4.33		134	3.75	
Union Labor	Annual Renewable Term	143	4.63		143	4.63	
New York Savings Bank	5 Year Renewable & Convertible Term	159	4.63		151	3.93	
New England Mutual	Yearly Renewable Term to Age 95 [RH]	147	4.96		135	4.27	
Metropolitan	One Year Term With Premium Adjustment	140	4.69		115	3.61	
National Life of Vermont	Yearly Renewable Term—100	139	5.12		124	4.39	
Phoenix Mutual	Annual Renewable Term to Age 70	148	5.18		125	4.30	
General American	Yearly Renewable Term to 95*	130	5.26		119	4.15	
Connecticut Mutual	Yearly Renewable Term	197	5.22		162	4.23	
Mutual of New York	Yearly Renewable Term	134	5.28		121	4.41	
Aid Association for Lutherans	Yearly Renewable Term	210	5.29		180	4.53	
Guardian Life	Yearly Renewable Term—Scheduled*	199	5.33		174	4.55	
Aetna	Flexi-Term	204	5.54		165	4.35	
Western & Southern Life	Annual Renewable & Convertible Term	179	5.19		154	4.47	
Massachusetts Mutual	5 Year Renewable Term	338	5.32		316	4.43	
Minnesota Mutual	Adjustable III	439	5.35		359	3.63	
Teachers Ins. & Annuity Assoc.	5 Year Renewable Term	208	5.46		208	5.46	
New York Life	Increasing Premium Term to Age 70	140	5.57		121	4.74	

Company	Product	Val 1	Val 2	Val 3	Val 4
Connecticut Mutual	Yearly Renewable Term—7	170	—	170	—
Minnesota Mutual	Convertible Annual Renewable Term	179	5.64	150	4.68
Home Life	Yearly Renewable Term to 75	169	5.81	169	5.81
General American	Yearly Renewable Term to 95	147	6.07	129	4.52
New England Mutual	Yearly Renewable Term to Age 95 [RU]	147	6.30	135	5.15
Northwestern Mutual	Term to Age 70—Increasing Premium	189	6.07	165	5.20
General American	Yearly Renewable Term to 70*	224	6.15	179	4.98
Massachusetts Mutual	Yearly Renewable Term	260	6.09	245	5.10
Mutual Benefit Life	Yearly Renewable Term	175	6.57	166	5.34
General American	Yearly Renewable Term to 70	239	6.65	189	5.29
Guardian Life	Yearly Renewable Term—Maximum*	199	7.46	174	6.11
John Hancock Mutual	Yearly Renewable Term	304	7.78	256	6.30
Metropolitan	5 Year Renewable & Convertible Term	397	6.90	332	5.58
Southern Farm Bureau	5 Year Renewable Term	406	6.99	343	5.26
Guardian Life	Yearly Renewable Term—Scheduled	293	7.85	267	7.08
Western & Southern Life	5 Year Renewable & Convertible Term	349	8.44	285	6.81
New England Mutual	5 Year Renewable & Convertible Term	374	8.51	292	6.33
Guardian Life	Yearly Renewable Term—Maximum	293	9.99	267	8.64

$200,000 Age 25 Nonparticipating

The 40 lowest-cost policies

COMPANY NAME	POLICY NAME	Male: First-year premium	Male: 10-year cost index	Female: First-year premium	Female: 10-year cost index
Massachusetts Indemnity & Life	Annual Renewable Term 100*	$121 / 0.83		$121 / 0.83	
First Colony	CA95*	208 / 1.04		218 / 1.09	
Federal Kemper	T95	210 / 1.05		210 / 1.05	
Massachusetts Indemnity & Life	Annual Renewable Term 100	155 / 1.11		155 / 1.11	
Fort Dearborn	Select Annual Renewable Term [RH]	231 / 1.18		229 / 1.17	
ITT Life	Guaranteed Re-entry Annual Renewable Term [RH]	167 / 1.19		165 / 1.14	
North Amer. Co. for Life & Health	Leveler—Current Premiums*	296 / 1.25		286 / 1.20	
Union Mutual	Yearly Renewable Term—70	228 / 1.32		206 / 1.19	
Northwestern National	LT—10 [RH]	267 / 1.34		265 / 1.33	
Northwestern National	LT—10 [RU]	267 / 1.34		265 / 1.33	
Alexander Hamilton	Annual Renewable Term 100	184 / 1.35		182 / 1.21	
Travelers	Yearly Renewable Term 10	245 / 1.54		251 / 1.52	
Integon	First Class Term	266 / 1.46		250 / 1.37	
Integon	First Class Term [RH]	267 / 1.47		251 / 1.38	
Integon	First Class Term [RU]	267 / 1.47		251 / 1.38	
Lincoln National	LNL—10	288 / 1.49		248 / 1.38	
American Agency Life	5 Year Renewable & Convertible Term*	288 / 1.49		282 / 1.42	
Old Line Life	LT—10 [RH]	298 / 1.49		298 / 1.49	
Jackson National Life	Yearly Renewable Term—100	265 / 1.54		265 / 1.52	
First Colony	Select 20 [RH]	231 / 1.57		237 / 1.58	
ITT Life	Guaranteed Re-entry Annual Renewable Term [RU]	167 / 1.19		165 / 1.14	

(Each row also carries Relative cost indicator symbols for 5-year, 10-year, and 20-year periods, for both Male and Female columns.)

American Agency Life	Ten Year Renewable & Convertible Term*	298	1.49	294	1.47
Franklin Life	Challenger 90*	254	1.52	270	1.56
Southwestern Life	Renaissance Annual Renewable Term II	299	1.52	251	1.30
Philadelphia Life	Electerm [RH]	302	1.52	302	1.51
Southwestern Life	Renaissance Renewable & Convertible Term	305	1.54	263	1.35
Continental Assurance Co.	Step 10	318	1.59	324	1.62
Old Line Life	CE82 [RH]	238	1.61	238	1.60
Fort Dearborn	Select Annual Renewable Term [RU]	231	1.71	229	1.63
First Colony	Select 20 [RU]	231	1.57	237	1.58
Life of Virginia	Yearly Renewable Term	282	1.59	254	1.43
Federal Kemper	SR22/84 [RH]	250	1.62	248	1.56
Old Line Life	LT—10 [RU]	298	1.49	298	1.49
Franklin Life	Challenger 90	278	1.66	292	1.69
Sun Life of Canada	Nova Yearly Renewable Term	327	1.66	307	1.56
Continental Assurance Co.	Adjustable Prem. Annual Renewable Term	314	1.68	316	1.62
United Investors	Vitalife Annual Renewable Term	327	1.69	275	1.44
State Mutual	Exeterm II—Term to Age 75 [RH]	309	1.70	285	1.57
North Amer. Co. for Life & Health	Leveler—Guaranteed Premiums*	296	1.71	286	1.69
Liberty National	Annually Renewable Term	331	1.71	286	1.48

The 6 highest-cost policies

Alexander Hamilton	5 Year Level Term	405	2.11	375	1.94
Guardsman	Yearly Renewable & Convertible Term	410	2.15	410	2.14
Old Line Life	Preferred Annual Renewable Term [RU]	345	2.27	339	2.17
ITT Life	5 Year Renewable & Convertible Term	409	2.30	390	2.14
Farmers New World	5 Year Renewable & Convertible Term	500	2.63	428	2.23
Crown Life	5 Year Renewable Term	568	2.88	536	2.72

$200,000 — Age 25 — Participating

COMPANY NAME	POLICY NAME	Male First-year premium	Male 10-year cost index	Female First-year premium	Female 10-year cost index
Metropolitan	One Year Term With Premium Adjustment	$201	1.06	$199	1.01
Teachers Ins. & Annuity Assoc.	5 Year Renewable Term	222	1.13	222	1.13
Northwestern Mutual	10 Year Term—Increasing Premium	221	1.15	199	1.03
Home Life	Yearly Renewable Term to 75	174	1.17	174	1.17
National Life of Vermont	Yearly Renewable Term—15	202	1.23	202	1.23
Union Central	Annual Renewable Term to 100	190	1.25	190	1.25
Southern Farm Bureau	Annual Renewable Term*	264	1.32	254	1.27
Equitable	Yearly Renewable Term	259	1.35	180	0.92
Northwestern Mutual	Term to Age 70—Increasing Premium	267	1.36	239	1.22
Massachusetts Mutual	Adjustable Premium Term	290	1.46	292	1.49
Bankers Life	One Year Term	302	1.42	258	1.21
Aetna	Flexi-Term	283	1.45	271	1.39
Massachusetts Mutual	Yearly Renewable Term	354	1.45	352	1.36
Massachusetts Mutual	5 Year Renewable Term	392	1.43	390	1.43
National Life of Vermont	Yearly Renewable Term—100	250	1.46	194	1.14
Phoenix Mutual	Annual Renewable Term to Age 70	250	1.55	257	1.55
General American	Yearly Renewable Term to 95*	232	1.56	214	1.46
Union Labor	Annual Renewable Term	237	1.56	237	1.56
Minnesota Mutual	Adjustable III	568	1.64	407	1.29
Prudential	Annually Increasing Premium Term to 70	363	1.75	289	1.33
Aid Association for Lutherans	Yearly Renewable Term	313	1.56	239	1.24
Mutual Benefit Life	Yearly Renewable Term	273	1.62	271	1.46

Company	Policy	Rate	Index					Rate	Index						
Minnesota Mutual	*Convertible Annual Renewable Term*	286	1.66	○	○	○	◐	262	1.52	◐	○	○	◐	—	○
Western & Southern Life	*Annual Renewable & Convertible Term*	329	1.66	○	○	○	○	307	1.55	○	○	○	○	○	○
John Hancock Mutual	*Preferred Yearly Renewable Term**	343	1.66	○	○	○	○	313	1.49	◐	○	○	○	◐	○
Connecticut Mutual	*Yearly Renewable Term—7*	261	—	—	—	—	—	261	—	—	—	—	—	—	—
General American	*Yearly Renewable Term to 95*	252	1.73	◐	●	○	◐	226	1.25	○	◐	●	●	○	○
New York Life	*Increasing Premium Term to Age 70*	281	1.69	○	◐	○	◐	293	1.73	◐	◐	◐	◐	○	○
General American	*Yearly Renewable Term to 70**	350	1.73	○	○	○	○	316	1.57	○	○	○	○	○	○
John Hancock Mutual	*Yearly Renewable Term*	363	1.78	◐	○	○	◐	333	1.61	○	○	○	○	○	○
Guardian Life	*Yearly Renewable Term—Scheduled**	357	1.79	○	○	○	○	309	1.55	○	○	○	○	○	○
Union Labor	*5 Year Level Term*	395	1.82	◐	◐	◐	◐	395	1.82	◐	◐	◐	◐	●	●
Mutual of New York	*Yearly Renewable Term*	326	1.87	◐	◐	◐	◐	322	1.84	◐	◐	◐	◐	●	◐
General American	*Yearly Renewable Term to 70*	376	1.88	◐	◐	◐	◐	332	1.66	◐	◐	◐	◐	●	◐
Connecticut Mutual	*Yearly Renewable Term*	380	1.90	◐	◐	◐	◐	322	1.62	◐	◐	◐	◐	●	◐
New England Mutual	**Yearly Renewable Term to age 95 [RH]**	361	1.94	●	●	●	●	343	1.85	◐	●	●	●	●	●
New England Mutual	**Yearly Renewable Term to Age 95 [RU]**	361	2.22	●	●	●	●	343	2.08	◐	●	●	●	●	●
Guardian Life	*Yearly Renewable Term-Maximum**	357	2.29	◐	●	●	◐	309	1.98	○	●	●	●	●	●
Southern Farm Bureau	*5 Year Renewable Term*	510	2.17	●	●	●	●	494	2.15	●	●	●	●	●	●
Metropolitan	*5 Year Renewable & Convertible Term*	600	2.24	●	●	●	●	563	2.10	●	●	●	●	●	●
New England Mutual	*5 Year Renewable & Convertible Term*	495	2.28	●	●	●	●	483	2.15	●	●	●	●	●	●
Guardian Life	*Yearly Renewable Term—Scheduled*	517	2.64	●	●	●	●	469	2.40	●	●	●	●	●	●
Western & Southern Life	*5 Year Renewable & Convertible Term*	567	2.84	●	●	●	●	549	2.74	●	●	●	●	●	●
Guardian Life	*Yearly Renewable Term—Maximum*	517	3.14	●	●	●	●	469	2.83	●	●	●	●	●	●

$200,000 — Age 35 — Nonparticipating

The 40 lowest-cost policies

COMPANY NAME	POLICY NAME	Male First-year premium	Male 10-year cost index	Female First-year premium	Female 10-year cost index
Massachusetts Indemnity & Life	Annual Renewable Term 100*	$137	1.22	$137	1.22
Fort Dearborn	Select Annual Renewable Term [RH]	255	1.42	261	1.45
North Amer. Co. for Life & Health	Leveler—Current Premiums*	330	1.42	316	1.35
First Colony	CA95*	306	1.53	252	1.26
Federal Kemper	T95	308	1.54	268	1.34
Massachusetts Indemnity & Life	Annual Renewable Term 100	179	1.73	179	1.73
Northwestern National	LT-10 [RH]	317	1.62	289	1.46
Northwestern National	LT-10 [RU]	317	1.62	289	1.46
Old Line Life	LT-10 [RH]	343	1.76	310	1.56
Jackson National Life	Yearly Renewable Term—100	273	1.90	269	1.62
ITT Life	Guaranteed Re-entry Annual Renewable Term [RH]	227	1.93	210	1.61
Continental Assurance Co.	Step 10	366	1.83	350	1.75
Lincoln National	LNL-10	310	1.84	316	1.75
Union Mutual	Yearly Renewable Term-70	244	1.85	230	1.69
Southwestern Life	Renaissance Renewable & Convertible Term	337	1.92	313	1.74
Travelers	Yearly Renewable Term 10	263	1.98	257	1.78
Philadelphia Life	Electerm [RH]	324	1.99	302	1.64
Integon	First Class Term [RH]	290	2.07	278	1.88
Integon	First Class Term	286	1.96	276	1.79
Southwestern Life	Renaissance Annual Renewable Term II	317	1.97	293	1.76
Integon	First Class Term [RU]	290	2.07	278	1.88

Relative cost columns (10-year premium, 5-year cost index, 10-year, 20-year) for both Male and Female are shown graphically with filled/half/open circles.

Old Line Life	CE82 [RH]	249	2.27	243	1.99
Fort Dearborn	Select Annual Renewable Term [RU]	255	2.28	261	2.14
Federal Kemper	SR22/84 [RH]	270	2.29	268	2.05
ITT Life	Guaranteed Re-entry Annual Renewable Term [RU]	227	1.93	210	1.61
Liberty National	Annually Renewable Term	360	2.09	322	1.92
Franklin Life	Challenger 90*	276	2.12	290	1.93
United Investors	Vitalife Annual Renewable Term	351	2.16	323	1.91
IDS	Yearly Renewable Term	361	2.18	355	2.15
Alexander Hamilton	Annual Renewable Term 100	228	2.19	202	1.66
Crown Life	Select Yearly Renewable Term	280	2.19	298	2.17
United Investors	Adjustable Annual Renewable Term	368	2.24	338	1.99
Old Line Life	Preferred Annual Renewable Term [RH]	383	2.27	365	2.02
First Colony	Select 20 [RH]	247	2.37	257	2.10
Life of Virginia	Yearly Renewable Term	308	2.17	280	1.94
American Agency Life	Ten Year Renewable & Convertible Term*	437	2.18	325	1.62
American Agency Life	5 Year Renewable & Convertible Term*	377	2.21	312	1.70
Great Southern	Termpacer	286	2.25	272	1.96
First Colony	CA99*	365	2.29	365	2.12
Sun Life of Canada	Nova Yearly Renewable Term	361	2.30	321	2.09

The 6 highest-cost policies

Alexander Hamilton	5 Year Level Term	501	2.98	451	2.64
Guardsman	Yearly Renewable & Convertible Term	458	3.07	458	2.52
ITT Life	5 Year Renewable & Convertible Term	573	3.71	487	2.98
Crown Life	5 Year Renewable Term	659	3.73	623	3.43
Old Line Life	Preferred Annual Renewable Term [RU]	383	3.74	365	3.04
Farmers New World	5 Year Renewable & Convertible Term	672	3.84	553	3.13

$200,000 — Age 35 — Participating

COMPANY NAME	POLICY NAME	Male First-year premium	Male 10-year cost index	Male Relative cost 5-year	Male Relative cost 10-year	Male Relative cost 20-year	Female First-year premium	Female 10-year cost index	Female Relative cost 5-year	Female Relative cost 10-year	Female Relative cost 20-year
Metropolitan	One Year Term with Premium Adjustment	$247	1.50	●	●	●	$233	1.33	●	●	●
Teachers Ins. & Annuity Assoc.	5 Year Renewable Term	272	1.58	●	●	●	272	1.58	●	●	●
Northwestern Mutual	10 Year Term—Increasing Premium	245	1.60	●	●	●	221	1.41	●	●	●
Equitable	Yearly Renewable Term	304	1.69	●	●	●	225	1.15	●	●	●
Union Central	Annual Renewable Term to 100	200	1.77	●	●	◐	192	1.46	●	●	●
Home Life	Yearly Renewable Term to 75	218	1.84	●	◐	◐	218	1.84	◐	●	◐
National Life of Vermont	Yearly Renewable Term—15	220	1.84	◐	◐	—	220	1.84	—	◐	—
Massachusetts Mutual	Adjustable Premium Term	314	2.01	◐	◐	●	316	1.75	●	●	●
Massachusetts Mutual	5 Year Renewable Term	486	1.72	◐	◐	●	460	1.41	◐	●	●
Southern Farm Bureau	Annual Renewable Term*	288	1.85	◐	◐	◐	278	1.78	◐	◐	◐
Bankers Life	One Year Term	316	1.94	◐	◐	◐	284	1.62	◐	●	◐
Aetna	Flexi-Term	325	1.98	◐	◐	◐	307	1.65	◐	●	◐
Northwestern Mutual	Term to Age 70—Increasing Premium	293	1.93	◐	◐	○	265	1.71	◐	◐	◐
Western & Southern Life	Annual Renewable & Convertible Term	341	1.98	○	◐	◐	317	1.80	◐	◐	◐
Massachusetts Mutual	Yearly Renewable Term	402	2.05	◐	○	○	398	1.61	○	◐	●
Prudential	Annually Increasing Premium Term to 70	381	2.14	○	○	●	339	1.76	◐	◐	◐
Union Labor	Annual Renewable Term	275	2.18	◐	○	◐	275	2.18	○	◐	◐
John Hancock Mutual	Preferred Yearly Renewable Term*	387	2.13	◐	○	◐	329	1.61	◐	◐	◐
General American	Yearly Renewable Term to 95*	254	2.19	○	○	◐	234	1.83	◐	○	◐
Guardian Life	Yearly Renewable Term—Scheduled*	371	2.19	○	○	○	319	1.86	○	○	◐
Phoenix Mutual	Annual Renewable Term to Age 70	292	2.15	○	○	○	284	1.94	○	○	○
National Life of Vermont	Yearly Renewable Term—100	270	2.20	◐	○	◐	226	1.78	○	●	◐

Minnesota Mutual	Adjustable III	782	2.21	●	●	○	656	1.71	◐	●	○
Minnesota Mutual	Convertible Annual Renewable Term	298	2.25	○	○	○	274	1.94	○	○	○
Connecticut Mutual	Yearly Renewable Term—7	277	—	○	—	—	277	—	◐	—	—
Aid Association for Lutherans	Yearly Renewable Term	362	2.28	○	◐	○	304	1.89	○	○	○
Mutual Benefit Life	Yearly Renewable Term	293	2.37	◑	○	●	291	1.90	●	◐	◐
Connecticut Mutual	Yearly Renewable Term	386	2.38	◐	○	○	332	1.98	○	○	○
John Hancock Mutual	Yearly Renewable Term	411	2.39	◐	○	○	353	1.87	◐	○	●
General American	Yearly Renewable Term to 95	280	2.49	○	◐	◑	248	1.97	◐	○	○
General American	Yearly Renewable Term to 70*	418	2.47	○	◐	◑	380	2.01	◐	○	○
New York Life	Increasing Premium Term to Age 70	293	2.53	●	●	●	309	2.21	○	●	●
New England Mutual	**Yearly Renewable Term to Age 95 [RH]**	375	2.60	◐	◑	○	367	2.24	●	○	◑
Mutual of New York	Yearly Renewable Term	334	2.63	◐	◑	◐	328	2.22	◐	◐	◑
General American	Yearly Renewable Term to 70	450	2.63	●	◑	◐	400	2.15	◐	◐	◑
Guardian Life	Yearly Renewable Term—Maximum*	371	3.21	○	◑	◐	319	2.74	○	○	○
Union Labor	5 Year Level Term	527	2.84	●	●	◑	527	2.84	●	●	●
Southern Farm Bureau	5 Year Renewable Term	650	3.02	●	●	●	604	2.76	●	●	●
New England Mutual	**Yearly Renewable Term to Age 95 [RU]**	375	3.09	●	●	●	367	2.58	◑	●	●
Metropolitan	5 Year Renewable & Convertible Term	838	3.12	●	●	●	756	2.81	●	●	●
Guardian Life	Yearly Renewable Term—Scheduled	565	3.44	●	●	●	513	3.10	●	●	●
New England Mutual	5 Year Renewable & Convertible Term	699	3.57	●	●	●	597	2.86	●	●	●
Western & Southern Life	5 Year Renewable & Convertible Term	663	3.74	●	●	●	639	3.31	●	●	●
Guardian Life	Yearly Renewable Term—Maximum	565	4.46	●	●	●	513	3.99	●	●	●

$200,000 — Age 45 — Nonparticipating

The 40 lowest-cost policies

COMPANY NAME	POLICY NAME	Male First-year premium	Male 10-year cost index	Female First-year premium	Female 10-year cost index
Fort Dearborn	Select Annual Renewable Term[RH]	$459	2.78	$461	2.62
Massachusetts Indemnity & Life	Annual Renewable Term 100*	263	3.18	263	3.18
Jackson National Life	Yearly Renewable Term-100	357	3.50	309	2.57
Lincoln National	LNL-10	530	3.70	408	2.90
Integon	First Class Term	491	3.98	387	3.17
Massachusetts Indemnity & Life	Annual Renewable Term 100	351	4.28	351	4.28
Integon	First Class Term [RH]	506	4.31	398	3.43
Integon	First Class Term [RU]	506	4.31	398	3.43
First Colony	CA95*	740	3.70	324	1.62
North Amer. Co. for Life & Health	Leveler—Current Premiums*	806	3.80	652	3.03
Northwestern National	LT-10 [RH]	733	3.85	552	2.90
Old Line Life	LT-10 [RH]	748	3.90	587	3.05
Federal Kemper	T95	780	3.90	626	3.13
Travelers	Yearly Renewable Term 10	432	3.94	372	3.28
Philadelphia Life	Electerm [RH]	574	4.11	414	2.90
Southwestern Life	Renaissance Renewable & Convertible Term	655	4.15	550	3.52
ITT Life	Guaranteed Re-entry Annual Renewable Term [RH]	483	4.28	388	3.42
Northwestern National	LT-10 [RU]	733	3.85	552	2.90
Liberty National	Annual Renewable Term	590	4.23	485	3.21
Southwestern Life	Renaissance Annual Renewable Term II	589	4.35	500	3.56
State Mutual	Exeterm II—Term to Age 75 [RH]	627	4.52	559	3.95

Relative cost columns (5-year, 10-year, 20-year) for both Male and Female are shown with graphic circle/pie symbols in the original table.

Federal Kemper	SR22/84 [RH]	430	4.56	386	3.94
Old Line Life	Preferred Annual Renewable Term [RH]	634	4.78	518	3.68
Continental Assurance Co.	Step 10	840	4.20	594	2.97
Crown Life	Select Yearly Renewable Term	453	4.48	415	3.80
Great Southern	Termpacer	391	4.50	338	3.28
Life of Virginia	Yearly Renewable Term	508	4.67	460	4.21
IDS	Yearly Renewable Term	605	4.71	595	4.06
Fort Dearborn	Select Annual Renewable Term [RU]	459	5.00	461	4.13
United Life & Accident	Dynamic Annual Renewable Term [RH]	469	5.09	437	4.28
Old Line life	CE82 [RH]	424	5.38	353	4.04
First Colony	Select 20 [RH]	403	5.48	375	4.78
United Investors	Vitalife Annual Renewable Term	635	4.83	471	3.58
United Investors	Adjustable Annual Renewable Term	650	4.91	486	3.65
Franklin Life*	Challenger 90 *	466	4.93	434	3.98
Alexander Hamilton	Annual Renewable Term 100	382	4.95	306	3.50
First Colony	CA99*	691	5.05	603	4.73
United Life & Accident	Dynamic Annual Renewable Term [RU]	469	5.09	437	4.28
ITT Life	Guaranteed Re-entry Annual Renewable Term [RU]	483	4.28	388	3.42
Union Mutual	Yearly Renewable Term 70	435	4.70	345	3.48
Travelers	5 Year Level Term	817	5.02	729	4.38

The 6 highest-cost policies

Alexander Hamilton	5 Year Level Term	1091	6.92	941	6.06
Guardsman	Yearly Renewable & Convertible Term	960	7.24	676	5.01
Crown Life	5 Year Renewable Term	1217	7.53	1085	6.58
ITT Life	5 Year Renewable & Convertible Term	1221	8.16	933	6.17
Farmers New World	5 Year Renewable & Convertible Term	1344	8.90	1061	6.97
Old Line Life	Preferred Annual Renewable Term [RU]	634	9.34	518	6.92

$200,000 Age 45 Participating

COMPANY NAME	POLICY NAME	Male First-year premium	Male 10-year cost index	Male Relative cost 5-year	Male Relative cost 10-year	Male Relative cost 20-year	Female First-year premium	Female 10-year cost index	Female Relative cost 5-year	Female Relative cost 10-year	Female Relative cost 20-year
National Life of Vermont	Yearly Renewable Term—15	$350	3.27			—	$350	3.27			—
Teachers Ins. & Annuity Assoc.	5 Year Renewable Term	555	3.63				555	3.63			
Southern Farm Bureau	Annual Renewable Term*	604	3.73				548	3.50			
Union Central	Annual Renewable Term to 100	380	3.76				282	2.99			
Northwestern Mutual	10 Year Term—Increasing Premium	507	3.81				431	3.22			
Equitable	Yearly Renewable Term	531	4.11				348	2.52			
Prudential	Annually Increasing Premium Term to 70	516	4.16				482	3.75			
Union Labor	Annual Renewable Term	495	4.25				495	4.25			
Massachusetts Mutual	Adjustable Premium Term	584	4.37				450	3.31			
Metropolitan	One Year Term With Premium Adjustment	465	4.22				366	3.14			
Guardian Life	Yearly Renewable Term—Scheduled*	591	4.30				489	3.53			
Connecticut Mutual	Yearly Renewable Term—7	453	—				453	—			—
National Life of Vermont	Yearly Renewable Term—100	434	4.52				374	3.79			
General American	Yearly Renewable Term to 95*	398	4.66				354	3.55			
Aetna	Flexi-Term	617	4.46				473	3.36			
New England Mutual	Yearly Renewable Term to Age 95 [RH]	513	4.59				465	3.90			
Home Life	Yearly Renewable Term to 75	474	4.81				474	4.81			
Massachusetts Mutual	5 Year Renewable Term	1082	4.07				938	3.13			
John Hancock Mutual	Preferred Yearly Renewable Term*	681	4.64				489	3.16			
Minnesota Mutual	Convertible Annual Renewable Term	506	4.74				416	3.87			
Connecticut Mutual	Yearly Renewable Term	698	4.77				558	3.78			
Bankers Life	One Year Term	654	4.54				545	3.60			

Western & Southern Life	Annual Renewable & Convertible Term	599	4.61		501	3.89		
Minnesota Mutual	Adjustable III	1621	4.67		1300	2.95		
Aid Association for Lutherans	Yearly Renewable Term	737	4.77		615	4.00		
Mutual of New York	Yearly Renewable Term	456	4.78		394	3.83		
Phoenix Mutual	Annual Renewable Term to Age 70	534	4.81		439	3.93		
Massachusetts Mutual	Yearly Renewable Term	818	5.11		760	3.70		
New York Life	Increasing Premium Term to Age 70	483	5.20		407	4.37		
Mutual Benefit Life	Yearly Renewable Term	523	5.36		479	4.10		
John Hancock Life	Yearly Renewable Term	807	5.40		615	3.92		
General American	Yearly Renewable Term to 95	468	5.47		394	4.06		
Northwestern Mutual	Term to Age 70—Increasing Premium	651	5.54		555	4.67		
New England Mutual	Yearly Renewable Term to Age 95 [RU]	513	5.92		465	4.78		
Guardian Life	Yearly Renewable Term—Maximum*	591	6.44		489	5.09		
General American	Yearly Renewable Term to 70*	804	5.70		626	4.53		
General American	Yearly Renewable Term to 70	864	6.20		664	4.84		
Southern Farm Bureau	5 Year Renewable Term	1512	6.44		1260	4.71		
Metropolitan	5 Year Renewable & Convertible Term	1515	6.52		1252	5.20		
Guardian Life	Yearly Renewable Term—Scheduled	965	6.83		863	6.05		
Western & Southern Life	5 Year Renewable & Convertible Term	1322	8.07		1064	6.44		
New England Mutual	5 Year Renewable & Convertible Term	1451	8.28		1123	6.10		
Guardian Life	Yearly Renewable Term—Maximum	965	8.96		863	7.61		

Alphabetical summary table

This table provides 10-year cost indexes for every term policy in our survey, including those not shown in the Ratings for space reasons. It is arranged alphabetically by company, and may serve to provide a rough idea of whether a company's term policies are low or high in cost. For more detailed information, see the Ratings on pages 182–205. Policies marked with an * are available to "preferred risks" only. Abbreviations: P = Participating; N = Nonparticipating; RH = Revertible policy analyzed on the assumption that the buyer stays healthy; RU = Revertible policy analyzed on the assumption that the buyer's health worsens midway through the period analyzed.

Company & policy name	Type	$50,000 Male/age 25	35	45	$50,000 Female/age 25	35	45	$200,000 Male/age 25	35	45	$200,000 Female/age 25	35	45
Aetna Life Insurance & Annuity													
Flexi-Term	P	○	○	○	◐	○	◐	◐	◐	◐	◐	◐	◐
Aid Association for Lutherans													
Yearly Renewable Term	P	◐	○	○	◐	○	○	○	○	○	○	○	○
Alexander Hamilton													
5 Year Level Term	N	○	○	◐	○	◐	◑	●	●	●○	●●	●●	●●
Annual Renewable Term 100	N	—	—	—	—	—	—	●○	●○	●●	●●	●●	●●
American Agency Life Insurance													
10 Year Renewable and Convertible Term*	N	●●	◐◐	◐◐	◐●	●●	●●	◐◐	◐●	○○	◐◐	◐◐	●●
5 Year Renewable and Convertible Term*	N	●●	◐◐	○○	●	●	●	◐	◐	○	●	◐	●●
Bankers Life (Iowa)													
One Year Term	P	—	—	—	—	—	—	◐	◐	○	◐	○	○
Connecticut Mutual Life Insurance													
Yearly Renewable Term	P	○	○	—	○	○	◐	○○	◐○	○○	○	○	○
Yearly Renewable Term-7	P	—	—	—	—	—	—	◐	◐	○	—	—	—
Continental Assurance													
Adjustable Premium Annual Renewable Term	N	○	○	○	●	○	○	○○	○●	○○	◐●	○◐	◐●
Step 10	N	◐	—	—	●	●	●	●●●	●●●	●●●	●●●	●●●	●●●
Crown Life Insurance													
Select Yearly Renewable Term	N	◐●●	○◐●	○◐●	●●●	○○●	○○●	●●●	●●●	●●●	●●●	●●●	○●●
Yearly Renewable Term	N	—	—	—	—	—	—	●	●	●	●	●	◐
5 Year Renewable Term	N	—	—	—	—	—	—	—	—	—	—	—	—
Equitable Life Assurance Society of the U.S.													
Yearly Renewable Term	P	—	—	—	—	—	—	●	●	●	●	●	●

Farmers New World Life Insurance
5 Year Renewable and Convertible Term — N

Federal Kemper Life Assurance
T95 — N
SR22/84 — RH
SR22/84 — RU

First Colony Life Insurance
CA95* — N
Select 20 — RH
CA99* — N
Select 20 — RU

Fort Dearborn
Annual Renewable Term — N
Select Annual Renewable Term — RH
Select Annual Renewable Term — RU

Franklin Life Insurance
Challenger 90* — N
Challenger 90 — N

General American Life Insurance
Yearly Renewable Term to 95* — P
Yearly Renewable Term to 70* — P
Yearly Renewable Term to 95 — P
Yearly Renewable Term to 70 — P

Great Southern
Termpacer — N

Guardian Life Insurance Co. of America
Yearly Renewable Term—Scheduled* [1] — P
Yearly Renewable Term—Scheduled [1] — P
Yearly Renewable Term—Maximum* [1] — P
Yearly Renewable Term—Maximum [1] — P

Guardsman Life Insurance
Yearly Renewable and Convertible Term — N

		$50,000						$200,000					
		Male / age			Female / age			Male / age			Female / age		
Company & policy name	Type	25	35	45	25	35	45	25	35	45	25	35	45
Home Life Insurance													
Yearly Renewable Term to 75	P	○	○	○	○	◑	●	●	◐	○	●	○	●
IDS Life Insurance													
Yearly Renewable Term	N	○	◑	○	○	○	○	○	○	○	○	○	○
Integon Life Insurance													
First Class Term	RH	—	—	—	—	—	—	●●●	●●●	●●●	●●●	●●●	●●●
First Class Term	RU	—	—	—	—	—	—	●●●	●●●	●●●	●●●	●●●	●●●
First Class Term	N	—	—	—	—	—	—	●●●	●●●	●●●	●●●	●●●	●●●
ITT Life [2]													
5 Year Renewable and Convertible Term	N	●	●	●	●	●	●	●●●	●●●	●●●	●●●	●●●	●●●
Guaranteed Re-entry Annual Renewable Term	RH	◑	—	—	—	—	—	●●●	●●●	●●●	●●●	●●●	●●●
Guaranteed Re-entry Annual Renewable Term	RU	—	—	—	—	—	—	●●●	●●●	●●●	●●●	●●●	●●●
Jackson National Life Insurance													
Yearly Renewable Term-100	N	—	—	—	—	—	—	◑	◐	●	○	◐	●
John Hancock Mutual Life Insurance													
Yearly Renewable Term	P	●	●	●	●	●	●	○○	○○	◐○	○○	○○	○○
Preferred Yearly Renewable Term*	P	—	—	—	—	—	—	○	○	○	○	○	●
Liberty National Life Insurance													
Annually Renewable Term	N	◐	◐	○	◐	◐	●	◐	○	●	◐	○	●
Life Insurance Co. of Virginia													
Yearly Renewable Term	N	◐	◐	●	◐	◐	●	●	●	●	●	◐	○
Lincoln National Life Insurance													
LNL-10	N	—	—	—	—	—	—	○○	○○	○○	○○	○○	◐○
Manufacturers Life Insurance													
Select 10	N	◐○	○○	○○	○○	◐●	●●	○○	◐○	◐○	●○○	○○	◐○
Yearly Renewable Term-70 –	N	●●	●●	●●	●●	●●	●●	●○●	●●●	●●●	●●●	●●●	●●●
Massachusetts Indemnity & Life Insurance [2]													
Annual Renewable Term 100	N	●●	—	—	—	—	—						
Modified Term	N	—	—	—	—	—	—						
Annual Renewable Term 100*	N	—	—	—	—	—	—						

Massachusetts Mutual Life Insurance
5 Year Renewable Term — P
Yearly Renewable Term — P
Adjustable Premium Term — P

Massachusetts Savings Bank Life Insurance
Yearly Renewable Term — P
5 Year Renewable Term — P

Metropolitan Life Insurance
One Year Term with Premium Adjustment — P
5 Year Renewable and Convertible Term — P

Minnesota Mutual Life Insurance
Adjustable III — P
Convertible Annual Renewable Term — P

Mutual Benefit Life Insurance
Yearly Renewable Term — P

Mutual Life Insurance Co. of New York
Yearly Renewable Term — P

National Life of Vermont
Yearly Renewable Term-15 — P
Yearly Renewable Term-100 — P

New England Mutual Life Insurance
Yearly Renewable Term to Age 95 — RH
Yearly Renewable Term to Age 95 — RU
5 Year Renewable and Convertible Term — P

New York Life Insurance
Increasing Premium Term to Age 70 — P

New York Savings Bank Life Insurance
5 Year Renewable and Convertible Term — P

North American Company for Life & Health Insurance
Leveler—Current Premiums* [1] — N
Leveler—Guaranteed Premiums* [1] — N

[1] This is a "flexible premium" policy; see text.
[2] This company is rated B+ for financial stability by Best's Insurance Reports, a trade source CU considers reliable. Unless you have independent knowledge of a company's financial condition, we advise buying from a company rated A or A+.

Continued

Alphabetical summary table
Continued

Company & policy name	Type	$50,000 Male/age			$50,000 Female/age			$200,000 Male/age			$200,000 Female/age		
		25	35	45	25	35	45	25	35	45	25	35	45
Northwestern Mutual Life Insurance													
10 Year Term—Increasing Premium	P												
Term to Age 70—Increasing Premium	P												
Northwestern National Life Insurance													
LT-10	RH												
LT-10	RU												
Old Line Life Insurance Co. of America													
LT-10	RH												
LT-10	RU												
Preferred Annual Renewable Term	RH												
CE82	RH												
CE82	RU												
Preferred Annual Renewable Term	RU												
Philadelphia Life Insurance													
Electerm	RH												
Electerm	RU												
Phoenix Mutual Life Insurance													
Annual Renewable Term to Age 70	P												
Prudential Insurance Co. of America													
Annually Increasing Premium Term to 70	P												
Southern Farm Bureau Life Insurance													
5 Year Renewable Term	P												
Annual Renewable Term*	P												
Southwestern Life													
Renaissance Renewable and Convertible Term	N												
Renaissance Annual Renewable Term II	N												
State Mutual Life Assurance Co. of America													
Yearly Renewable Flexterm Level Term	N												
Execterm II—Term to Age 75	RH												
Execterm II—Term to Age 75	RU												

Sun Life of Canada
Nova Yearly Renewable Term — N

Teachers Insurance & Annuity Association of America
5 Year Renewable Term — P

Transamerica Occidental Life Insurance
Trendsetter 20 — N

Travelers Insurance
5 Year Level Term — N
Yearly Renewable Term-10 — N

Union Central
Annual Renewable Term to 100 — P

Union Labor [3]
Annual Renewable Term — P
5 Year Level Term — P

Union Mutual Life Insurance
Yearly Renewable Term-70 — N

United Investors
Vitalife Annual Renewable Term — N
Adjustable Annual Renewable Term — N

United Life & Accident
Yearly Renewable Term — N
Dynamic Annual Renewable Term — RH
Dynamic Annual Renewable Term — RU

Washington National
Annual Renewable Term 90 — N

Western & Southern Life Insurance
Annual Renewable and Convertible Term — P
5 Year Renewable and Convertible Term — P

[3] *This company is rated B for financial stability by Best's Insurance Reports.*

Ratings

(as published in *Consumer Reports*, July 1986)

Whole life insurance

Listed in order of estimated overall cost, based on 5-year, 10-year, and 20-year interest-adjusted cost index and 10-year-interest-adjusted net payment index, weighted equally. Policies marked with an asterisk are available to "preferred risks" only. All rates shown are for nonsmokers. Information was gathered in the latter part of 1985.

Age 25 — $50,000 — Male

Company Name	Policy Name	First-year premium	20-year cost index	Relative cost (5-year / 10-year / 20-year cost index / 20-year payment index)	Rate of return 5-year	10-year	20-year
Participating policies							
New York Savings Bank	Whole Life *	$388	−2.80	● ● ● ●	−4.00%	10.72%	11.91%
Phoenix Mutual	Whole Life	502	−2.29	● ◐ ◐ ●	2.56	7.75	9.87
New England Mutual	Ordinary Life *	443	−2.11	● ● ● ●	−5.16	5.74	9.78
Northwestern Mutual	Extra Ordinary Life (EOL)	374	−2.05	● ● ○ ●	−4.13	6.40	9.40
Massachusetts Savings Bank	Straight Life	370	−0.51	● ● ● ●	5.27	7.49	8.85
Teachers Ins. & Annuity Assoc.	Ordinary Life	164	−0.31	● ● ● ●	−31.98	8.35	11.77
Manufacturers Life	Graded Premium Whole Life	249	−0.54	◐ ◐ ○ ●	−25.55	3.99	8.76
Mutual of New York	Moneyconomizer	401	−0.41	● ○ ○ ○	−3.77	5.31	8.40
Prudential	Modified Life 5 *	418	−1.23	● ● ◐ ○	−31.69	3.84	8.47
Northwestern Mutual	90 Life	604	−1.06	◐ ◐ ○ ◐	−6.83	4.57	8.12
Manufacturers Life	Premier Life	302	0.30	◐ ○ ○ ◐	−23.47	3.07	8.33

Prudential	Modified Life 3*	451	-1.31	-24.79	3.39	8.35
Crown Life	Advance	462	-0.36	-19.20	2.28	8.05
Massachusetts Mutual	Convertible Whole Life	572	-2.00	-11.60	3.90	8.85
Prudential	Estate 25—Whole Life*	506	-1.46	-19.40	3.14	8.34
Metropolitan	Whole Life Policy	462	-0.64	-20.65	2.33	7.79
New York Life	Whole Life	549	-0.54	-21.66	3.35	7.81
Mutual Benefit Life	Ordinary Life—1985	481	-1.51	-28.04	3.01	9.01
Connecticut Mutual	Econolife Preferred	512	0.36	-16.16	0.25	6.52
Crown Life	Prove	290	0.69	-63.44	-2.42	7.67
Manufacturers Life	Estate Protector	488	-0.45	-23.77	2.10	7.85
Bankers Life Co.	Special Whole Life*	584	-0.35	-14.08	3.27	7.17
Continental Assurance Co.	EVP96	466	-0.31	-39.09	-0.75	8.19
Equitable	Whole Life 50	604	0.25	-5.96	1.66	6.65
Bankers Life Co.	Life Paid-Up at Age 65 Money Saver*	661	-0.39	-13.80	2.63	6.89
Sun Life of Canada	Sun Permanent Life	514	0.11	-33.81	-1.48	7.44
Sun Life of Canada	Nova Whole Life	476	0.13	-27.17	-0.73	7.16
Great-West Life	Life at 95 X-Series	373	2.05	-45.30	-5.23	4.66
John Hancock Mutual	Preferred Risk Whole Life*	524	0.08	-22.80	2.46	7.00
Aid Association for Lutherans	Estate Life	509	1.66	-6.59	0.87	5.09
Aid Association for Lutherans	Whole Life	588	2.22	-10.31	-0.36	4.47
Connecticut Mutual	Econolife	569	2.11	-19.40	-2.41	4.62

Nonparticipating policies

Federal Kemper	RL-1	158	1.17	-11.68	5.21	8.68
Executive Life	Irreplaceable Life II	315	-3.43	-1.63	8.59	10.97
N. Amer. Co. for Life & Health	The Stabilizer—Current*	256	2.30	-63.53	-5.34	3.88
Federal Kemper	RL-2	496	5.35	-2.02	-4.47	-0.20
N. Amer. Co. for Life & Health	The Stabilizer—Guaranteed*	256	5.40	-77.49	-19.31	-3.26
Crown Life	Low Cost Life Preferred	424	4.22	-47.15	-7.74	1.02

Age 25 — $50,000 — Female

Participating policies

COMPANY NAME	POLICY NAME	First-year premium	20-year cost index	Relative cost 5-year	Relative cost 10-year	Relative cost 20-year	payment index	Rate of return 5-year	Rate of return 10-year	Rate of return 20-year
New York Savings Bank	Whole Life*	$312	-2.83	●	●	●		-5.99%	11.33%	12.86%
Phoenix Mutual	Whole Life	441	-2.31	◐	●	◐		3.73	8.24	10.26
Northwestern Mutual	Extra Ordinary Life (EOL)	347	-2.59	●	●	○		-1.05	7.93	9.92
New England Mutual	Ordinary Life*	443	-2.28	●	●	○		-4.65	5.96	9.69
Massachusetts Savings Bank	Straight Life	370	-0.51	●	●	●		5.27	7.49	8.85
Teachers Ins. & Annuity Assoc.	Ordinary Life	164	-0.31	●	●	●		-31.98	8.35	11.77
Mutual of New York	Monyconomizer	327	-0.16	◐	◐	◐		-2.69	5.85	8.36
Northwestern Mutual	90 Life	574	-1.66	◐	◐	◐		-4.76	5.76	8.62
Prudential	Modified Life 5*	373	-0.87	●	◐	◐		-34.82	4.50	8.39
Manufacturers Life	Premier Life	258	0.70	○	○	●		-33.08	1.39	7.51
Bankers Life Co.	Special Whole Life*	535	-1.34	○	◐	◐		-10.55	5.31	8.14
Prudential	Estate 25—Whole Life*	447	-1.03	◐	◐	◐		-19.64	4.02	8.27
Prudential	Modified Life 3*	402	-0.92	○	◐	◐		-26.13	4.21	8.26
Crown Life	Advance	398	0.03	○	○	●		-21.06	2.10	7.71
Manufacturers Life	Graded Premium Whole Life	225	0.47	◐	◐	●		-44.19	-0.48	7.04
Massachusetts Mutual	Convertible Whole Life	560	-2.24	○	○	●		-10.83	4.27	8.89
New York Life	Whole Life	494	-0.40	○	○	○		-12.39	3.23	7.68
Connecticut Mutual	Econolife Preferred	431	0.68	◐	◐	◐		-16.63	0.12	6.01
Crown Life	Prove	247	1.01	●	◐	●		-66.90	-3.92	6.81
Mutual Benefit Life	Ordinary Life—1985	469	-1.75	○	○	○		-27.14	3.47	9.05
Bankers Life Co.	Life Paid-Up at Age 65 Money Saver*	613	-1.37	◐	◐	●		-10.82	4.36	7.71

Company	Policy		Rating		−25.44 col	col	col
Metropolitan	*Whole Life Policy*	419	−0.51	◐○○	−25.44	1.87	7.71
Equitable	*Whole Life 50*	528	0.28	◐◐◑	−6.50	1.73	6.63
Continental Assurance Co.	*EVP96*	452	−0.59	●●◑	−37.89	−0.10	8.28
John Hancock Mutual	*Preferred Risk Whole Life **	491	−0.57	●○○	−20.41	3.83	7.55
Sun Life of Canada	*Sun Permanent Life*	489	−0.39	●●○	−31.86	−0.28	7.87
Sun Life of Canada	*Nova Whole Life*	450	−0.38	●●○	−25.11	0.46	7.56
Manufacturers Life	*Estate Protector*	428	0.33	●●◑	−35.27	−0.58	6.89
Aid Association For Lutherans	*Estate Life*	492	1.31	◑●●	−5.30	1.51	5.23
Great-West Life	*Life at 95 X-Series*	370	1.99	●◑●	−45.13	−5.32	4.22
Aid Association For Lutherans	*Whole Life*	569	1.85	○●●	−9.15	0.24	4.60
Connecticut Mutual	*Econolife*	489	2.23	●◑◑	−20.81	−3.36	4.00

Nonparticipating policies

Company	Policy		Rating				
Federal Kemper	*RL-1*	144	1.32	◐●○	−21.04	2.36	7.06
Executive Life	*Irreplaceable Life II*	261	−1.99	◐●◐	−5.00	7.04	10.42
N. Amer. Co. For Life & Health	*The Stabilizer—Current**	208	2.06	○◐◑	−100.00	−5.67	3.39
Federal Kemper	*RL-2*	449	5.16	○○◑	−3.25	−5.62	−1.16
Crown Life	*Low Cost Life Preferred*	407	3.88	●●◑	−45.83	−6.98	1.07
N. Amer. Co. For Life & Health	*The Stabilizer—Guaranteed**	208	5.84	●●◐	−100.00	−27.01	−7.26

Age 25 | $200,000 | Male

COMPANY NAME	POLICY NAME	First-year premium	20-year cost index	Relative cost: 5-year	Relative cost: 10-year	Relative cost: 20-year	Relative cost: Payment index	Rate of return: 5-year	Rate of return: 10-year	Rate of return: 20-year
Participating policies										
Phoenix Mutual	*Whole Life*	$1948	-2.59	◉	◉	◉	○	3.96%	8.56%	10.34%
New England Mutual	*Ordinary Life**	1695	-2.48	◉	◉	◉	○	-3.36	6.78	10.37
Northwestern Mutual	*Extra Ordinary Life (EOL)*	1434	-2.35	◉	◉	◉	○	-2.40	7.34	9.85
Mutual of New York	*Monyconomizer*	1452	-1.16	◉	◉	○	◓	0.47	7.79	9.83
Teachers Ins. & Annuity Assoc.	*Ordinary Life*	554	-0.81	◉	◉	◒	◉	-23.81	13.28	14.46
John Hancock Mutual	*Preferred 100**	1654	-1.56	◓	◉	◓	○	-12.32	6.93	9.38
Manufacturers Life	*Premier Life*	1064	-0.42	◉	◓	◒	◉	-17.49	6.68	10.30
Manufacturers Life	*Benefit Builder IV*	3376	-5.13	◓	◉	◉	●	-1.21	7.20	9.27
Northwestern Mutual	*Select 100*	2018	-2.70	○	◉	◉	◒	-9.16	6.33	9.79
Equitable	*Whole Life 50*	2072	-1.47	◉	◓	◓	◒	0.22	5.41	8.85
Manufacturers Life	*Graded Premium Whole Life*	934	-0.85	◉	◓	◒	◓	-22.98	5.36	9.40
Bankers Life Co.	*Century 100**	2047	-1.59	○	◓	◓	○	-11.58	5.76	9.02
Massachusetts Mutual	*Convertible Whole Life*	2196	-2.45	○	◓	◉	●	-10.00	4.86	9.42
Mutual Benefit Life	*Ordinary Life—1985*	1783	-2.21	●	◓	◉	○	-25.03	4.90	10.08
Northwestern Mutual	*90 Life*	2356	-1.36	◓	◓	○	◒	-5.78	5.22	8.51
Prudential	*Estate 25—Whole Life**	1950	-1.84	◒	○	◓	○	-17.87	4.05	8.83
Prudential	*Modified Life 5**	1598	-1.61	●	◓	◓	○	-29.98	4.90	9.03
Crown Life	*Advance*	1756	-0.82	○	○	◒	◓	-16.98	3.66	8.83
Connecticut Mutual	*Econolife Preferred*	1848	-0.63	◓	○	◒	○	-11.86	3.00	8.12
Manufacturers Life	*Benefit Builder I*	2160	-1.89	◒	◓	◓	●	-12.57	5.10	8.92
Prudential	*Modified Life 3**	1731	-1.68	●	○	◓	○	-23.20	4.35	8.86

Company	Policy			(rating symbols)				
Manufacturers Life	Estate Protector	1802	-1.20	◑○○○○○	-20.55	4.11	8.99
New York Life	Whole Life	2121	-0.92	○○○◑○○	-10.18	4.27	8.33
Crown Life	Prove	1069	0.24	○○◑●●○	-60.24	0.02	8.97
Great-West Life	Life at 95 X-Series	1171	0.44	○◑◑●●○	-35.17	1.56	8.31
Sun Life of Canada	Nova Whole Life	1655	-1.11	◑◑◑○○○	-21.61	2.81	9.09
Metropolitan	Whole Life Policy	1776	-1.01	◑◑●○○◑	-19.00	3.34	8.32
Continental Assurance Co.	EVP96	1742	-0.92	●●●○●◑	-36.12	1.21	9.28
Sun Life of Canada	Sun Permanent Life	1879	-0.76	●●●◑●◑	-30.11	1.06	8.90
Aid Association for Lutherans	Estate Life	1962	1.28	◑●●●●●	-5.13	1.69	5.53
Bankers Life Co.	Special Whole Life*	2289	-0.58	●●◑●●●	-13.29	3.75	7.44
Bankers Life Co.	Life Paid-Up at Age 65 Money Saver*	2600	-0.61	●●◑◑●●	-13.12	3.04	7.12
Connecticut Mutual	Econolife	2066	1.06	●●●●●●	-15.64	-0.01	6.00
Aid Association for Lutherans	Whole Life	2307	1.99	●●●●●●	-9.58	0.07	4.71

Nonparticipating policies

Company	Policy			(rating symbols)				
Federal Kemper	RL-1	482	0.42	●●●●○●	10.64	17.16	14.65
Executive Life	Irreplaceable Life II	1186	-3.81	○◑●◑○◑	1.09	10.03	11.64
N. Amer. Co. for Life & Health	The Stabilizer—Current*	899	1.67	○○◑●○◑	-58.70	-1.65	5.69
Crown Life	Low Cost Life Preferred	1413	2.78	○◑●◑◑○	-40.64	-3.39	3.19
Federal Kemper	RL-2	1834	4.07	●●●◑●●	1.13	-1.77	1.72
N. Amer. Co. for Life & Health	The Stabilizer—Guaranteed*	899	4.95	○●●●●○	-76.15	-17.80	-2.56

Age 25 — $200,000 — Female

Participating policies

Company name	Policy name	First-year premium	20-year cost index	Relative cost — 5-year cost index	10-year	20-year	payment index	Rate of return — 5-year	10-year	20-year
Northwestern Mutual	Extra Ordinary Life (EOL)	$1326	−2.89	●	●	○	◑	0.88%	8.95%	10.41%
Phoenix Mutual	Whole Life	1702	−2.61	●	◑	◑	◑	5.36	9.19	10.80
New England Mutual	Ordinary Life *	1695	−2.65	●	◑	◑	○	−2.83	7.02	10.29
Bankers Life Co.	Century 100 *	1854	−2.59	◑	◑	◑	○	−7.18	8.32	10.27
John Hancock Mutual	Preferred 100 *	1552	−2.17	◑	◑	◑	●	−9.49	8.52	10.04
Mutual of New York	Monyconomizer	1158	−0.91	●	◑	●	●	2.95	9.09	10.21
Teachers Ins. & Annuity Assoc.	Ordinary Life	554	−0.81	◑	●	●	●	−23.81	13.28	14.46
Manufacturers Life	Benefit Builder IV	3338	−5.32	○	◑	◑	◑	−0.81	7.38	9.28
Northwestern Mutual	Select 100	1906	−3.26	◑	◑	◑	◑	−6.96	7.55	10.30
Manufacturers Life	Premier Life	858	−0.17	○	●	◑	◑	−23.65	7.19	10.62
Northwestern Mutual	90 Life	2236	−1.96	◑	◑	○	○	−3.62	6.45	9.03
Equitable	Whole Life 50	1768	−1.44	○	◑	◑	◑	0.86	6.19	9.27
Prudential	Modified Life 3 *	1534	−1.30	○	◑	◑	◑	−24.29	5.35	8.88
Massachusetts Mutual	Convertible Whole Life	2148	−2.69	●	◑	◑	◑	−9.18	5.25	9.46
Mutual Benefit Life	Ordinary Life—1985	1735	−2.45	○	◑	○	○	−24.03	5.41	10.15
Prudential	Estate 25—Whole Life *	1711	−1.41	◑	◑	◑	◑	−17.82	5.11	8.86
Connecticut Mutual	Econolife Preferred	1544	−0.21	●	●	●	●	−11.85	2.91	7.75
Prudential	Modified Life 5 *	1417	−1.24	○	○	○	○	−32.88	5.73	9.05
Crown Life	Advance	1503	−0.42	◑	◑	◑	◑	−18.33	3.78	8.66
Crown Life	Prove	898	0.56	●	●	●	●	−62.80	−0.70	8.49
Manufacturers Life	Benefit Builder I	2116	−2.11	○	◑	◑	◑	−11.82	5.46	8.94

Company	Policy			Ratings			
Sun Life of Canada	Nova Whole Life	1553	-1.62	◐ ○ ○	-19.08	4.24	9.62
Bankers Life Co.	Special Whole Life*	2096	-1.57	○ ○ ●	-9.65	5.85	8.44
New York Life	Whole Life	1901	-0.78	○ ○ ○	-10.69	4.29	8.29
Great-West Life	Life at 95 X-Series	1159	0.38	○ ●	-34.90	1.51	7.84
Bankers Life Co.	Life Paid-Up at Age 65 Money Saver*	2407	-1.59	● ○	-10.07	4.81	7.97
Sun Life of Canada	Sun Permanent Life	1779	-1.26	● ● ◐	-27.87	2.42	9.43
Manufacturers Life	Graded Premium Whole Life	838	0.16	○ ● ●	-41.74	1.00	7.72
Continental Assurance Co.	EVP96	1688	-1.19	● ● ○	-34.83	1.89	9.39
Metropolitan	Whole Life Policy	1600	-0.88	◐ ◐ ●	-23.55	3.04	8.31
Manufacturers Life	Estate Protector	1574	-0.36	● ● ●	-31.90	1.62	8.11
Aid Association for Lutherans	Estate Life	1892	0.93	◐ ● ●	-3.77	2.36	5.68
Connecticut Mutual	Econolife	1762	1.26	◐ ● ●	-16.67	-0.70	5.50
Aid Association for Lutherans	Whole Life	2233	1.62	◐ ● ●	-8.38	0.69	4.85

Nonparticipating policies

Company	Policy			Ratings			
Federal Kemper	RL-1	428	0.58	● ● ●	7.44	17.76	14.34
Executive Life	Irreplaceable Life II	971	-2.36	● ● ◐	-1.45	8.94	11.29
N. Amer. Co. for Life & Health	The Stabilizer—Current*	717	1.48	◐ ● ◐	-100.00	-0.93	5.66
Federal Kemper	RL-2	1646	3.61	● ◐ ◐	0.31	-2.55	1.64
Crown Life	Low Cost Life Preferred	1352	2.49	● ○ ○	-39.15	-2.60	3.22
N. Amer. Co. for Life & Health	The Stabilizer—Guaranteed*	717	5.41	● ● ●	-100.00	-25.55	-6.54

Age 35 **$50,000** **Male**

Participating policies

COMPANY NAME	POLICY NAME	First-year premium	20-year cost index	Relative cost: 5-year cost index	20-year	10-year	5-year payment index	Rate of return: 5-year	10-year	20-year
New York Savings Bank	Whole Life*	$617	-3.64	●	●	●	●	-0.36%	10.49%	11.70%
Phoenix Mutual	Whole Life	745	-3.12	●	●	●	●	2.83	8.04	10.10
Massachusetts Savings Bank	Straight Life	569	-1.31	●	◐	◐	●	9.46	9.64	9.97
New England Mutual	Ordinary Life*	682	-2.89	○	●	●	○	-4.58	5.80	9.88
Northwestern Mutual	Extra Ordinary Life (EOL)	558	-2.78	●	●	●	○	-3.17	6.61	9.56
Mutual of New York	Monyconomizer	594	-0.73	●	●	●	●	-1.87	6.29	9.00
Equitable	Whole Life 50	746	-1.24	◐	◐	◐	○	-4.91	4.89	8.54
Teachers Ins. & Annuity Assoc.	Ordinary Life	346	0.64	●	●	●	●	-16.55	4.65	8.93
Prudential	Modified Life 5*	578	-2.16	◐	●	●	◐	-21.16	5.02	9.44
Manufacturers Life	Graded Premium Whole Life	372	0.11	●	●	●	○	-13.98	4.63	8.35
Prudential	Estate 25—Whole Life*	669	-2.49	◐	●	●	○	-12.49	4.00	9.20
Northwestern Mutual	90 Life	875	-1.34	●	◐	●	○	-5.62	4.90	8.35
New York Life	Whole Life	778	-1.04	◐	●	●	○	-6.90	4.54	8.41
Manufacturers Life	Premier Life	504	0.79	○	●	●	●	-13.45	3.82	8.15
Massachusetts Mutual	Convertible Whole Life	800	-2.77	◐	●	●	○	-9.36	4.48	9.18
Prudential	Modified Life 3*	637	-2.01	○	◐	◐	●	-16.58	4.51	9.04
Crown Life	Advance	693	-0.48	○	●	●	○	-12.59	3.53	8.41
Mutual Benefit Life	Ordinary Life—1985	727	-1.43	◐	●	●	○	-14.54	3.56	8.70
Metropolitan	Whole Life Policy	689	-0.42	○	○	◐	○	-12.02	3.44	7.80
Crown Life	Prove	456	0.51	○	○	◐	●	-28.01	1.97	8.82
Bankers Life Co.	Special Whole Life*	841	-0.67	○	◐	◐	○	-8.41	4.60	7.75

Connecticut Mutual	Econolife Preferred	773	0.10	○	○	○	-12.60	1.84	7.34
Bankers Life Co.	Life Paid-Up at Age 65 Money Saver*	1001	-0.85	◑	○	●	-8.55	3.73	7.24
Sun Life of Canada	Sun Permanent Life	789	-0.25	◑	○	◑	-21.08	1.24	8.18
Manufacturers Life	Estate Protector	748	0.26	◑	◑	○	-13.59	3.29	7.48
Great-West Life	Life at 95 X-Series	556	2.26	◑	●	◑	-22.78	-0.27	6.29
John Hancock Mutual	Preferred Risk Whole Life*	754	0.08	●	●	◑	-13.02	3.31	7.42
Continental Assurance Co.	EVP96	741	0.21	◑	◑	○	-20.38	0.61	7.70
Sun Life of Canada	Nova Whole Life	716	0.26	●	◑	○	-19.26	0.96	7.51
Aid Association for Lutherans	Estate Life	733	2.61	◑	●	●	-5.05	1.44	5.31
Aid Association for Lutherans	Whole Life	819	3.03	○	●	●	-7.91	0.34	4.99
Connecticut Mutual	Econolife	850	2.60	●	●	●	-15.55	-0.64	5.47

Nonparticipating policies

Executive Life	Irreplaceable Life II	510	-5.54	◑	●	○	-0.99	8.30	10.83
Federal Kemper	RL-1	274	1.59	●	◑	◐	-6.11	6.75	9.43
N. Amer. Co. for Life & Health	The Stabilizer Current*	395	2.95	○	○	○	-20.77	0.90	5.65
Crown Life	Low Cost Life Preferred	583	5.16	●	◑	●	-20.34	-1.75	2.81
N. Amer. Co. for Life & Health	The Stabilizer—Guaranteed*	395	7.65	◑	●	●	-31.61	-10.84	-1.15
Federal Kemper	RL-2	746	8.32	○	●	●	-1.82	-3.97	-0.12

Age 35   **$50,000**   **Female**

Participating policies

COMPANY NAME	POLICY NAME	First-year premium	20-year cost index	Relative cost (5-yr / 10-yr / 20-yr, payment index)	5-year payment index	Rate of return 10-year	Rate of return 20-year
New York Savings Bank	Whole Life *	$492	-3.32	● ◐ ● ● ● ●	-4.09%	9.39%	11.36%
Phoenix Mutual	Whole Life	657	-3.21	● ● ● ● ◐ ●	2.62	7.70	9.78
Massachusetts Savings Bank	Straight Life	569	-1.31	● ● ● ◐ ● ●	9.46	9.64	9.97
Northwestern Mutual	Extra Ordinary Life (EOL)	513	-3.68	● ● ● ○ ● ○	-1.50	7.19	9.54
Mutual of New York	Monyconomizer	470	-0.33	● ◐ ◐ ● ○ ●	-2.18	5.27	8.16
New England Mutual	Ordinary Life *	682	-3.31	● ● ● ● ◐ ○	-5.46	5.09	9.27
Bankers Life Co.	Special Whole Life *	769	-2.17	◐ ● ● ○ ◐ ○	-5.76	5.95	8.25
Manufacturers Life	Graded Premium Whole Life	311	-0.32	● ○ ● ● ● ●	-19.17	3.80	8.18
Northwestern Mutual	90 Life	825	-2.34	◐ ◐ ● ○ ◐ ●	-4.33	5.44	8.38
Prudential	Modified Life 5 *	506	-1.38	● ● ● ○ ◐ ●	-26.06	4.76	8.56
Teachers Ins. & Annuity Assoc.	Ordinary Life	346	0.64	◐ ◐ ○ ○ ◐ ●	-16.55	4.65	8.93
Prudential	Estate 25—Whole Life *	591	-1.66	◐ ○ ◐ ◐ ◐ ●	-15.10	3.86	8.41
Equitable	Whole Life 50	647	-0.29	◐ ◐ ◐ ● ● ○	-7.38	3.27	7.30
Manufacturers Life	Premier Life	401	0.84	◐ ◐ ○ ● ● ○	-19.21	2.05	7.24
Mutual Benefit Life	Ordinary Life—1985	691	-2.15	◐ ◐ ◐ ○ ◐ ○	-13.87	3.70	8.45
Prudential	Modified Life 3 *	567	-1.67	◐ ● ● ○ ◐ ○	-20.86	3.39	8.44
New York Life	Whole Life	696	-1.03	○ ○ ◐ ○ ● ○	-9.03	3.91	7.84
Massachusetts Mutual	Convertible Whole Life	774	-3.29	○ ● ◐ ● ◐ ●	-9.22	4.33	8.81
Bankers Life Co.	Life Paid-Up at Age 65 Money Saver *	930	-2.32	◐ ○ ○ ○ ○ ◐	-6.50	4.78	7.64
Manufacturers Life	Estate Protector	608	-0.33	◐ ◐ ○ ○ ◐ ○	-18.40	2.50	7.49
Crown Life	Advance	584	0.02	◐ ◐ ○ ○ ● ○	-15.37	1.94	7.43

Connecticut Mutual	Econolife Preferred	638	0.35	○	◐	◐	○	−14.74	0.44	6.51
Crown Life	Prove	382	1.07	○	◉	●	◐	−37.98	−1.31	7.08
John Hancock Mutual	Preferred Risk Whole Life*	701	−0.98	◐	○	○	○	−11.47	3.98	7.48
Metropolitan	Whole Life	607	−0.58	◐	◐	○	○	−14.53	2.65	7.34
Sun Life of Canada	Sun Permanent Life	759	−0.85	●	●	○	○	−20.80	1.11	7.75
Continental Assurance Co.	EVP96	707	−0.46	●	●	○	○	−19.87	−0.60	7.34
Aid Association for Lutherans	Estate Life	709	1.69	◐	●	●	●	−4.40	1.54	5.06
Great-West Life	Life at 95 X-Series	555	2.24	●	●	◐	◐	−24.49	−1.81	4.91
Sun Life of Canada	Nova Whole Life	708	0.11	◐	●	●	●	−20.16	0.07	6.68
Aid Association for Lutherans	Whole Life	799	2.60	●	●	●	◐	−7.91	0.10	4.56
Connecticut Mutual	Econolife	715	2.68	●	●	●	◐	−18.22	−2.37	4.47

Nonparticipating policies

Executive Life	Irreplaceable Life II	412	−4.80	○	●	◐	○	−1.45	8.31	10.78
Federal Kemper	RL-1	232	1.42	○	◉	◐	◐	−10.47	4.00	7.44
N. Amer. Co. for Life & Health	The Stabilizer—Current*	318	2.72	○	◐	○	○	−33.58	−2.73	4.02
Crown Life	Low Cost Life Preferred	546	4.33	●	◐	●	○	−19.25	−1.47	2.51
Federal Kemper	RL-2	663	7.28	○	●	◐	●	−2.88	−4.78	−0.63
N. Amer. Co. for Life & Health	The Stabilizer—Guaranteed*	318	8.53	●	●	●	◐	−52.39	−20.73	−5.72

Age 35 **$200,000** **Male**

Participating policies

Company Name	Policy Name	First-year premium	20-year cost index	Payment index 5-year	Payment index 10-year	Payment index 20-year	Rate of return 5-year	Rate of return 10-year	Rate of return 20-year
Phoenix Mutual	Whole Life	$2920	-3.42	●	●	◐◐	3.73%	8.57%	10.42%
Equitable	Whole Life 50	2668	-2.81	●	●	◐◐	-0.44	7.56	10.15
Northwestern Mutual	Extra Ordinary Life (EOL)	2170	-3.08	●	●	○	-2.06	7.22	9.87
Mutual of New York	Moneyconomizer	2224	-1.48	●	●	●	0.85	7.90	9.96
New England Mutual	Ordinary Life *	2653	-3.26	●	●	○	-3.46	6.46	10.27
Manufacturers Life	Benefit Builder IV	5248	-6.48	●	●	●	0.68	7.19	8.77
Bankers Life Co.	Century 100 *	3052	-2.08	●	●	○	-6.27	6.59	9.25
John Hancock Mutual	Preferred 100 *	2426	-1.68	●	●	○	-3.44	7.11	9.27
Manufacturers Life	Premier Life	1798	-0.30	●	●	●	-8.45	6.83	9.87
Prudential	Modified Life 5 *	2237	-2.53	◐	◐	●	-19.93	5.77	9.85
Manufacturers Life	Graded Premium Whole Life	1426	-0.19	●	○	●	-12.30	5.48	8.76
Teachers Ins. & Annuity Assoc.	Ordinary Life	1284	0.14	◐	◐	●	-13.55	6.49	9.97
Prudential	Estate 25—Whole Life *	2600	-2.87	○	○	◐	-11.37	4.66	9.56
Northwestern Mutual	Select 100	2940	-2.87	○	◐	◐	-6.84	6.17	9.58
Connecticut Mutual	Econolife Preferred	2836	-1.17	◐	◐	◐	-9.04	4.14	8.73
Prudential	Modified Life 3 *	2473	-2.38	◐	○	●	-15.46	5.18	9.41
New York Life	Whole Life	3037	-1.41	○	○	○	-5.89	5.16	8.78
Massachusetts Mutual	Convertible Whole Life	3108	-3.22	○	◐	○	-8.25	5.14	9.58
Manufacturers Life	Benefit Builder I	3322	-2.43	○	◐	○	-6.24	5.71	8.84
Mutual Benefit Life	Ordinary Life—1985	2727	-2.32	◐	○	○	-12.01	5.12	9.60
Great-West Life	Life at 95 X-Series	1871	0.50	●	●	●	-15.52	4.29	8.88

Northwestern Mutual	90 Life	3440	−1.64	−4.92	5.33	8.62
Sun Life of Canada	Nova Whole Life	2535	−1.37	−14.43	4.01	9.25
Crown Life	Advance	2681	−0.93	−11.21	4.39	8.92
Manufacturers Life	Estate Protector	2792	−0.74	−10.84	4.98	8.49
Crown Life	Prove	1736	0.06	−25.87	3.33	9.60
Bankers Life Co.	Special Whole Life*	3318	−0.90	−7.86	4.93	7.94
Metropolitan	Whole Life Policy	2682	−0.80	−10.94	4.10	8.16
Sun Life of Canada	Sun Permanent Life	2961	−1.22	−18.45	3.01	9.26
Aid Association for Lutherans	Estate Life	2843	1.73	−3.39	2.38	5.83
Bankers Life Co.	Life Paid-Up at Age 65 Money Saver*	3957	−1.07	−8.11	4.00	7.40
Continental Assurance Co.	EVP96	2836	−0.42	−18.57	1.75	8.36
Aid Association for Lutherans	Whole Life	3231	2.80	−7.39	0.65	5.16
Connecticut Mutual	Econolife	3126	1.23	−12.34	1.43	6.70

Nonparticipating policies

Federal Kemper	RL-1	944	0.83	2.34	11.52	12.02
Executive Life	Irreplaceable Life II	1966	−5.91	0.54	9.12	11.23
N. Amer. Co. for Life & Health	The Stabilizer—Current*	1393	2.01	−15.21	4.21	7.40
Crown Life	Low Cost Life Preferred	1971	3.28	−13.76	2.13	4.84
Federal Kemper	RL-2	2832	6.74	0.21	−1.92	1.51
N. Amer. Co. for Life & Health	The Stabilizer—Guaranteed*	1439	7.18	−28.86	−9.77	−0.66

Age 35 — $200,000 — Female

Participating policies

COMPANY NAME	POLICY NAME	First-year premium	Relative cost 20-year cost index	Relative cost 5-year	Relative cost 10-year	Relative cost 20-year	Payment index	Rate of return 5-year	Rate of return 10-year	Rate of return 20-year
Northwestern Mutual	Extra Ordinary Life (EOL)	$1990	○	●	●	●	−3.98	−0.32%	7.82%	9.86%
Bankers Life Co.	Century 100*	2763	◐	●	●	●	−3.57	−3.17	8.19	9.87
Phoenix Mutual	Whole Life	2568	◐	●	●	◐	−3.51	3.62	8.29	10.13
John Hancock Mutual	Preferred 100*	2254	●	●	●	●	−2.71	−1.75	7.84	9.33
Equitable	Whole Life 50	2270	○	●	○	◐	−1.87	−2.23	6.34	9.12
Mutual of New York	Moneyconomizer	1730	●	●	◐	◐	−1.08	1.28	7.27	9.32
Manufacturers Life	Benefit Builder IV	5150	◐	●	◐	●	−6.97	0.78	7.13	8.62
Manufacturers Life	Graded Premium Whole Life	1184	●	○	◐	◐	−0.62	−17.27	4.80	8.66
Manufacturers Life	Premier Life	1400	●	○	◐	◐	−0.18	−13.27	5.65	9.24
Northwestern Mutual	Select 100	2752	◐	●	◐	◐	−3.81	−5.53	6.69	9.59
Northwestern Mutual	90 Life	3240	●	●	◐	◐	−2.64	−3.60	5.89	8.65
Bankers Life Co.	Special Whole Life*	3031	●	○	◐	●	−2.40	−5.16	6.31	8.46
New England Mutual	Ordinary Life*	2653	◐	●	◐	●	−3.69	−4.38	5.73	9.64
Metropolitan	Whole Life Policy	2354	●	○	●	●	−0.96	−16.22	5.67	9.64
Teachers Ins. & Annuity Assoc.	Ordinary Life	1284	○	○	◐	○	0.14	−13.55	6.49	9.97
Mutual Benefit Life	Ordinary Life—1985	2583	◐	●	○	◐	−3.04	−11.26	5.28	9.35
Prudential	Estate 25—Whole Life*	2290	●	●	○	●	−2.04	−13.83	4.62	8.83
Prudential	Modified Life 5*	1951	○	●	◐	◐	−1.75	−24.69	5.61	9.03
Connecticut Mutual	Econolife Preferred	2328	●	○	○	●	−0.77	−10.98	2.88	7.96
Manufacturers Life	Benefit Builder I	3218	●	◐	◐	○	−2.63	−6.09	5.57	8.30
New York Life	Whole Life	2709	○	◐	◐	○	−1.41	−7.92	4.59	8.23

Company	Policy			Rating				
Manufacturers Life	Estate Protector	2252	-1.23	◑ ◑ ◑	-15.38	4.37	8.57
Crown Life	Advance	2246	-0.43	◑ ○ ◑	-13.72	2.96	8.02
Massachusetts Mutual	Convertible Whole Life	3004	-3.74	○ ◑ ●	-8.09	4.99	9.20
Bankers Life Co.	Life Paid-Up At Age 65 Money Saver*	3675	-2.54	○ ○ ●	-6.03	5.06	7.80
Prudential	Modified Life 3*	2192	-2.05	● ● ◑	-19.63	4.15	8.86
Great-West Life	Life at 95 X-Series	1867	0.48	○ ○ ◑	-17.65	2.47	7.28
Crown Life	Prove	1437	0.62	○ ● •	-35.42	0.36	8.00
Sun Life of Canada	Sun Permanent Life	2841	-1.82	◑ ● ◑	-18.13	2.89	8.81
Sun Life of Canada	Nova Whole Life	2505	-1.52	● ○ ○	-15.48	3.02	8.32
Continental Assurance Co.	EVP96	2702	-1.09	● ● ○	-18.02	1.76	8.00
Aid Association for Lutherans	Estate Life	2762	1.31	◑ ● ◑	-3.39	2.10	5.37
Connecticut Mutual	Econolife	2618	1.47	● ● ◑	-14.89	-0.21	5.73
Aid Association for Lutherans	Whole Life	3151	2.37	◑ ● ●	-7.39	0.40	4.73

Nonparticipating policies

Company	Policy			Rating				
Executive Life	Irreplaceable Life II	1572	-5.17	◑ • ○	0.46	9.33	11.26
Federal Kemper	RL-1	780	0.68	● ● •	-1.01	9.26	10.13
N. Amer. Co. for Life & Health	The Stabilizer—Current*	1135	2.05	◑ ◑ ◑	-28.87	0.20	5.51
Crown Life	Low Cost Life Preferred	1833	2.52	○ ○ ○	-12.60	2.38	4.46
Federal Kemper	RL-2	2502	5.71	● ● ●	-0.66	-2.50	1.18
N. Amer. Co. for Life & Health	The Stabilizer—Guaranteed*	1135	8.07	● ◑ ◑	-50.31	-19.76	-5.26

Age 45 — $50,000 — Male

Participating policies

COMPANY NAME	POLICY NAME	First-year premium	20-year cost index	20-yr cost index 5-year	10-year	20-year	Payment index 5-year	10-year	20-year	Rate of return 5-year	10-year	20-year
New York Savings Bank	Whole Life*	$1031	-2.68	●	●	●	◐	●	●	-0.30%	10.16%	11.60%
Phoenix Mutual	Whole Life	1142	-2.30	●	●	●	◐	◐	●	2.91	8.24	10.53
New England Mutual	Ordinary Life*	1056	-2.27	●	●	●	◐	◐	●	-3.01	6.56	10.42
Massachusetts Savings Bank	Straight Life	927	-0.88	●	●	◐	◐	●	◐	12.63	11.52	11.26
Northwestern Mutual	Extra Ordinary Life (EOL)	884	-2.53	●	●	●	○	●	◐	-0.11	7.63	10.13
Equitable	Whole Life 50	1078	-0.95	●	●	●	◐	◐	●	-2.52	6.81	9.80
Mutual of New York	Monyconomizer	947	0.39	●	●	○	●	◐	●	-0.63	7.29	9.77
Prudential	Modified Life 5*	850	-1.21	●	●	●	●	◐	●	-18.20	5.79	10.16
Manufacturers Life	Premier Life	825	2.39	●	◐	◐	●	◐	●	-7.36	5.88	9.08
New York Life	Whole Life	1192	-0.44	●	◐	◐	○	◐	◐	-4.74	5.63	9.30
Manufacturers Life	Graded Premium Whole Life	545	2.48	●	●	◐	◐	◐	◐	-11.38	5.71	8.87
Prudential	Estate 25—Whole Life*	1031	-1.42	◐	◐	◐	◐	◐	●	-11.48	4.85	9.67
Crown Life	Advance	1045	0.44	○	◐	○	◐	◐	●	-9.42	5.08	9.36
Bankers Life Co.	Special Whole Life*	1291	0.57	●	◐	○	◐	◐	◐	-5.13	5.40	8.38
Teachers Ins. & Annuity Assoc.	Ordinary Life	636	2.73	●	◐	○	●	◐	●	-12.52	4.94	9.10
Massachusetts Mutual	Convertible Whole Life	1213	-2.24	◐	◐	○	◐	◐	◐	-8.13	5.32	9.80
Prudential	Modified Life 3*	930	-0.95	◐	◐	○	◐	◐	◐	-13.89	4.65	9.57
Northwestern Mutual	90 Life	1343	0.03	◐	●	○	◐	◐	◐	-3.99	5.45	8.75
Crown Life	Prove	760	1.94	○	○	○	◐	◐	◐	-19.83	3.90	9.76
Connecticut Mutual	Econolife Preferred	1213	1.38	○	◐	◐	○	◐	◐	-11.09	2.81	8.10
Manufacturers Life	Estate Protector	1121	2.01	○	◐	◐	○	○	◐	-8.53	4.41	8.04

Company	Policy											
Great-West Life	Life at 95 X-Series	858	3.83	○			●	-14.57	2.99	7.92
Bankers Life Co.	Life Paid-Up at Age 65 Money Saver*	1707	-0.98	◑	◑	◑	●	-5.47	4.04	7.35
Mutual Benefit Life	Ordinary Life—1985	1172	0.75	◑	◑	○	◑	-10.58	3.58	8.49
Metropolitan	Whole Life Policy	1150	1.67	○	◑	○	◑	-8.85	3.39	7.83
John Hancock Mutual	Preferred Risk Whole Life*	1160	1.82	○	◑	○	◑	-8.18	4.04	7.90
Continental Assurance Co.	EVP96	1137	1.59	◑	●	○	○	-12.40	2.02	8.39
Aid Association for Lutherans	Estate Life	1067	4.52	◉	●	●	●	-2.27	2.77	6.22
Sun Life of Canada	Nova Whole Life	1125	1.85	●	●	◑	○	-15.37	2.28	8.14
Sun Life of Canada	Sun Permanent Life	1266	2.23	●	●	●	○	-19.29	1.43	8.01
Aid Association for Lutherans	Whole Life	1237	4.91	●	●	●	●	-6.49	0.90	5.59
Connecticut Mutual	Econolife	1332	5.19	●	●	●	●	-14.22	0.12	5.98

Nonparticipating policies

Company	Policy											
Executive Life	Irreplaceable Life II	864	-8.22	◉	●	◑	◑	-0.91	8.55	10.92
Federal Kemper	RL-1	517	3.40	●	◉	◑	◉	-3.48	8.91	10.79
Federal Kemper	RL-2	1187	1.02	◑	◑	◑	○	-1.56	7.73	9.70
N. Amer. Co. for Life & Health	The Stabilizer—Current*	749	7.16	○	◑	●	○	-17.99	0.44	5.10
Crown Life	Low Cost Life Preferred	870	8.10	◑	●	●	◑	-10.67	1.41	3.92
N. Amer. Co. for Life & Health	The Stabilizer—Guaranteed*	749	13.15	●	●	●	●	-25.23	-8.29	-0.46

Age 45 — $50,000 — Female

COMPANY NAME	POLICY NAME	First-year premium	20-year cost index	Relative cost 5-year	10-year	20-year	Payment index	Rate of return 5-year	10-year	20-year
Participating policies										
New York Savings Bank	Whole Life*	$799	-3.40	●	●	●	●	-2.18%	9.48%	11.24%
Phoenix Mutual	Whole Life	975	-3.12	●	●	◐	◐	2.22	7.52	9.71
Massachusetts Savings Bank	Straight Life	927	-0.88	●	●	◐	●	12.63	11.52	11.26
Mutual of New York	Monyconomizer	719	-0.14	●	●	○	◐	-2.44	5.83	8.84
Northwestern Mutual	Extra Ordinary Life (EOL)	799	-4.24	●	●	●	●	0.09	7.36	9.53
New York Life	Whole Life	1004	-1.53	●	◐	◐	○	-5.19	5.14	8.67
New England Mutual	Ordinary Life*	1056	-3.73	◐	●	●	◐	-5.30	5.08	9.36
Bankers Life Co.	Special Whole Life*	1165	-2.08	●	◐	◐	◐	-3.34	6.19	8.42
Equitable	Whole Life 50	909	-0.77	○	●	○	○	-6.39	4.43	8.43
Massachusetts Mutual	Convertible Whole Life	1128	-3.94	○	◐	◐	●	-8.00	5.09	9.20
Northwestern Mutual	90 Life	1248	-1.87	●	●	◐	●	-3.53	5.41	8.27
Manufacturers Life	Graded Premium Whole Life	477	1.65	◐	○	○	◐	-16.11	2.98	7.37
Bankers Life Co.	Life Paid-Up at Age 65 Money Saver*	1582	-3.63	◐	◐	●	●	-4.19	4.66	7.52
Prudential	Estate 25—Whole Life*	887	-1.46	○	○	◐	◐	-15.87	2.99	8.58
Prudential	Modified Life 5*	764	-0.95	◐	○	◐	●	-25.78	4.22	8.71
Manufacturers Life	Premier Life	667	2.03	●	◐	●	●	-15.32	2.32	7.39
John Hancock Mutual	Preferred Risk Whole Life*	1050	-0.52	○	◐	●	◐	-7.14	4.32	7.66
Teachers Ins. & Annuity Assoc.	Ordinary Life	636	2.73	○	○	●	◐	-12.52	4.94	9.10
Prudential	Modified Life 3*	860	-1.13	◐	◐	○	○	-21.04	2.32	8.38
Continental Assurance Co.	EVP96	1014	-0.87	○	◐	◐	◐	-10.80	2.58	8.20
Crown Life	Advance	899	0.90	◐	○	◐	◐	-15.23	1.78	7.53

Company	Policy									
Connecticut Mutual	*Econolife Preferred*	974	1.10	○	○	○	○	−14.44	0.56	6.89
Crown Life	*Prove*	623	1.89	◑	○	●	◐	−30.14	−0.35	7.73
Manufacturers Life	*Estate Protector*	943	1.25	◑	○	●	◐	−12.65	2.77	7.07
Aid Association for Lutherans	*Estate Life*	994	2.92	●	◑	●	●	−2.31	2.41	5.57
Metropolitan	*Whole Life Policy*	990	0.83	◑	○	●	◑	−11.06	2.29	6.94
Mutual Benefit Life	*Ordinary Life—1985*	1083	1.84	○	●	●	●	−10.33	3.38	6.58
Aid Association for Lutherans	*Whole Life*	1114	3.33	●	●	●	●	−5.56	1.15	5.31
Great-West Life	*Life at 95 X-Series*	836	3.39	●	●	●	○	−17.73	0.43	5.71
Sun Life of Canada	*Sun Permanent Life*	1191	0.73	●	◑	●	◑	−19.62	0.80	7.13
Sun Life of Canada	*Nova Whole Life*	1085	1.05	●	●	●	●	−16.97	0.84	6.81
Connecticut Mutual	*Econolife*	1093	4.63	●	●	●	●	−18.03	−2.37	4.73

Nonparticipating policies

Company	Policy									
Executive Life	*Irreplaceable Life II*	674	−7.04	●	●	◐	○	−1.57	7.99	10.65
Federal Kemper	*RL-1*	437	2.79	●	◑	●	◐	−10.14	4.23	7.65
N. Amer. Co. for Life & Health	*The Stabilizer—Current**	573	5.35	◐	○	◑	◑	−26.10	−2.76	3.95
Crown Life	*Low Cost Life Preferred*	776	6.11	○	○	●	◑	−9.84	1.42	3.31
Federal Kemper	*RL-2*	1042	13.01	●	●	●	●	−3.64	−5.44	−1.84
N. Amer. Co. for Life & Health	*The Stabilizer—Guaranteed**	573	13.85	●	●	●	●	−40.06	−17.81	−4.70

Age 45 — $200,000 — Male

Participating policies

COMPANY NAME	POLICY NAME	First-year premium	Relative cost — 20-year cost index	5-year cost index	10-year cost index	20-year payment index	10-year payment index	5-year payment index	Rate of return 5-year	10-year	20-year
Equitable	Whole Life 50	$3960	-2.70	●	●	●	◐	1.16%	9.05%	11.23%	
Phoenix Mutual	Whole Life	4508	-2.60	●	●	●	◐	3.53	8.61	10.76	
Mutual of New York	Monyconomizer	3636	-0.36	●	○	●	◐	1.17	8.38	10.46	
Northwestern Mutual	Extra Ordinary Life (EOL)	3476	-2.83	●	●	●	●	0.65	8.05	10.36	
Bankers Life Co.	Century 100*	4769	-1.17	◐	●	●	●	-2.71	7.48	9.81	
Manufacturers Life	Benefit Builder IV	7840	-6.68	●	◐	◐	●	2.67	7.37	8.47	
New England Mutual	Ordinary Life*	4149	-2.65	◐	◐	○	●	-2.23	7.02	10.71	
Manufacturers Life	Premier Life	3004	0.91	●	◐	●	○	-2.90	8.58	10.73	
John Hancock Mutual	Preferred 100*	3810	-0.33	◐	○	●	○	0.64	7.34	9.59	
Prudential	Modified Life 5*	3324	-1.59	○	◐	●	◐	-17.27	6.35	10.48	
Northwestern Mutual	Select 100	4636	-1.51	◐	◐	●	◐	-3.95	6.71	9.84	
Connecticut Mutual	Econolife Preferred	4504	-0.36	○	◐	●	◐	-7.76	4.99	9.50	
Prudential	Estate 25—Whole Life*	4051	-1.80	◐	◐	●	●	-10.72	5.32	9.95	
Manufacturers Life	Benefit Builder I	4942	-1.06	◐	○	●	●	-1.77	6.77	8.98	
New York Life	Whole Life	4691	-0.82	○	○	●	◐	-4.05	6.07	9.58	
Crown Life	Advance	4092	-0.01	○	○	●	●	-8.45	5.69	9.75	
Great-West Life	Life at 95 X-Series	3061	1.98	○	◐	◐	●	-9.26	6.30	9.93	
Manufacturers Life	Graded Premium Whole Life	2120	2.17	◐	◐	●	●	-10.08	6.37	9.20	
Teachers Ins. & Annuity Assoc.	Ordinary Life	2444	2.23	◐	◐	●	●	-10.82	6.01	9.74	
Massachusetts Mutual	Convertible Whole Life	4760	-2.69	◐	○	●	●	-7.34	5.80	10.10	
Prudential	Modified Life 3*	3647	-1.33	◐	◐	●	◐	-13.05	5.15	9.86	

Company	Policy						
Northwestern Mutual	*90 Life*	5312	−0.27	○	−3.50	5.76	8.96
Sun Life of Canada	*Nova Whole Life*	4111	−0.09	◑	−11.50	4.77	9.65
Manufacturers Life	*Estate Protector*	4228	0.73	○	−6.01	5.97	9.02
Crown Life	*Prove*	2951	1.49	◐	−18.47	4.76	10.28
Bankers Life Co.	*Special Whole Life**	5117	0.34	○	−4.74	5.64	8.53
Mutual Benefit Life	*Ordinary Life—1985*	4449	−0.45	◐	−8.36	4.96	9.34
Sun Life of Canada	*Sun Permanent Life*	4717	0.51	◑	−16.22	3.50	9.32
Bankers Life Co.	*Life Paid-Up at Age 65 Money Saver**	6784	−1.20	●	−5.21	4.20	7.45
Continental Assurance Co.	*EVP96*	4414	0.92	◑	−11.05	2.86	8.89
Metropolitan	*Whole Life Policy*	4526	1.29	◐	−8.16	3.82	8.09
Aid Association for Lutherans	*Estate Life*	4191	4.14	◐	−1.53	3.19	6.47
Aid Association for Lutherans	*Whole Life*	4904	4.70	●	−6.12	1.12	5.71
Connecticut Mutual	*Econolife*	4952	3.31	●	−11.24	2.06	7.20

Nonparticipating policies

Company	Policy						
Executive Life	*Irreplaceable Life II*	3382	−8.60	○	0.04	9.06	11.18
Federal Kemper	*RL-1*	1916	2.64	◉	1.03	11.52	12.32
N. Amer. Co. for Life & Health	*The Stabilizer—Current**	2779	6.09	○	−14.58	2.51	6.27
Crown Life	*Low Cost Life Preferred*	3021	7.65	○	−6.81	3.66	5.18
Federal Kemper	*RL-2*	4596	13.63	●	−0.23	−2.64	0.15
N. Amer. Co. for Life & Health	*The Stabilizer—Guaranteed**	2779	12.57	◑	−22.86	−7.44	−0.08

Age 45 — $200,000 — Female

Participating policies

COMPANY NAME	POLICY NAME	First-year premium	20-year cost index	Relative cost (5/10/20-yr cost & payment index symbols)	5-year payment index	10-year rate of return	20-year rate of return
Bankers Life Co.	Century 100*	$4265	-3.82	(symbols)	-0.65%	8.40%	9.88%
Phoenix Mutual	Whole Life	3840	-3.42	(symbols)	2.90	7.93	9.96
Northwestern Mutual	Extra Ordinary Life (EOL)	3134	-4.54	(symbols)	0.86	7.77	9.75
John Hancock Mutual	Preferred 100*	3448	-2.50	(symbols)	1.47	7.54	9.19
Equitable	Whole Life 50	3290	-2.49	(symbols)	-2.39	6.87	9.92
Mutual of New York	Monyconomizer	2724	-0.89	(symbols)	-0.20	7.17	9.65
Manufacturers Life	Benefit Builder IV	7606	-7.85	(symbols)	2.36	7.09	8.16
Northwestern Mutual	Select 100	4278	-3.30	(symbols)	-3.65	6.54	9.25
Bankers Life Co.	Special Whole Life*	4617	-2.31	(symbols)	-2.94	6.44	8.58
New England Mutual	Ordinary Life*	4149	-4.11	(symbols)	-4.59	5.50	9.62
New York Life	Whole Life	3941	-1.91	(symbols)	-4.42	5.62	8.97
Manufacturers Life	Premier Life	2410	0.74	(symbols)	-10.95	5.00	8.94
Massachusetts Mutual	Convertible Whole Life	4420	-4.39	(symbols)	-7.21	5.56	9.50
Northwestern Mutual	90 Life	4932	-2.17	(symbols)	-3.03	5.72	8.47
Manufacturers Life	Benefit Builder I	4728	-2.13	(symbols)	-2.67	5.93	8.06
Prudential	Modified Life 5*	2981	-1.32	(symbols)	-24.87	4.80	9.05
Connecticut Mutual	Econolife Preferred	3602	-0.37	(symbols)	-11.15	2.69	8.20
Manufacturers Life	Graded Premium Whole Life	1846	1.34	(symbols)	-14.85	3.64	7.70
Prudential	Estate 25—Whole Life*	3473	-1.83	(symbols)	-15.04	3.50	8.87
Continental Assurance Co.	EVP96	3922	-1.54	(symbols)	-9.38	3.44	8.71
Manufacturers Life	Estate Protector	3542	0.10	(symbols)	-10.15	4.32	8.01

Company	Policy								
Teachers Ins. & Annuity Assoc.	*Ordinary Life*	2444	2.23	○	◐	●	−10.82	6.01	9.74
Bankers Life Co.	*Life Paid-Up at Age 65 Money Saver**	6284	−3.85	◐	●	◐	−3.91	4.83	7.61
Prudential	*Modified Life 3**	3364	−1.51	◐	○	◐	−20.23	2.83	8.67
Sun Life of Canada	*Nova Whole Life*	3951	−0.89	◐	○	○	−13.32	3.17	8.18
Crown Life	*Advance*	3504	0.45	◐	○	◐	−14.18	2.44	7.93
Mutual Benefit Life	*Ordinary Life—1985*	4091	0.64	○	◐	◐	−8.09	4.75	7.44
Crown Life	*Prove*	2401	1.44	◐	◐	●	−28.63	0.64	8.30
Great-West Life	*Life at 95 X-Series*	2973	1.54	○	●	◐	−12.98	3.38	7.42
Sun Life of Canada	*Sun Permanent Life*	4417	−0.99	●	○	○	−16.58	2.83	8.38
Aid Association for Lutherans	*Estate Life*	3903	2.54	◑	●	●	−1.58	2.82	5.80
Metropolitan	*Whole Life Policy*	3883	0.46	◐	◐	◐	−10.31	2.75	7.20
Aid Association for Lutherans	*Whole Life*	4411	3.11	●	●	●	−5.17	1.37	5.44
Connecticut Mutual	*Econolife*	4050	3.02	●	●	●	−15.09	−0.45	5.88

Nonparticipating policies

Company	Policy								
Executive Life	*Irreplaceable Life II*	2622	−7.41	◐	●	○	−0.42	8.61	10.95
Federal Kemper	*RL-1*	1596	2.03	◐	○	●	−5.75	6.77	9.04
Crown Life	*Low Cost Life Preferred*	2625	3.77	○	○	○	−3.32	5.11	5.28
N. Amer. Co. for Life & Health	*The Stabilizer—Current**	2117	4.48	○	○	◐	−22.82	−0.72	5.05
Federal Kemper	*RL-2*	4016	11.39	●	●	●	−2.23	−3.91	−0.45
N. Amer. Co. for Life & Health	*The Stabilizer—Guaranteed**	2117	13.33	●	●	◐	−38.25	−17.15	−4.39

Ratings

(as published in Consumer Reports, August 1986)

Universal life Insurance

Listed in order of estimated overall quality, based on cash value and surrender value for 5, 10, and 20 years (see text). Rates shown are for male buyers. Policies marked with an asterisk are available to "preferred risks" only.

Age 25 **$60,000**

The table compares policies across two groups — **8% interest rate** and **Recent interest rate** — each with **Cash value** and **Surrender value** ratings (5-year average, 10-year sum, 20-year sum). The **Recent interest rate** group also includes a **Rate** column. Quality ratings are shown as Harvey-ball circles.

COMPANY NAME	POLICY NAME	Rate
Woodmen of the World	Adjustable Life	10.15
United Presidential	10/20	10.00
USAA Life	Universal Life	10.25
Alexander Hamilton	Irresistible Newlife II	11.00
Central Life	Universal Life	10.00
Philadelphia Life	Spectralife	10.25
Security-Connecticut	Designer III	10.40
Southwestern Life	Vision Universal Life	9.50
Acacia Mutual	Flex I	9.92
Jefferson National	Super Universal Life	10.00
Aetna	Aeconoflex	10.00

Company	Product	Rating
State Mutual	Exceptional Life	8.75
Century Life	Universal Life	10.25
Hartford Life & Accident	Easy Solution	10.25
IDS	UL 100	9.50
Aid Association for Lutherans	Horizon	10.50
Inter-State Assurance	Flexlife II—Standard Plus	10.50
Integon	Flexible Premium Adj. Life	11.00
Liberty Life	Answer/Ultra	10.00
New York Life	Target Life II	11.00
Southern Farm Bureau	Flexible Premium Life*	10.00
Life of Virginia	Contender Plus*	10.20
First Colony	Life One Plus	9.75
Equitable	Flexible Prem. Adj. Whole Life	9.50
Western-Southern	Capitalife	10.25
Lincoln National	Advocate II*	10.50
Valley Forge	Series II Universal Life*	10.25
Penn Mutual	Security Builder II	10.00
Ohio National	Optimalife II	9.50
Sun Life of Canada	Sun Lifemaster II	9.75
Great Southern	Lifetime Universal Life	10.00
Virginia Life of New York	Contender II*	9.71
Nationwide	Flexible Premium Life	10.50
Maccabees Mutual	Prestige Life	9.00
Kemper Investors	The Individualist	10.00
Penn Insurance & Annuity	Independence Builder II	8.25
Union Central	Adjustable Life	10.00
Prudential	Appreciable Life	9.00
Metropolitan	Flexible-Premium Life	9.25

Age 25 $100,000

| | | 8% interest rate | | | | | Recent interest rate | | | | | |
| | | Cash value | | | Surrender value | | Cash value | | | Surrender value | | |
COMPANY NAME	POLICY NAME	5-year average	10-year sum	20-year sum	5-year average	10-year sum	5-year average	10-year sum	20-year sum	5-year average	10-year sum	Rate
Woodmen of the World	Adjustable Life											10.15
Alexander Hamilton	Irresistible Newlife II											11.00
Central Life	Universal Life											10.00
USAA Life	Universal Life											10.25
United Presidential	10/20											10.00
Aetna	Aeconoflex											10.00
Security-Connecticut	Designer III											10.40
Southwestern Life	Vision Universal Life											9.50
Philadelphia Life	Spectralife											10.25
State Mutual	Exceptional Life											8.75
Hartford Life & Accident	Easy Solution											10.25
Jefferson National	Super Universal Life											10.00
Acacia Mutual	Flex I											9.92
Century Life	Universal Life											10.25
IDS	UL100											9.50
Inter-State Assurance	Flexlife II—Standard Plus											10.50
Aid Association for Lutherans	Horizon											10.50
First Colony	Life One Plus											9.75
Connecticut Mutual	Adjustable Life											10.00
Ohio National	Optimalife II											10.50
Integon	Flexible Premium Adj. Life											11.00

Company	Product									Rating
Liberty Life	Answer/Ultra									10.00
Travelers	Executive Universal Life Plus									10.00
Western-Southern	Capitalife									10.25
Equitable	Flexible Prem. Adj. Whole Life									9.50
Valley Forge	Series II Universal Life*									10.25
Great Southern	Lifetime Universal Life									10.00
Lincoln National	Advocate II*									10.50
Sun Life of Canada	Sun Lifemaster II									9.75
New York Life	Target Life II									11.00
Southern Farm Bureau	Flexible Premium Life*									10.00
Penn Mutual	Security Builder II									10.00
Nationwide	Flexible Premium Life									10.50
Life of Virginia	Contender Plus*									10.20
Kemper Investors	The Individualist									10.00
Penn Insurance & Annuity	Independence Builder II									8.25
Maccabees Mutual	Prestige Life									9.00
Union Central	Adjustable Life									10.00
Metropolitan	Flexible-Premium Life									9.25
Virginia Life of New York	Contender II*									9.71
Prudential	Appreciable Life									9.00

Age 35 $60,000

COMPANY NAME	POLICY NAME	Rate
Woodmen of the World	Adjustable Life	10.15
USAA Life	Universal Life	10.25
United Presidential	10/20	10.00
Security-Connecticut	Designer III	10.40
Central Life	Universal Life	10.00
Alexander Hamilton	Irresistible Newlife II	11.00
Philadelphia Life	Spectralife	10.25
Southwestern Life	Vision Universal Life	9.50
Jefferson National	Super Universal Life	10.00
State Mutual	Exceptional Life	8.75
Aetna	Aeconoflex	10.00
Acacia Mutual	Flex I	9.92
Century Life	Universal Life	10.25
IDS	UL 100	9.50
Inter-State Assurance	Flexlife II—Standard Plus	10.50
Hartford Life & Accident	Easy Solution	10.25
Aid Association for Lutherans	Horizon	10.50
Liberty Life	Answer/Ultra	10.00
Integon	Flexible Premium Adj. Life	11.00
Equitable	Flexible Prem. Adj. Whole Life	9.50
Lincoln National	Advocate II *	10.50

Company	Product	Rating
Valley Forge	Series II Universal Life*	10.25
Life of Virginia	Contender Plus*	10.20
Western-Southern	Capitalife	10.25
Southern Farm Bureau	Flexible Premium Life*	10.00
First Colony	Life One Plus	9.75
Sun Life of Canada	Sun Lifemaster II	9.75
Penn Mutual	Security Builder II	10.00
Ohio National	Optimalife II	9.50
New York Life	Target Life II	11.00
Great Southern	Lifetime Universal Life	10.00
Maccabees Mutual	Prestige Life	9.00
Nationwide	Flexible Premium Life	10.50
Penn Insurance & Annuity	Independence Builder II	8.25
Union Central	Adjustable Life	10.00
Kemper Investors	The Individualist	10.00
Virginia Life of New York	Contender II*	9.71
Metropolitan	Flexible-Premium Life	9.25
Prudential	Appreciable Life	9.00

Age 35 $100,000

COMPANY NAME	POLICY NAME	8% interest rate							Recent interest rate							Rate
		Cash value 5-year average	10-year average	20-year sum	10-year sum	5-year sum	Surrender value 20-year sum	10-year average 5-year average	Cash value 5-year average	10-year average	20-year sum	10-year sum	5-year sum	Surrender value 20-year sum	10-year average 5-year average	
Woodmen of the World	Adjustable Life															10.15
USAA Life	Universal Life															10.25
Central Life	Universal Life															10.00
Security-Connecticut	Designer III															10.40
Aetna	Aeconoflex															10.00
Alexander Hamilton	Irresistible Newlife II															11.00
United Presidential	10/20															10.00
State Mutual	Exceptional Life															8.75
Southwestern Life	Vision Universal Life															9.50
Philadelphia Life	Spectralife															10.25
Connecticut Mutual	Adjustable Life															10.00
Jefferson National	Super Universal Life															10.00
Inter-State Assurance	Flexlife II—Standard Plus															10.50
Liberty Life	Answer/Ultra															10.00
Ohio National	Optimalife II															10.50
Valley Forge	Series II Universal Life *															10.25
Century Life	Universal Life															10.25
Equitable	Flexible Prem. Adj. Whole Life															9.50
Hartford Life & Accident	Easy Solution															10.25
Lincoln National	Advocate II *															10.50
Western-Southern	Capitalife															10.25

Company	Product											
Great Southern	Lifetime Universal Life											10.00
Aid Association for Lutherans	Horizon											10.50
Integon	Flexible Premium Adj. Life											11.00
Sun Life of Canada	Sun Lifemaster II											9.75
IDS	UL100											9.50
Acacia Mutual	Flex I											9.92
Nationwide	Flexible Premium Life											10.50
First Colony	Life One Plus											9.75
Penn Mutual	Security Builder II											10.00
Union Central	Adjustable Life											10.00
Maccabees Mutual	Prestige Life											9.00
Southern Farm Bureau	Flexible Premium Life *											10.00
Life of Virginia	Contender Plus *											10.20
Penn Insurance & Annuity	Independence Builder II											8.25
New York Life	Target Life II											11.00
Kemper Investors	The Individualist											10.00
Travelers	Executive Universal Life Plus											10.00
Metropolitan	Flexible-Premium Life											9.25
Virginia Life of New York	Contender II *											9.71
Prudential	Appreciable Life											9.00

Age 45 $60,000

Columns are grouped under **8% interest rate** and **Recent interest rate**, each with **Cash value** and **Surrender value** sub-columns. The sub-column labels (reading across) are: 5-year average, 10-year sum, 20-year sum, 5-year average, 10-year average (under 8% interest rate) and 5-year average, 10-year sum, 20-year sum, 5-year average, 10-year average, Rate (under Recent interest rate). The individual cell ratings are shown as graphical (filled/partial/empty circle) symbols.

COMPANY NAME	POLICY NAME	Rate
USAA Life	Universal Life	10.25
Woodmen of the World	Adjustable Life	10.15
Security-Connecticut	Designer III	10.40
Central Life	Universal Life	10.00
United Presidential	10/20	10.00
Alexander Hamilton	Irresistible-Newlife II	11.00
State Mutual	Exceptional Life	8.75
Philadelphia Life	Spectralife	10.25
Valley Forge	Series II Universal Life*	10.25
Southwestern Life	Vision Universal Life	9.50
Hartford Life & Accident	Easy Solution	10.25
Jefferson National	Super Universal Life	10.00
Century Life	Universal Life	10.25
Life of Virginia	Contender Plus*	10.20
Aetna	Aeconoflex	10.00
Lincoln National	Advocate II*	10.50
Maccabees Mutual	Prestige Life	9.00
New York Life	Target Life II	11.00
Equitable	Flexible Prem Adj. Whole Life	9.50
Inter-State Assurance	Flexlife II—Standard Plus	10.50
Penn Mutual	Security Builder II	10.00

Company	Product								Rating
Liberty Life	Answer/Ultra								10.00
Aid Association for Lutherans	Horizon								10.50
Ohio National	Optimalife II								9.50
IDS	UL100								9.50
Union Central	Adjustable Life								10.00
Acacia Mutual	Flex I								9.92
First Colony	Life One Plus								9.75
Integon	Flexible Premium Adj. Life								11.00
Western-Southern	Capitalife								10.25
Sun Life of Canada	Sun Lifemaster II								9.75
Penn Insurance & Annuity	Independence Builder II								8.25
Southern Farm Bureau	Flexible Premium Life*								10.00
Metropolitan	Flexible Premium Life								9.25
Nationwide	Flexible Premium Life								10.50
Kemper Investors	The Individualist								10.00
Virginia Life of New York	Contender II*								9.71
Great Southern	Lifetime Universal Life								10.00
Prudential	Appreciable Life								9.00

Age 45 — $100,000

		8% interest rate						Recent interest rate		
		Cash value			Surrender value			Cash value	Surrender value	
COMPANY NAME	POLICY NAME	5-year average	10-year sum	20-year sum	5-year average	10-year sum	20-year sum	5-year average	10-year sum	Rate
USAA Life	Universal Life									10.25
Security-Connecticut	Designer III									10.40
Central Life	Universal Life									10.00
Woodmen of the World	Adjustable Life									10.15
Alexander Hamilton	Irresistible Newlife II									11.00
Aetna	Aeconoflex									10.00
United Presidential	10/20									10.00
State Mutual	Exceptional Life									8.75
Valley Forge	Series II Universal Life*									10.25
Connecticut Mutual	Adjustable Life									10.00
Philadelphia Life	Spectralife									10.25
Southwestern Life	Vision Universal Life									9.50
Hartford Life & Accident	Easy Solution									10.25
Liberty Life	Answer/Ultra									10.00
Century Life	Universal Life									10.25
Equitable	Flexible Prem. Adj. Whole Life									9.50
Ohio National	Optimalife II									10.50
Lincoln National	Advocate II*									10.50
Maccabees Mutual	Prestige Life									9.00
Inter-State Assurance	Flexlife II-Standard Plus									10.50
Jefferson National	Super Universal Life									10.00

Company	Product								Rating
New York Life	*Target Life II*								11.00
Nationwide	*Flexible Premium Life*								10.50
Great Southern	*Lifetime Universal Life*								10.00
Western-Southern	*Capitalife*								10.25
Sun Life of Canada	*Sun Lifemaster II*								9.75
Life of Virginia	*Contender Plus* *								10.20
Penn Mutual	*Security Builder II*								10.00
IDS	*UL100*								9.50
Metropolitan	*Flexible-Premium Life*								9.25
First Colony	*Life One Plus*								9.75
Union Central	*Adjustable Life*								10.00
Aid Association for Lutherans	*Horizon*								10.50
Penn Insurance & Annuity	*Independence Builder II*								8.25
Integon	*Flexible Prem. Adj. Life*								11.00
Acacia Mutual	*Flex I*								9.92
Southern Farm Bureau	*Flexible Premium Life* *								10.00
Kemper Investors	*The Individualist*								10.00
Travelers	*Executive Universal Life Plus*								10.00
Virginia Life of New York	*Contender II* *								9.71
Prudential	*Appreciable Life*								9.00

Appendix B

Calculating Interest-Adjusted Net Cost Indexes

Use the following procedure to calculate the interest-adjusted net cost indexes for a new policy or for an existing policy you want to replace. If you're figuring the index for a new policy, Year 1 in the following steps means the first year of the new policy, so enter the values for that year. If you're figuring the index for an existing policy, Year 1 means the current policy year. So if you are actually in the fifth year of the policy, you would enter the policy values for the fifth year in the space for Year 1.

If the anniversary date for your old policy is within the next six months, evaluate the policy as of the next anniversary date. If the anniversary date is more than six months away, use the policy values for last year's anniversary.

Calculating a twenty-year interest-adjusted net cost index:

STEP 1. First you accumulate twenty years' worth of premiums at 5-percent interest. These premiums are shown in your policy or on the statement supplied by the insurer. If the premium is the same for each year, as it will be for most whole life policies, you can simplify this step. Just multiply the premium by 34.719 and enter the result as the total for step 1.

Year	Premium for year		Interest factor		Result
1	_____	×	2.653	=	_____
2	_____	×	2.527	=	_____
3	_____	×	2.407	=	_____
4	_____	×	2.292	=	_____
5	_____	×	2.183	=	_____
6	_____	×	2.079	=	_____
7	_____	×	1.980	=	_____
8	_____	×	1.885	=	_____
9	_____	×	1.796	=	_____
10	_____	×	1.710	=	_____
11	_____	×	1.629	=	_____
12	_____	×	1.551	=	_____
13	_____	×	1.477	=	_____
14	_____	×	1.407	=	_____
15	_____	×	1.340	=	_____
16	_____	×	1.276	=	_____
17	_____	×	1.215	=	_____
18	_____	×	1.157	=	_____
19	_____	×	1.102	=	_____
20	_____	×	1.050	=	_____
			Total	=	_____

The total in step 1 represents the accumulated value of your premiums at 5-percent interest.

STEP 2. If you have a participating policy, you'll also need to accumulate the policy's illustrated dividends at 5-percent interest. The dividends for a new policy are shown on the ledger statement the agent or company provided for you. If you're making this calculation for an existing policy, don't rely on the dividend scale provided when you purchased the policy. Because dividend projections change over time, you should obtain an updated ledger statement from the company. Enter the dividends on the lines shown on page 250.

Year	Dividend		Interest factor		Result
1	_____	×	2.527	=	_____
2	_____	×	2.407	=	_____
3	_____	×	2.292	=	_____
4	_____	×	2.183	=	_____
5	_____	×	2.079	=	_____
6	_____	×	1.980	=	_____
7	_____	×	1.885	=	_____
8	_____	×	1.796	=	_____
9	_____	×	1.710	=	_____
10	_____	×	1.629	=	_____
11	_____	×	1.551	=	_____
12	_____	×	1.477	=	_____
13	_____	×	1.407	=	_____
14	_____	×	1.340	=	_____
15	_____	×	1.276	=	_____
16	_____	×	1.215	=	_____
17	_____	×	1.157	=	_____
18	_____	×	1.102	=	_____
19	_____	×	1.050	=	_____
20	_____	×	1.000	=	_____
			Total	=	_____

The total represents the accumulated value of the dividends at 5-percent interest. Now you are ready to calculate the actual cost index.

STEP 3. Calculate the interest-adjusted increase in your policy's cash surrender value as follows:

(A) Enter the current cash surrender value, if any (plus the terminal dividend, if any). You can find this number in the policy or on the statement the company provided for you. If you're evaluating a new policy, its current cash surrender value will be zero. $_____

(B) Multiply the amount in (A) by 2.653 and enter the result here. (It will still be zero for a new policy.) $_____

(C) Enter the illustrated cash surrender value (plus the terminal dividend, if any) the policy will have twenty years from now. This number is found in the policy or in the statement you received from the company. If you are calculating an index for a new policy, simply enter the twentieth-year cash surrender value. If you are figuring an index for a replacement policy, and are now in the fifth year of the policy, for example, use the value for the twenty-fifth anniversary of the policy. $_____

(D) Subtract (B) from (C). The difference represents the interest-adjusted increase in cash value over the next twenty years. (For a new policy, it will be the twentieth-year surrender value only.) $_____

STEP 4. Now you're ready to calculate the actual interest-adjusted cost for the policy by completing the following:

$$\frac{P - D - C}{34.719} = \text{interest-adjusted net cost}$$

Where P is the total of accumulated premiums from step 1, D is the total of accumulated dividends from step 2, and C is the interest-adjusted increase in cash value from step 3.

STEP 5. To calculate the index on a per $1,000 basis, divide the step 4 result by the policy's face amount minus the current cash surrender value, each expressed in thousands (for example, use $100 for a $100,000 policy). The current cash surrender value for a new policy will be zero, so you simply divide by the number of thousands of face amount. An existing policy will likely have a cash surrender value.

Result from
step 4

_____

Face amount
− current cash
surrender value

STEP 6. If you're calculating an index for an   Old index:
existing policy, compare the index you got in step   —————
5 with the index an agent shows you for a new
policy, provided of course that the new policy is of
the same type as the old. The indexes can be used
even if the policies' face amounts are different. If
you are calculating an index for a new policy, simply
compare it with indexes for other policies.

New
index:

—————

Calculating a twenty-year interest-adjusted net payment index:

You may want also to calculate an interest-adjusted net payment
index for the policy you're thinking of buying. You can use the same
procedure we've just outlined, but you'll need to make a couple of
adjustments. Omit step 3 and use the following formula in step 4:

$$\frac{P-D}{34.719}$$

Calculating a ten-year interest-adjusted net cost index:

You may want to compare policies over a shorter period than twenty
years. In fact, given the wide swings in interest rates over the past
several years, calculating a ten-year cost index may be more realistic.
If your old company won't supply the ten-year index, here's how to
do it yourself. (Again, you can use this procedure for either a new or
an existing policy.)

Follow the steps we outlined for calculating a twenty-year index,
except substitute the tenth-year figure in each place that requires a
twentieth-year figure. You also need to use different factors for accumulating and totaling premiums and dividends. When you accumulate premiums at 5 percent, use the following factors:

Year	Premium for year		Interest factor		Result
1	——————	×	1.629	=	————
2	——————	×	1.551	=	————

3	_____	×	1.477	=	_____
4	_____	×	1.407	=	_____
5	_____	×	1.340	=	_____
6	_____	×	1.276	=	_____
7	_____	×	1.215	=	_____
8	_____	×	1.157	=	_____
9	_____	×	1.102	=	_____
10	_____	×	1.050	=	_____
			Total	=	_____

In step 2, when you accumulate dividends at 5 percent, use these factors:

Year	Dividend		Interest factor		Result
1	_____	×	1.551	=	_____
2	_____	×	1.477	=	_____
3	_____	×	1.407	=	_____
4	_____	×	1.340	=	_____
5	_____	×	1.276	=	_____
6	_____	×	1.215	=	_____
7	_____	×	1.157	=	_____
8	_____	×	1.102	=	_____
9	_____	×	1.050	=	_____
10	_____	×	1.000	=	_____
			Total	=	_____

You'll also need to make some changes in step 3. In step 3 (B), p. 250, use the factor 1.629 instead of 2.653. And be sure to substitute the tenth-year cash surrender value for the twentieth-year cash surrender value.

You'll need to make one more change in step 4. In the denominator (bottom) of the fraction, substitute the factor 13.207 for the 34.719 factor used in calculating the twenty-year cost index.

Appendix C

States with Cost Disclosure Regulations

Alabama	New Hampshire
Arizona	New Jersey
Arkansas	New Mexico
California	New York
Connecticut	North Carolina
Delaware	North Dakota
Florida	Ohio
Georgia	Oregon
Illinois	Pennsylvania
Indiana	Rhode Island
Iowa	South Carolina
Kansas[a]	South Dakota
Maine	Tennessee
Maryland	Texas
Massachusetts	Utah
Missouri	Vermont
Montana	Washington
Nebraska	West Virginia
Nevada	Wisconsin

[a] Buyer's guide and cost indexes not required.

Appendix D

States with Policy Replacement Regulations

Alabama	New Hampshire
Arizona	New Jersey
Colorado	New Mexico
Delaware	New York
Florida	North Carolina
Georgia	Ohio
Hawaii	Oregon
Idaho	Pennsylvania
Illinois	Rhode Island
Indiana	South Carolina
Iowa	South Dakota
Kansas	Tennessee
Kentucky	Utah
Maryland	Vermont
Michigan	Virginia
Mississippi	Washington
Missouri	West Virginia
Montana	Wisconsin
Nebraska	Wyoming
Nevada	

Oklahoma has recently enacted a statutory procedure to cover replacement. Massachusetts has enacted a law that directs the state insurance commissioner to promulgate model replacement regulations of the National Association of Insurance Commissioners (NAIC).

Appendix E

State Insurance Regulators

Alabama	135 S. Union St. #160 Montgomery, AL 36130-3401	205-269-3550
Alaska	P.O. Box D Juneau, AK 99811	907-465-2515
Arizona	801 E. Jefferson, 2nd Floor Phoenix, AZ 85034	602-255-5400
Arkansas	400 University Tower Bldg. 12th and University St. Little Rock, AR 72204	501-371-1325
California	100 Van Ness Ave. San Francisco, CA 94102	415-557-3245
Colorado	303 W. Colfax Ave. Denver, CO 80204	303-866-3201

Connecticut	165 Capitol Ave. State Office Bldg. Room 425 Hartford, CT 06106	203-566-5275
Delaware	841 Silver Lake Blvd. Dover, DE 19901	302-736-4251
District of Columbia	614 H St. N.W. North Potomac Bldg. Suite 512 Washington, DC 20001	202-727-7419
Florida	State Capitol Plaza Level Eleven Tallahassee, FL 32399-0300	904-488-3440
Georgia	2 Martin L. King Jr. Dr. Floyd Memorial Bldg. 704 W. Tower Atlanta, GA 30334	404-656-2056
Hawaii	P.O. Box 3614 Honolulu, HI 96811	808-548-5450
Idaho	700 West State St. Boise, ID 83720	208-334-2250
Illinois	320 W. Washington St. Springfield, IL 62767	217-782-4515
Indiana	311 W. Washington St. Suite 300 Indianapolis, IN 46204-2787	317-232-2386
Iowa	Lucas State Office Bldg. 6th Floor Des Moines, IA 50319	515-281-5705
Kansas	420 S.W. 9th St. Topeka, KS 66612	913-296-7801
Kentucky	229 W. Main St. P.O. Box 517 Frankfort, KY 40602	502-564-3630

Louisiana	P.O. Box 44214 Baton Rouge, LA 70804 *or* 950 North 5th St. Baton Rouge, LA 70801	504-342-5328
Maine	State Office Bldg. State House, Station 34 Augusta, ME 04333	207-289-3101
Maryland	501 St. Paul Place (Stanbalt Bldg.) 7th Floor-South Baltimore, MD 21202	301-333-6300
Massachusetts	100 Cambridge St. Boston, MA 02202	617-727-3333
Michigan	611 W. Ottawa St. 2nd Floor North Lansing, MI 48933	517-373-9273
Minnesota	500 Metro Square Bldg. 5th Floor St. Paul, MN 55101	612-296-6907
Mississippi	1804 Walter Sillers Bldg. P.O. Box 79 Jackson, MS 39205	601-359-3569
Missouri	301 W. High St. 6 North P.O. Box 690 Jefferson City, MO 65102-0690	314-751-2451
Montana	126 N. Sanders Mitchell Bldg. Room 270, P.O. Box 4009 Helena, MT 59601	406-444-2040
Nebraska	301 Centennial Mall South State Capitol Bldg. P.O. Box 94699 Lincoln, NE 68509	402-471-2201

Nevada	Nye Bldg. 201 South Fall St. Carson City, NV 89701	702-885-4270
New Hampshire	169 Manchester St. P.O. Box 2005 Concord, NH 03301	603-271-2261
New Jersey	201 East State St. CN 325 Trenton, NJ 08625	609-292-5363
New Mexico	PERA Bldg. P.O. Drawer 1269 Santa Fe, NM 87504-1269	505-827-4535
New York	160 W. Broadway New York, NY 10013	212-602-0429
North Carolina	Dobbs Bldg. P.O. Box 26387 Raleigh, NC 27611	919-733-7343
North Dakota	Capitol Bldg. Fifth Floor Bismarck, ND 58505	701-224-2440
Ohio	2100 Stella Court Columbus, OH 43266-0566	614-466-3584

Oklahoma	P.O. Box 53408
	Oklahoma City, OK
	  73152-3408
	  or
	1901 North Walnut
	Oklahoma City, OK 73105
		405-521-2828

Oregon	158-12th St. NE Salem, OR 97310	503-378-4271
Pennsylvania	Strawberry Square 13th Floor Harrisburg, PA 17120	717-787-5173
Rhode Island	100 North Main St. Providence, RI 02903	401-277-2246

South Carolina	1612 Marion St. P.O. Box 100105 Columbia, SC 29202-3105	803-737-6117
South Dakota	Insurance Building 910 E. Sioux Ave. Pierre, SD 57501	605-773-3563
Tennessee	1808 West End Ave. 14th Floor Nashville, TN 37219-5318	615-741-2241
Texas	1110 San Jacinto Blvd. Austin, TX 78701-1998	512-463-6329
Utah	P.O. Box 45803 Salt Lake City, UT 84145	801-530-6400
Vermont	State Office Building Montpelier, VT 05602	802-828-3301
Virginia	700 Jefferson Building P.O. Box 1157 Richmond, VA 23209	804-786-3741
Washington	Insurance Building AQ21 Olympia, WA 98504	206-753-7301
West Virginia	2100 Washington St., E Charleston, WV 25305	304-348-3394
Wisconsin	P.O. Box 7873 Madison, WI 53707 *or* 123 W. Washington Ave. Madison, WI 53702	608-266-0102
Wyoming	Herschler Building 122 West 25th St. Cheyenne, WY 82002	307-777-7401

Appendix F

States with Life Insurance Guaranty Associations

Alabama	Nebraska
Arizona	Nevada
Connecticut	New Hampshire
Delaware	New Mexico
Florida	New York
Georgia	North Carolina
Hawaii	North Dakota
Idaho	Oklahoma
Illinois	Oregon
Indiana	Pennsylvania
Iowa	Rhode Island
Kansas	South Carolina
Kentucky	Texas
Maine	Utah
Maryland	Vermont
Massachusetts	Virginia
Michigan	Washington
Minnesota	West Virginia
Mississippi	Wisconsin
Montana	

Appendix G

Where to Find the Companies

The following list is a directory of the life insurance companies that submitted policies for our 1986 study. The address of each company is included, as well as the names of those states where that particular company sells its policies.

Acacia National Life, 51 Louisiana Ave. N.W., Washington, DC 20001. DC and all states except AK, HI, ME, NH, NY, SD, VT, and WY.

Aetna Life, 151 Farmington Ave., Hartford, CT 06156. All states plus DC.

Aid Association for Lutherans, 4321 N. Ballard Rd., Appleton, WI 54919. All states plus DC.

Alexander Hamilton Life, 33045 Hamilton Blvd., Farmington Hills, MI 48018. All states except NY.

American Agency Life, 6660 W. Broad St., Richmond, VA 23230. DC and all states except HI, IA, KY, MN, NJ, NY, ND, VT.

Bankers Life, 711 High St., Des Moines, IA 50307. All states plus DC.

Central Life Assurance, 611 Fifth Ave., Des Moines, IA 50309. All states except AK, AR, CT, HI, LA, MA, ME, MS, NV, NH, NJ, NY, RI, SC.

Century Life, Heritage Way, Waverly, IA 50677. AZ, CA, CO, DE, DC, FL, ID, IL, IN, IA, MI, MN, MT, NE, ND, OH, OR, PA, SD, TX, WA, WI.

CNA, CNA Plaza, Chicago, IL 60685. All states.

Connecticut Mutual Life, 140 Garden St., Hartford, CT 06154. All states plus DC.

Crown Life, 120 Bloor St. W., Toronto, Ontario M4W 1B8. All states except NY; subsidiary American Crown Life is licensed in NY.

Equitable Life Assurance, 1285 Ave. of Americas, New York, NY 10019. All states plus DC.

Executive Life Insurance, 11444 W. Olympic Blvd., Los Angeles, CA 90064. DC plus all states except CT, ME, NH, NY, VT, WV.

Farmers New World Life, 3003 77th Ave. S.E., Mercer Island, WA 98040. AZ, AK, CA, CO, ID, IL, IN, IA, KN, MI, MN, MO, MT, NE, NV, NM, ND, OH, OK, OR, SD, TX, UT, WA, WI, WY.

Federal Kemper Life, Long Grove, IL 60049. DC and all states except NY.

First Colony Life, 700 Main St., Lynchburg, VA 24504. All states except NY.

Fort Dearborn Life, 233 N. Michigan Ave., Chicago, IL 60601. All states except NY, NH, ME.

Franklin Life Company, Franklin Sq., Springfield, IL 62713. DC and all states except NY; subsidiary Franklin United is licensed in NY.

General American Life, 700 Market St., St. Louis, MO 63101. All states except NY and DC.

Great Southern Life, 3121 Buffalo Speedway, Houston, TX 77251. All states except CT, DC, MA, ME, NY, ND, SD, NH, RI, VT, WY.

Great-West Life Assurance, 7400 E. Orchard Rd., Englewood, CO 80111. DC and all states except NY and RI.

Guardian Life of America, 201 Park Ave. So., New York, NY 10003. All states plus DC.

Guardsman Life, 3737 Westown Pkwy., West Des Moines, IA 50265. All states except ME, NY, NJ, WV, PA.

Hartford Life Insurance, Hartford Plaza, Hartford, CT 06115. All states plus DC.

Home Life Insurance, 253 Broadway, New York, NY 10007. DC and all states.

IDS Life, IDS Tower, Minneapolis, MN 55474. All states plus DC.

Integon Life, 500 W. Fifth St., Winston-Salem, NC 27152. All states except CT, HI, MA, ME, NH, NY, RI, VT.

Inter-State Assurance, 1206 Mulberry St., Des Moines, IA 50309. AL, AR, AZ, CA, DE, DC, FL, GA, HI, ID, IL, IN, IA, KN, LA, MN, MS, MT, MO, NE, NV, NM, ND, OH, OK, SC, SD, UT, WV, WI, WY.

ITT, 600 S. County Rd. 18, Minneapolis, MN 55426. DC and all states except NJ, NY.

Jackson National Life, 5901 Executive Dr., Lansing, MI 48910. All states except CT, MD, ME, NY, NC, WY; subsidiary Jackson National Life of Texas is licensed in TX.

Jefferson National Life, One Virginia Ave., Indianapolis, IN 46204. All states except AL, AR, CA, CT, ME, MD, MA, NH, NJ, NY, OH, PA, RI, WY.

John Hancock Mutual Life, John Hancock Plaza, Boston, MA 02117. All states plus DC.

Kemper Investors Life, 120 S. LaSalle St., Chicago, IL 60603. All states except NY, MT.

Liberty Life, 2000 Wade Hampton Blvd., Greenville, SC 29615. All states except HI, ID, MA, MN, MT, NV, NH, NJ, NY, ND, PA, WY.

Liberty National, P.O. Box 2612, Birmingham, AL 35202. All states except NY.

Life Insurance Co. of Virginia, 6610 W. Broad St., Richmond, VA 23230. DC and all states except HI, ME, NY; business in NY written by Virginia Life of NY.

Lincoln National Life, 1300 So. Clinton St., Fort Wayne, IN 46801. DC and all states except NY.

Maccabees Mutual Life, 25800 Northwestern Hwy., Southfield, MI 48037. DC and all states except AK and NY.

Manufacturers Life Insurance, 200 Bloor St. E., Toronto, Ontario M4W 1E5. DC and all states except NY.

Massachusetts Indemnity and Life, 3130 Wilshire Blvd., Santa Monica, CA 90406. All states except NY.

Massachusetts Mutual Life, 1295 State St., Springfield, MA 01111. All states plus DC.

Massachusetts Savings Bank Life Insurance, P.O. Box 4046, Woburn, MA 01888. Only MA.

Metropolitan Life, One Madison Ave., New York, NY 10010. All states plus DC.

Minnesota Mutual Life, 400 N. Robert St., St. Paul, MN 55101. DC and all states except NY.

Mutual Benefit Life, 520 Broad St., Newark, NJ 07101. All states plus DC.

Mutual Life of New York, 1740 Broadway, New York, NY 10019. All states plus DC.

National Life of Vermont, National Life Dr., Montpelier, VT 05604. All states plus DC.

Nationwide Life, One Nationwide Plaza, Columbus, OH 43216. All states except AR, CT, HI, MT, NJ, MN, NY.

New England Mutual Life, 501 Boylston St., Boston, MA 02117. All states plus DC.

New York Life, 51 Madison Ave., New York, NY 10010. All states plus DC.

N.Y. Savings Bank Insurance, 200 Park Ave., New York, NY 10166. Only NY.

North American Co. For Life & Health, 222 S. Riverside Plaza, Chicago, IL 60606. All states except NY.

Northwestern Mutual Life, 720 E. Wisconsin Ave., Milwaukee, WI 53202. All states plus DC.

Northwestern National Life, 20 Washington Ave. So., Minn., MN 55440. All states except NY.

Ohio National, 237 William Howard Taft Road, Cincinnati, OH 45219. DC and all states except AL, AK, CT, HI, MA, ME, NH, NY, OK, RI, VT.

Old Line Life, P.O. Box 401, Milwaukee, WI 53201. DC plus all states except NY.

Penn Insurance & Annuity, 510 Walnut St., Philadephia, PA 19172. All states except ME, MA, NH, NJ, NY, NC, RI, SD, VT.

Penn Mutual Life, Independence Sq., Philadelphia, PA 19172. All states plus DC.

Philadelphia Life, One Independence Mall, Philadelphia, PA 19106. All states except NY.

Phoenix Mutual Life, One American Row, Hartford, CT 06115. DC and all states except HI.

Prudential Insurance Co. of America, 745 Broad St., Newark, NJ 07101. All states plus DC.

Security-Connecticut Life, 20 Security Dr., Avon, CT 06001. All states except MN, NJ.

Southern Farm Bureau, P.O. Box 78, Jackson, MS 39205. AL, AK, FL, GA, KY, LA, MS, NC, SC, TX, VA. ·

Southern Life, P.O. Box 2699, Dallas, TX 75221. AL, AZ, AK, CA, CO, DE, DC, FL, GA, ID, IL, IN, IA, KS, KT, LA, MA, MS, MI, NE, NV, NJ, NM, NC, OH, OK, OR, PA, SC, TN, TX, VT, VA, WA, WV, WY.

Southwestern Life, Southwestern Life Bldg., Dallas, TX 75201. All states except AK, HI, ME, MA, MN, NH, NY, ND, RI, SD, WI.

State Mutual, 440 Lincoln St., Worcester, MA 01605. DC and all states except HI.

Sun Life of Canada, 1 Sun Life Executive Park, Wellesley Hills, MA 02181. All states except NY.

Teachers Insurance & Annuity, 730 Third Ave., New York, NY 10017. AL, AR, CA, CO, CT, DE, FL, GA, HI, ID, IL, KY, ME, MD, MA, MN, MS, MT, NE, NV, NM, NY, NC, OH, OR, SD, TX, WA, WV, WI, WY.

Transamerica Occidental, P.O. Box 2101, Terminal Annex, Los Angeles, CA 90051. DC and all states except NY.

Travelers Insurance, One Tower Sq.-15NB, Hartford, CT 06183. All states.

Union Central Life, P.O. Box 179, Cincinnati, OH 45231. All states plus DC.

Union Labor Life, 111 Massachusetts Ave. N.W., Washington, DC 20001. DC and all states except SD.

Union Mutual, 2211 Congress St., Portland, ME 04122. All states except MA, NJ, NY, NC.

United Investors Life, 2001 3rd Ave. So., Birmingham, AL 35255-5926. DC and all states except NY.

United Life & Accident, One Granite Pl., Concord, NH 03303. All states except NY.

United Presidential Life, 217 Southway Blvd. E., Kokomo, IN 46902. DC and all states except AK, AR, CT, HI, NH, NJ, NY, VT, WV, WY.

USAA, USAA Bldg., San Antonio, TX 78288. All states plus DC.

Valley Forge Life, CNA Insurance Companies, CNA Plaza, Chicago, IL 60685. All states except NJ and NY.

Washington National, 1630 Chicago Ave., Evanston, IL 60201. All states except NY.

Western & Southern Life, 400 Broadway, Cincinnati, OH 45202. DC and all states except AK, CT, ME, MA, NH, NJ, NY, RI, VT.

Woodmen of the World Life, 1700 Farnam St., Omaha, NE 68102. All states.

Glossary

Insurance Terms at a Glance

This glossary will help you understand many of the basic life insurance concepts and terms. Refer to the various chapters for more detailed information.

Accidental-death benefit. Rider that provides for payment of double (or triple) the face amount of a life insurance policy if the insured's death results from an accident. Sometimes called double (or triple) indemnity.

Actuary. Person who designs products or systems for insurance companies by using the theories of interest and probability.

Assumed interest rate. Minimum interest rate required on variable life policies. Investments backing a policyholder's cash value account must earn this rate in order to cover the insurance company's costs and still provide the initial coverage selected by the policyholder.

Backloaded policy. Policy that has surrender charges assessed against its cash value when the policyholder surrenders or terminates it. The insurance company covers its expenses from these charges.

Beneficiary. Person designated in a life insurance policy to receive the death benefit when the insured dies. There can be one or more beneficiaries.

Cash surrender value. Amount of cash a policyholder receives if he or she actually terminates (surrenders) a life insurance policy. This amount is net of any surrender charges and outstanding policy loans.

Cash value. Money that accumulates in a whole life, universal life, or variable life policy during the time the policy is in force. A policyholder may borrow against the accumulated amount.

Claim. Request filed with an insurance company for payment due under the provisions of an insurance policy.

Conversion clause. Provision found in most term policies guaranteeing the policyholder the right to exchange or convert the term insurance policy for a cash value type of policy without needing to show evidence of insurability (usually a current medical report).

Cost-of-living rider. Rider, usually offered with universal life policies, that automatically increases a policy's death benefit in relation to increases in the consumer price index. Companies usually set limits on the amount a policyholder's coverage can increase.

Crediting rate. Interest rate (sometimes called the *current rate*) that companies currently credit to cash values for universal life and current assumption whole life policies. The rate generally reflects market conditions, and may be competitive with rates offered by other financial instruments. A crediting rate is not the same as a rate of return, which reflects expenses and gives policyholders a true picture of what their investment actually earns.

Direct recognition. Method insurance companies use to "recognize" the effect that policy loans have in calculating the dividends they pay to policyholders.

Dividend interest rate. Interest rate an insurance company figures into its formula for determining its dividends. The rate reflects the performance of the company's investments.

Dividend options. Ways in which the dividends of a participating policy can be used by the policyholder.

Dividends. On participating policies, a nonguaranteed return of part of the premium intended to reflect a company's favorable operating experience. Dividends are usually expressed as dollars per $1,000 of coverage. The size of a dividend reflects a company's expense, mortality, and investment experience. Dividends are not taxed when they are paid because the Internal Revenue Service considers them refunds of previous overpayments of premiums.

Dividend scale. Schedule of illustrated dividends that will be paid under a particular participating policy if the assumptions that underlie the scale are fully realized by the company. Illustrated dividends may be based on a company's current expense, mortality, and investment experience, or they may be based on what the company hopes that experience will be. Dividends are never guaranteed.

Double indemnity. *See* Accidental-death benefit.

Equivalent level annual dividend. Dividend figure that reflects the levelized annual equivalent of a series of (nonlevel) dividends. It is intended to show the relative importance of illustrated dividends with interest-adjusted net cost indexes. The equivalent level annual dividend added to the interest-adjusted net cost index gives a "worst case" scenario—the cost of a policy if the company fails to pay any dividends.

Evidence of insurability. Medical and other information provided to an insurance company that allows the company to decide whether a policyholder or would-be policyholder is a good risk—i.e., insurable.

Excess interest. Amount of interest an insurance company has earned on its investments beyond what it needs to cover its expenses and the cost of claims. These earnings are shared with policyholders in a variety of ways depending on the kind of policy a person owns.

Expense charges. Charges a company assesses against a policy to cover such things as administrative costs and agents' commissions. These charges may be taken in the form of frontloads or backloads (surrender charges).

Face amount. Contractually stated policy amount to be paid when the insured dies. *See* Accidental-death benefit.

Frontloaded policy. Policy that has charges assessed directly against the premiums a policyholder pays.

General account. Insurance company's overall investment account that contains the assets that back the cash value accumulations of policyholders. The money in the account is invested in a variety of instruments ranging from short-term Treasury bills to long-term corporate bonds. Insurers have less investment flexibility with general account assets than with separate account assets.

Group life insurance. Life insurance plans often available at one's place of employment or through a particular organization. Term insurance is usually offered through these plans, but occasionally universal life policies are also available. Rates for group policies may be lower than rates for policies purchased individually. The master contract for this insurance is held by the employer or the organization rather than the employee or member.

Guaranteed insurability. Rider usually offered on cash value policies that gives a policyholder the right to buy additional cash value insurance at specified times in the future. The additional insurance is available at standard rates even if a policyholder's health has deteriorated.

Guaranteed rate. Minimum interest rate an insurance company guarantees to credit to a policyholder's cash values on universal life or current assumption whole life policies.

Illustration. *See* Ledger statement.

Indeterminate premium. Premium for a life insurance policy that may change over the life of the policy, but never goes higher than a maximum amount specified in the policy. Whether the premium goes up or down depends on the company's operating experience, including interest earned on investments.

Insured. Person on whose life an insurance policy is written.

Interest-adjusted method. Way of calculating the relative cost of similar life insurance policies over a given period of time that takes into account a policy's premiums, illustrated dividends, and future cash value as well as the timing of such cash flows. Timing is important because consumers prefer to have a dollar today rather than the same dollar next year, and this method reflects the fact that money has a time value. The method also makes assumptions about the length of time a policy will be in force, the dividends to be paid, and probable interest rate.

Interest-adjusted net cost index. Dollar figure derived by the interest-adjusted method used to compare the costs of similar policies. The index gives the average annual cost of a life insurance policy assuming the premiums and dividends (if any) are paid as illustrated. The index also assumes the policy is surrendered at the end of the stated time period and that money is valued at some stated interest rate, typically 5 percent. Also called the *surrender cost index*.

Interest-adjusted net payment index. Dollar figure derived by the interest-adjusted method used to compare the costs of similar policies. This index indicates the average annual outlay (premium less dividend) for a policy assuming premiums and dividends (if any) are paid as illustrated. The index also assumes that the policy is not surrendered and that money is valued at a stated interest rate, typically 5 percent. The net cost and net payment indexes for term policies are usually the same because term policies generally have no cash surrender value.

Ledger statement. Computer-generated printout that gives a prospective policyholder information about a particular policy. It may include such items as premiums, illustrated dividends (if any), cost indexes, and cash and cash surrender values at various durations. The values for current assumption whole life and universal life policies may be illustrated using a variety of interest rates. The ledger statement may also include important warnings and explain the basis for any dividends used in the projections. Sometimes called an *illustration*.

Level premium. Premium that stays the same or is fixed for the entire time the policy is in force, or for a specific number of years.

Linton yield. Method of imputing a rate of return to a cash value policy. The calculation assumes you are duplicating a cash value policy with a term policy and savings fund arrangement. The Linton yield is the rate of return that makes the savings fund equal to a whole life policy's cash value. Actuaries assume certain rates for the insurance protection when they perform the calculation. The lower the rates used, the lower the yields.

Maturity date. Time at which the insurance coverage of a cash value policy ends and the policyholder, if still alive, is paid the policy's face amount. At this point the cash value equals the policy's face amount.

Mortality charges. Charges a company makes against the policy to cover the policy's share of the cost of death claims—the cost of providing the insurance protection. Charges are often expressed as cost per $1,000 of coverage. Also called *cost of insurance*.

Nonforfeiture options. Choices available to a policyholder who surrenders a cash value policy before the maturity date. Most policies offer three options: a lump-sum cash payment (the cash surrender value), a reduced amount of paid-up cash value insurance, or paid-up term insurance for the policy's death benefit.

Nonparticipating policy. Policy that does not pay dividends. Also called a *nonpar policy*.

Ordinary life. Term often applied to level premium whole life policies.

Paid-up additions. Additional, usually small, amounts of single-premium whole life insurance protection purchased with dividends. Companies do not deduct expense charges from the dividends used to buy this extra insurance.

Paid-up life insurance. Life insurance coverage that will remain in effect but for which the policyholder pays no further premiums. Once a policy is paid up, the cash value continues to accumulate and the company continues to pay dividends if the policy is participating.

Participating policy. Policy that pays dividends to the policyholder. Also called a *par policy*.

Policy. Contract of insurance between the policyholder and the insurance company.

Policyholder. Person who actually owns the policy. May not be the same as the person whose life the policy insures.

Policy loan. Loan made by a life insurance company to the owner of a cash value policy. The cash value serves as collateral for the loan, which is made from the company's funds. If a policyholder dies while the loan is outstanding, the amount of the loan plus any unpaid interest is deducted from the policy's face amount in order to reimburse the company for the loan.

Premium. Money paid by a policyholder—usually annually, semiannually, quarterly, or monthly—for insurance coverage. Premiums are usually lowest if paid annually or through a plan whereby the insurance company automatically debits your checking account for the premium.

Rate of return. Number expressed as a percent that represents what policyholders actually earn on their cash values. The number is net of all fees and expenses charged by the insurance company.

Rating tables. Tables that companies use to classify the risks policyholders present to the insurance company. Such tables furnish the amount of any extra premium that an unhealthy person will have to pay for insurance coverage.

Renewable term insurance. Term life insurance—usually for a period of one or five years—that guarantees the policyholder, without presenting evidence of insurability, the right to continue the coverage for successive, equal time periods. Each time the coverage is renewed, the premium increases because the person whose life is insured is older. Companies allow renewals until age 65 or 70.

Rider. Optional benefit included in a life insurance policy for which the policyholder pays an additional charge. *See* Accidental-death benefit, Cost-of-living rider, Guaranteed insurability, and Waiver of premium.

Separate account. On variable life policies, the account or accounts into which the monies backing a policyholder's cash values are invested. The accounts often invest in a single type of financial instrument.

Single-premium variable life. Type of variable life insurance that calls for a policyholder to pay one premium, after which the policy is paid up. Monies backing a policyholder's cash values are put into a separate account, and the size of the death benefit fluctuates with the investment performance of the separate account or accounts. The policy is sold more as an investment than as life insurance.

Single-premium whole life. Type of whole life insurance that calls for a policyholder to pay one premium, after which the policy is paid up. The policy is sold more as an investment than as life insurance because the policyholder can generate tax-free income by borrowing the interest earned on the cash values. The death benefit is fixed.

Surrender. To terminate or cancel a life insurance policy before its maturity date and receive the policy's cash surrender value. The policyholder may exercise one of the nonforfeiture options at the time of surrender.

Target premium. Minimum premium a policyholder must pay on a universal life policy to cover the cost of insurance protection and keep the policy in force.

Terminal dividend. Dividend paid by some life insurance companies at the time a policy is surrendered, ends in a death claim, or matures.

Universal life. Type of cash value insurance that allows policyholders to vary their premiums from time to time and allows them to increase or decrease coverage. The policies' cash values vary depending on the interest rate the company credits. Under one option the death benefit is level; under another, it rises.

Vanishing premium. Option on a cash value policy that allows the policyholder to stop paying premiums after a certain number of years. For the premium to vanish, dividends and cash values must be high enough to cover the cost of future premiums.

Variable life. Life insurance policy in which the assets backing a policyholder's cash value grow in a separate account rather than in the insurance company's general account. The separate account assets are invested in stocks, bonds, money market funds, or other such instruments. Death benefits on traditional variable life policies fluctuate with the investment performance of the separate accounts, but will never fall below the policy's initial face amount. Cash values are not guaranteed.

Variable universal life. A type of cash value insurance policy in which the death benefit is fixed but premiums can be flexible. The cash values, however, rise and fall with the performance of the investments that policyholders choose for their accounts.

Waiver of premium. Rider that waives the payment of future premiums if the insured becomes disabled. Riders may have different definitions of what constitutes a disability.

Whole life. Cash value policy designed to cover a policyholder for a lifetime. All elements of the policy—the cash value, death benefit, and the premium—are fixed when the policy is issued. Cash values grow according to a schedule spelled out in the policy. Such insurance may or may not pay dividends.

Index